COMPETING
AGAINST AMERICA

COMPETING AGAINST AMERICA

WHY CANADA HAS FALLEN BEHIND IN THE RACE FOR TALENT AND WEALTH (AND WHAT TO DO ABOUT IT)

MICHAEL ALEXANDER

John Wiley & Sons Canada, Ltd.

Library and Archives Canada Cataloguing in Publication Data

Alexander, Michael, 1956-
          Competing against America : why Canada has fallen behind in the race for talent and wealth (and what to do about it) / Michael Alexander.

Includes index.
ISBN-13 978-0-470-83512-8
ISBN-10 0-470-83512-5

1. Canada—Economic conditions—1991- 2. Canada—Economic conditions—1971-1991. 3. Cost and standard of living—Canada. 4. Competition—Canada. I. Title.

HC115.A44 2005   330.971'071   C2005-903747-4

Production Credits:
Cover design: Adrian So
Interior text design: Tia Seifert

Printer: Tri-Graphic Printing Ltd.

John Wiley & Sons Canada, Ltd.
6045 Freemont Blvd.
Mississauga, Ontario
L5R 4J3

Printed in Canada

10 9 8 7 6 5 4 3 2 1

In memory of my grandfather, Jack Beardall—radio pioneer, entrepreneur, enthusiast—who made everything possible

It appears, you blessed man, that [justice] been rolling around at our feet from the beginning and we couldn't see it after all, but were quite ridiculous. As men holding something in their hand sometimes seek what they're holding, we too didn't look at it but turned our gaze somewhere far off, which is also perhaps the reason it escaped our notice.

—Socrates to Glaucon and Adeimantus, Book IV, Plato's *Republic*

CONTENTS

Preface

Canada is on the brink of losing the chance to catch up to the United States in the global race for talent and wealth. Recent economic studies have established that Canada's standard of living has been declining since the early 1980s and is now 20% lower than America's.

To encourage debate about how to deal with this situation, I decided to write this book, which began to take shape in mind over twenty years ago, when I first began to feel that the country was moving in the wrong direction. The idea I had then was that the Canadian state was relinquishing basic liberal democratic principles that leveled the playing field to promote equality of opportunity in favor of misguided illiberal principles that rigged the game to produce equality of result. I predicted that this trend—manifested in policies such as multiculturalism, pay equity, employment equity, deficit spending and regional equalization—would eventually undermine our economic performance. The recent economic findings that attest to our declining standard of living have confirmed my worst fears. My goal in this book is to call into question the ideas and policies that initiated our decline as the first step in devising a new policy framework that will allow us to restore productivity and achieve our economic potential.

I am by training a lawyer and a political scientist, and by temperament, a thinker. I spent several years studying both law and political philosophy at the graduate level in Canada and the United States, and briefly, in France. Although I'm inclined to take a scholarly approach to the analysis of political and economic issues, this book is not an academic treatise. Neither is it a rant. It draws on my academic knowledge of jurists and political philosophers and it's tempered by practical experiences gained by working in five federal election campaigns and three provincial campaigns. Ultimately, the book represents what I think about the economic and political challenges that we face as we move into the 21st century. My hope is that the book will have value for those who want to improve our standard of living while remaining true to the equal opportunity ideal, which holds that justice consists in allowing every individual to compete for opportunities on the basis of talent and merit.

Acknowledgments

I developed the idea for my first book, *How to Inherit Money*, when I was having a phone conversation with my good friend, Patrick Graham, who then was also one of my business partners. Patrick liked the idea and encouraged me to pursue it. When I was giving thought to writing *Competing Against America* several years later, Patrick again played an important role. When he was in Toronto briefly, taking a break from working as an international correspondent in Iraq, we sat down for an evening and talked about the project. He *insisted* that I write the book. After many years of conversation, he remarked that he knew my ideas so well that he could write the book himself. If he knew my thinking that well, he argued, then surely I wouldn't have any trouble getting my ideas down on paper. So, I started writing.

Our mutual friends, Ron Leblanc and Diane Robinson, enthusiastically embraced the project and cheered me on while I scribbled away. Without the encouragement of Patrick, Ron and Diane, this book would never have been written. I am immensely thankful for their support.

I also wish to thank the following friends and colleagues who read sample chapters, made helpful suggestions and also provided support and encouragement: Dr. Emmanuel Frantzis, Dr. Taras Babiak,

Frank Klees, M.P.P., Lynne Gallagher, Robert Paul, Dr. Richard Myers, David Marsden, Martin Perelmuter and Pallavi Valabhji. Pallavi has been particularly helpful in making suggestions regarding both style and substance.

I would also like to express my gratitude for the support and encouragement of Dr. James Breech, Denise Castonguay, Alex and Linda Moir, Alexandra Bezeredi, Mitra Manesh, Symbha and Alyne Ruremesha, Mark Gray, Willie Fennell, Ted Fennell, Osborne Colson, Fiona Robinson, Gloria Robinson, Jules Ruhinda, Lisa Pieterse, Ken and Paulette Ormsby, William and Helen Dimitroff, Tracy Quan, Emilio Reyes Leblanc, William Eigles, Margaret Bebell, Herb Charles, the late Ruth Charles, and the late Elizabeth Armstrong.

Finally, I would like to extend special thanks to my editor at Wiley and Sons, Don Loney. Don's sound judgment has improved the book immeasurably and his positive attitude kept me in good spirits when the deadlines began to loom. I would also like to thank Robert Harris, Wiley's manager of trade publications, as well as Don and everyone on the editorial board at Wiley, for taking a chance on this project. The risk they've taken is in the spirit of the book.

These acknowledgements do not indicate that anyone mentioned above is in agreement with the ideas contained in the book.

Myth One

CANADA IS
"THE BEST PLACE TO LIVE"

The Politicians' Mantra

During the 1990s, Canadian politicians never seemed to tire of re-minding everyone that the United Nations (UN) had declared Canada as "the best place in the world to live." And, indeed, for seven consecutive years (1994–2000), Canada was ranked first on the annual United Nations Human Development Index, which compares all countries based on the criteria of life expectancy, educational achievement and personal income. Most Canadians took great pride in their UN standing because it reinforced their long-standing belief that Canada offers a higher quality of life than the United States and many of the European democracies. Unlike its democratic rivals, Canada had successfully combined a high standard of living with a willingness to use government to improve the lives of the disadvantaged.

While many of my fellow Canadians were celebrating Canada's first-place finish on the UN list, the statement that "Canada is the best place to live" was bothering me. I thought: If Canada has such a high level of literacy (one of the measures on the UN list), why were our leaders making a statement that was patently ungrammatical? No one lives a country; one lives *in* a country.

I also had a more serious problem with the UN findings—the UN criteria provide a very limited picture of a nation's level of development. Consider the statistics on income. The federal Liberals have frequently quoted UN reports to buttress their claim that Canada's economic performance has been outstanding. That claim, however, skewed, or even misrepresented the findings. Canada finished first mostly due to its strong showing on the measures relating to life expectancy and education. In fact, during the 1990s, Canada's real per capita income did not rank first in the world, didn't even come close.[1] Another problem with the criteria is that they tell us very little about the justice of a particular society. A nation can achieve a high ranking on life expectancy, education and income and yet deny essential freedoms to its citizens. Look for China to move up dramatically on the list by the end of this decade.

My deepest concern about the "best place" mantra is that it encourages complacency. Our political leaders have used it to justify their hold on power and their unwillingness to face up to corruption, mismanagement and obvious inequities. For instance, a billion dollars goes missing from Human Resources and Development Canada. *Don't worry*. Canada is the best place to live. The federal Gun Registry is $1.8 billion over budget and was never necessary in the first place. *Don't worry*. Homeless people are showing up on the streets of Toronto in record numbers. *Don't worry*. Thousands of Canadians, many of them highly educated, are moving to the United States each year in search of better opportunities and higher earning power. *Don't worry*. The United States is now spending twice as much as Canada on a per capita basis on post-secondary education. *Don't worry*. Canada is the best place to live. Fortunately, all of this hollow talk about Canada's quality of life vanished in 2001, when Canada slipped from first to sixth on the UN's list. Currently, we're in the fourth spot, after dropping to eighth in 2003. In spite of our fall in the standings, most Canadians are still feeling pretty good about the country, primarily because they believe the economy is moving in the right direction. An Ipsos-Reid consumer poll published in March 2005 revealed that three-quarters of Canadians would describe the economy as "good." One-quarter of Canadians believes the economy will improve over the next year. And those who believe that they or their family members might lose their jobs represent a mere 17% of the sample: that's the lowest figure in a decade.[2]

It's not difficult to imagine why many Canadians are optimistic about the economy. Since 1997 Canada has had one of the highest economic growth rates among all Western nations, posting an average gain of around 2.5% per year. Inflation has rarely risen above 2%. After reaching almost 12% in 1993, unemployment has steadily declined and now hovers at around 7%. Our exports to the United States have gradually increased and now account for over 25% of our Gross Domestic Product.[3] At the time of writing, we have a rising dollar and historically low interest rates that have allowed millions of Canadians to become first-time homeowners.

Even though recent events inspire confidence, if we examine economic trends in both Canada and the United States, a very different picture emerges. Studies presented in the fall of 2002 at the TD Bank's Economic Forum on Canada's Standard of Living convincingly demonstrated that Canada's economic performance has been declining relative to that of the United States during the past 20 years. Many experts believe that our standard of living is now at least 20% lower than America's. In other words, one American dollar will buy 20% more in goods or services in the United States than a Canadian dollar will buy in goods and services in Canada. You can see this very concretely in the cars people can afford. In 2004, the most popular passenger car in the United States was Toyota's mid-size flagship, the Camry; in Canada it was the Honda Civic, an inexpensive compact.[4]

In part, our decline can be attributed to the fact that Canadian workers have been producing wealth less efficiently than American workers during the last 20 years. This is expressed by economists as a lag in unit labor costs. By examining the gross output of goods and services in both countries, economists have determined that Canadian workers have been producing, on average, fewer goods and services per hour than American workers since the early 1980s. Today, this means that a factory worker in Ohio who earns $20.00 per hour produces more goods every hour than a Canadian worker receiving an equivalent wage, which at current rates of exchange (June 2005) would be around $25. So, even though our economy has been growing and our exports to the United States have been increasing steadily under the Free Trade Agreement, our lower productivity has been nixing some of our gains.

At the same time that Canada has been losing ground economically, the very people we need to improve our economic performance have been relocating to the South. Our doctors, engineers, computer scientists and professors have been emigrating to the United States in large numbers. During the 1990s, the total number of Canadians emigrating to the United States annually was over 21,000 and may have been as high as 40,000. The brain drain is both *a cause* and *an effec*t of our declining prosperity.[5]

What the Ruling Elites Would Have Us Believe

Put simply, the real cause of Canada's decline is a lot of bad thinking. And that bad thinking is reflected in a cluster of myths perpetuated by the ruling elites—about how government should be involved in our lives. By ruling elites I mean certain groups of bureaucrats, judges, lawyers, politicians, professors and journalists. Behind every policy that holds Canada back is an idea borrowed by these elites from this cluster.

So, my diagnosis of Canada's problem is that our political culture, comprised of ruling elites that determine our laws and set our policies, is in a malaise. My foremost concern is that the ruling elites fail to grasp the essential meaning of equal opportunity and therefore fail to make the connection between the guarantee of equal opportunity and the improvement of our economic performance. Our decision makers should be doing everything possible to expand the freedom to create and pursue opportunities; instead they are supporting policies that restrict it. This is the problem of our time.

The TD Economic Forum on Canadian Standard of Living held in the fall of 2002 concluded that Canada is in decline due to a leadership vacuum: "Canada currently has no unifying consensus on where it wants to go. No national leader in recent memory has been able to unite Canadians behind a clear and enabling vision of what our common future should look like."[6] Why has no one generated a common vision that would motivate us to embrace meaningful economic and political reform? Why have we been twiddling our thumbs while smaller nations with fewer advantages, such as Ireland, Norway and Luxembourg, have surpassed our standard of living? The answer is not that our leaders have no vision; it's that they have a mind-numbing vision that is stifling our potential and economic productivity.

What Can We Do?

The remedy is clear. We must critically examine the basic tenets that form our political culture if we hope to create a climate of healthy debate and forward thinking that will engender practices and policies that will improve our economic performance, keep our talented people at home and enhance our quality of life. In pursuit of that aim, I have identified ten myths that have produced our most unjust and unproductive policies. These myths have become so deeply ingrained that they are often accepted at face value. However, when analyzed and put to the test, they prove to be false and even corrosive.

1. Canada is "the best place to live."
2. Canada is a productive and prosperous nation.
3. Multiculturalism promotes peace and prosperity.
4. Employment equity promotes equal opportunity.
5. Pay equity promotes equal pay.
6. Private property is not a fundamental right.
7. Canadians have a social democratic bias.
8. Doing is more important than thinking.
9. A compassionate society is a just society.
10. The success of the individual depends on the success of the group.

These myths must be rejected if we hope to become truly competitive in the 21st century. In the course of examining these myths, I will show how they inform the policies that currently prevent us from achieving our potential as individuals and as a nation. At the same time, I will draw lessons from the American experience, illustrate how core political beliefs in the United States differ from our own and how they have produced policies that have given the United States its astounding lead in the race for talent, capital and economic power.

In examining American ideas and policies, I am not advocating that we should embrace them as a panacea. Rather, they need to be studied because, whatever flaws they may have, they aim at achieving the goal of equal opportunity. Thus, they aim at meritocracy and its natural companion, national prosperity. American political culture should be our touchstone, not only because it has produced policies that have made America enormously powerful, but also because it can point Canadians in the direction of questioning the homegrown ideas and policies that hold us back. To attain the twin goals of meritocracy and prosperity, we do not have to become "American." However, we must study America to get a perspective on our own problems and begin the task of crafting uniquely Canadian policies that allow us to achieve the same goals.

How Did We Get Here?

To understand why our economic decline is so unexpected, we need to return to the fall of 1988. Prime Minister Mulroney called a federal election, which became a public referendum on his government's decision to sign the Free Trade Agreement (FTA) with the United States earlier that same year.

The basic aim of the FTA was to gradually repeal the tariff on imported goods that had protected Canadian business from American competition for more than 110 years. During the election, the Liberals and the New Democratic Party (NDP) vigorously attacked the agreement. John Turner led the opposition charge, claiming that it contained flaws that would put Canadian business at a competitive disadvantage and undermine Canadian sovereignty. The prime minister defended the agreement, principally on the ground that it would pave the way to sustained prosperity by giving Canadian business unprecedented access to the American market. With an economy that had been growing rapidly for the last five years, some Canadians were feeling optimistic and in the mood to take the greatest economic risk since the provinces entered into Confederation in 1867. The Conservatives garnered 43% of the popular vote, enough to give Mulroney his second straight majority in the House of Commons, and to put to rest, at least formally, any doubts about public support for the agreement. In 1992, with the addition of Mexico as a signatory, the FTA was replaced by the North American Free Trade Agreement (NAFTA), which established a commitment to further reduce barriers to trade and investment throughout North America by 2008.

Prior to the FTA, the long-standing tariff on imported goods, first established in 1878 as part of the National Policy of Sir John A. Macdonald's Conservative government, had given us two distinct economic advantages. It gave our manufacturers a competitive edge over their American rivals because imported goods became more expensive due to the imposition of the tariff. It also gave us a guarantee of foreign investment, since some American manufacturers established factories within Canada to avoid the tariff. However, the National Policy also resulted in two serious disadvantages. In response, America established a tariff on Canadian goods and restrictions on Canadian investment. (The only exception to the mutual tariff restrictions was the Canada–U.S. Auto Pact of 1965, which eliminated tariffs on cars, trucks, buses, tires and automotive parts on two conditions: for every car a U.S. company sold in Canada, one had to be built in Canada; and every car built by a U.S. company in Canada had to have 60% Canadian content in terms of parts and labor.)[7]

By initiating a process for eliminating most of the tariffs and investment barriers in each country, the FTA and NAFTA took away Canada's advantages. Canadian manufacturers were forced to compete head-on with their American rivals, and American businesses were no longer compelled to invest in Canada. At the same time, however, it eliminated the disadvantages. Canadian manufacturers and investors gained unrestricted access to America's vast market.

Unfortunately, the increased prosperity that free trade promised did not arrive as quickly as planned. This was due, in part, to the fact that our governments had not prepared us for the challenge of competing against the United States. When NAFTA was signed, public spending was still out of control. Both the federal and provincial governments were running deficits, which were adding to government debt at alarming rates and causing inflation to skyrocket. To keep inflation at bay and attract the capital needed to finance the deficits and the interest on the debt, the Bank of Canada was forced to maintain relatively high interest rates. This meant that some Canadian businesses couldn't afford to borrow the funds they needed to lower the costs of production, either by modernizing their facilities or expanding capacity. As a result, they couldn't gain an edge on pricing and compete effectively against their American rivals.

Our ability to compete against American business was dealt a further blow when the country plunged into the worst recession since the Great Depression. The stock and real estate markets collapsed, interest rates exceeded 18% and unemployment reached 12%. (Needless to say, the United States had to battle this recession as well, but it didn't last as along or bite as hard south of the border.)

If these developments weren't bad enough, the corporate response to the reduction of trade and investment barriers around the world—globalization—produced economic reversals for individuals and communities across Canada. Major corporations decided to cut costs by "downsizing" the ranks of management. Hundreds of thousands of highly trained people, who thought they had secure, permanent jobs, suddenly found themselves unemployed and wondering how long their savings would last. Mergers and acquisitions, a response to increased global competition, accelerated redundancy at all levels of employment, as did the application of new labor-saving computer technologies. And plants relocated to the United States, Mexico and the Far East, where labor costs were lower. These changes decimated smaller communities that had been built around one or two successful industries. In larger centers, the effects were less evident, but equally devastating for those employed in industries where these forces were in play.

By the mid-1990s, understandably, many Canadians were having second thoughts about free trade. However, by the late 1990s, these doubts had been put to rest by renewed growth, lower interest rates, balanced budgets and rising employment. Now, public confidence in free trade and our economic future are extremely high, and the anti-free trade movement, which showed its violent face at the Free Trade Summit in Quebec City in 2001, has virtually disappeared. Today, though, the question is whether public confidence is still justified, since we now know that Canada is losing the economic race with the United States. How should we respond to the news that Canada's standard of living is 20% lower than America's?

The Challenge We Face

In a speech to the Canadian Club in the fall of 2001, Charlie Baillie, then CEO and Chairman of TD Bank Financial Group, argued that we could substantially improve our economic performance if we made a concerted, strategic effort to outperform the Americans. He stated, "[O]ur goal should be to increase our standard of living so that in 15 years it is not just equal to the United States, but it is better." However, just to catch up, he argued, we would have to grow 1.6 percentage points faster than the United States every year for the next 15 years. As daunting as that task seemed, it did not stop others from joining the chorus.

Baillie's ambitious plan was applauded the next day by Paul Martin, then Minister of Finance, who declared: "I think we can do it. You've got to begin with policy, but ultimately people have to believe; then there is nothing that can stop them." In its daily editorial, the *National Post* endorsed the idea: "There is no reason Canadians should not set high standards. And the fact that we have underachieved for so long is all the more reason we should begin to change course immediately."[8]

In pursuit of the goal of exceeding American economic performance, Baillie called on 50 academics, policy analysts and business leaders from across the country to present proposals for economic reform at the TD Economic Forum on Canada's Standard of Living held in the fall of 2002. The participants presented proposals for both private-sector and public-sector reform, although, as the Conference Board noted in its summary of the proceedings, a majority of the participants favored public-sector solutions. These included measures such as

- Eliminating capital taxes
- Reducing personal and corporate taxes
- Reducing public debt
- Increasing investment in business programs in colleges and universities
- Increasing investment in urban infrastructure
- Establishing subsidy programs that protect individuals and regions from the effects of rapid economic change.

Some of the leading private-sector solutions included

- Encouraging companies to compete in global markets
- Finding new ways of adding value to natural resource production
- Using employment criteria that focus on general abilities rather than specific skills
- Establishing training programs that encourage continuous learning
- Creating manufacturing processes that encourage continuous product improvement
- Investing more money in research and development.[9]

While I agree with the TD commentators that many of these proposals should be adopted if we hope to equal America's economic performance, I believe we must develop a broader notion of reform before we can achieve that goal.

The Pursuit of Excellence

Today Canadians are not simply facing the challenge of outperforming the American economy. That challenge is just part of a broader one being faced by the entire world. The advent of global free trade has forced every nation to discover and pursue the economic activities at which it naturally excels. Success for all nations depends on pursuing excellence in areas where they enjoy a comparative advantage. This has had an enormous impact on the individual. To compete globally, every country must summon the best from its own people. This, in turn, has put tremendous pressure on individuals to improve their efficiency and output.

Needless to say, the arrival of high technology in the workplace has also put a new emphasis on individual achievement. In high-technology environments, employees must constantly upgrade their skills. Every employee must pursue excellence or risk receiving a pink slip.

This imperative, given to us by global competition and high technology, compels us to ask how Canadians can pursue excellence on a corporate and individual level. But this question in turn raises a more fundamental question: What do we mean by excellence? For the majority of commentators at the TD Forum, excellence meant producing wealth more efficiently. While everyone can agree that it's desirable to increase collective wealth, a wealthier society is not necessarily a better society. We cannot measure the success of a society simply by its level of prosperity. Some of the world's wealthiest regimes have been tyrannical. Nor can we judge the quality of an individual by his or her wealth. Gangster Sam Giancana was worth hundreds of millions of dollars but, given his many iniquities, no decent person would dare suggest that he was an excellent man. Clearly, societies and individuals must have moral worth, both must be regarded as just, before either can be called truly excellent. So, if Canada is to pursue excellence—as it must—we need to consider new policies that will enhance our prosperity and also secure justice for every citizen.

The State's Highest Goal: To Combine Justice and Prosperity

Economic growth is easily measured. It is defined by the yearly increase in the value of all goods and services produced by a nation. That measure, however, tells us very little about the practice of justice in a nation. For example, it does not tell us whether citizens are guaranteed fundamental rights such as freedom of the person (personal security), freedom of speech, freedom of religion, freedom of association and the freedom to own and transmit private property. Together, these rights support the most important right of all—the freedom to pursue happiness, however understood. Yet, in the economic realm, that freedom can never be fully realized unless the state also establishes the principle of equal opportunity, which holds that opportunities should be distributed on the basis of individual merit rather than on irrelevant group criteria such as race, religion or gender. Although justice and prosperity are distinct qualities that must be measured by different criteria, they are intimately linked nonetheless. Only when the state guarantees equal opportunity will each citizen enjoy the freedom to choose a vocation and succeed in it in accordance with ability and hard work. Only then will each individual seek to maximize his or her own wealth, and only then will the wealth of the whole increase.

So, when addressing the issue of how Canada can pursue excellence and improve its economic performance, we must also examine the degree to which Canada guarantees equal opportunity to its people; that is, the degree to which Canada is a meritocracy. The meritocratic ideal is extraordinary because it offers the best guarantee of collective prosperity and the only guarantee of individual justice.

The Broader Meaning of Equal Opportunity

Equal opportunity is perfected when everyone truly enjoys the right to succeed in a chosen vocation in accordance with hard work and ability. This freedom exists when the state guarantees that access to educational and employment opportunities will not be restricted by prejudice or personal bias. It follows that the guarantee of equal opportunity can be reduced to freedom from discrimination, or, put another way, the equal protection of the law. But, in fact, that is just one of the conditions needed to establish an equal opportunity society. The legal guarantee of non-discrimination is fine as far as it goes; however, since it is a formal guarantee, it does not affect the actual social and economic conditions that promote or hinder the advancement of individuals. As the Parisian novelist, Anatole France, once wrote, "The law, in its majestic equality, forbids the rich as well as the poor to sleep under the bridges, to beg in the street, and to steal bread."

Properly understood, the guarantee of equal opportunity is actualized when three conditions exist. First, the state must enforce the principle of non-discrimination in the distribution of opportunities. For example, the state will prohibit public and private employers from denying positions to anyone based on race, gender, sexual orientation, culture or religion. Second, people must have access to certain public and private goods and services that give them the boost they need to get into the race for opportunity. Some of these goods and services are obvious—a stable home environment, safe neighborhoods, good schooling, adequate health care, financial assistance for the poor and disadvantaged. There are many others.

The modern political debate for the last 50 years revolves around how much of a role the state should play in providing these goods. Conservatives tend to rely on the market to provide them; Liberals tend to rely on government. Today, the issue of whether the federal government should fund a national daycare program is really an equal opportunity issue. Recent research has proven that the quality of a child's mental development and life prospects depends on the stimulation the child receives from birth to the age of three. Those who favor national daycare argue that it will promote the equal opportunity ideal in two basic ways. It will reduce the child-rearing load on low-income parents, particularly low-income single parents, and allow them to compete for opportunities in the full-time workforce. At the same time, it will ensure that their children receive the daily care and support they need to develop their full potential as human beings and future members of the workforce. I do not necessarily favor national public daycare as the way to ensure that all children receive the nurturing they deserve. I do believe, however, that a government that is truly devoted to the principle of equal opportunity has a clear interest in establishing policies that assist families in achieving that goal.

The final condition needed to perfect the equal opportunity ideal is the widespread belief that opportunities should be earned and distributed on the basis of merit. Some critics of liberal societies argue that there is no such thing as merit, that decision making in the workplace is inherently biased by personal preferences, and so we need not concern ourselves with the idea of merit. It's a phantasm created by decision makers to cover up their arbitrary practices. That argument, however, defies the realities of the workplace. It's true that some hiring and promotion decisions in the workplace are made for arbitrary reasons. But that doesn't mean that an objective standard for measuring individual merit doesn't exist. It just means that some employers choose to ignore it.

Every job has a particular end in view. If you're a litigation lawyer who specializes in commercial disputes, you'll have to demonstrate a solid working knowledge of commercial law, corporate law and civil procedure, as well as a clear understanding of how business is done on a transactional level; you'll have to prove you can win cases; and you'll have to show that you're capable of turning out enough work to meet the firm's billable hour targets. Those requirements translate into employment criteria against which a candidate for hiring or promotion can be judged. Whether those criteria are properly applied is another matter.

The same approach can be used to develop criteria of merit for teachers, nurses, carpenters, morticians and stone masons. Every job has a particular function or end, which dictates the skills that are needed to achieve it, and those skills determine the criteria of merit that should govern employment decisions. This approach wouldn't seem to apply to entrepreneurs, since they seem to define merit on their own terms. However, that is only appearance. Every self-employed person is successful because he or she has an insight into what the public needs or wants. That insight must be reduced to the provision of a service or a product. Providing either will require that the entrepreneur and his or her team offer a particular set of skills. Those skills then translate, as they do for employees, into criteria of merit. But, in this case, the market will be the ultimate judge of whether the entrepreneur has met the criteria and deserves to succeed.

The idea of merit goes hand in hand with the concept of equal opportunity. However, for equal opportunity to become a reality, it must become inscribed in the hearts of the people. They must believe in it so completely that they freely promote it every day in their dealings with others in schools, the workplace, government, political parties and community organizations. Unfortunately, this isn't happening on a consistent basis in Canada today. That's because many Canadians seem to be confused about what equal opportunity means in theory and in practice.

My Perspective

Since this book has a great deal to say about politics and governance, readers will want to know more about my perspective. Am I a Liberal or a Conservative? Or am I a crypto-Republican, who secretly wants Canada to model itself on the United States? I could best be described as a small "c" conservative, but not in the sense that I believe that all social and economic problems can be solved by relying on market forces. I'm a conservative in the sense that I believe in conserving the fundamental principles of liberal democratic justice that have guided the political and economic development of Western nations. Those nations, which include Canada, the United States, Australia and the member states of the European Union (EU), are described as Western because they govern themselves by those principles. They all believe that government can rule only with the consent of the people (that's the democratic part); they also believe that the state should protect fundamental human rights, the primary goal of civil society is economic prosperity and everyone should be free to live in accordance with his or her own conception of the good (those are the liberal parts).[10]

When considering major political issues, I often look for guidance from the writers and philosophers who played a major role in developing the leading principles that guide liberal democratic life: Hobbes, Locke, Montesquieu, Kant, de Tocqueville, J.S. Mill and the Federalists. I turned to these thinkers while studying law and political science at the graduate level at the University of Toronto, the University of Chicago and Columbia University. Their thought informs every chapter in this book.

Since political life in North America takes place within this broad agreement about the goals of liberal democracy, political disputes are often narrowly drawn and based on popular trends in thinking generated by the media and political parties rather than on sober reflection on the meaning of our founding principles. And that's understandable. To many, it might seem absurd to resolve political issues in the 21st century by examining ideas that were developed in the 18th century. Given all the radical changes that have been wrought by the collapse of communism, globalization and the microchip, it's hard to believe that these writers could teach us something that is relevant to the demands of daily life. Beyond the commonsense objection, we have to face the challenges posed by historical and cultural relativism. In today's universities, certain schools of thought deny that it's possible to learn anything important from historical texts. According to the relativist view, writers such as Locke and Kant created ideas that were determined by the historical and cultural circumstances of their own time and place. Their ideas may have been right for their situation but not for ours; so, the relativists argue, it's impossible to use their works to guide our political reflections. Then there is the challenge of post-modernism, which denies that we can gain access to the meaning of an historical text. Post-modernists believe that our sensibilities have been shaped so thoroughly by our circumstances that we can't even begin to understand how to read a text that was shaped by entirely different circumstances.

These views may or may not be true. However, they all share a common weakness. They discourage anyone from reading historical texts with an open mind and considering that they might contain truths about the human condition. This problem was neatly summarized by Canadian speechwriter, Mari Silverstein, who once said that the post-modernists are skeptical about everything except their own skepticism.

I choose to proceed on the assumption that the writers who gave us liberal democracy deserve the benefit of the doubt—for two reasons. First, they claimed to have discovered the starting point for discovering principles of justice that are universal, in the sense that they are applicable in all times and places. The *Declaration of Independence* begins with the words, "We hold these truths to be self-evident, that all men are created equal, that they are endowed by their Creator with certain unalienable rights, that among these are life, liberty and the pursuit of happiness." This language is not indicative of American arrogance; rather it reveals that the framers of the Constitution were influenced by the liberal philosophers, who claimed to have discovered the truth that justice is secured only when government protects the natural rights of its citizens. If we are to take our own tradition seriously, we need to begin by opening ourselves to the possibility that these principles embody the truth about political justice and that they deserve our allegiance (see Chapter 7). The second reason that I choose to work within the liberal democratic tradition is that it is *our* tradition. Even if that tradition is open to question or might be improved upon, to understand ourselves—what we have valued and should still value—we must begin by understanding the higher principles by which we have chosen to govern our lives. We must begin by being true to ourselves.

If we hope to realize our economic potential as a nation, we must begin by giving every individual a chance to realize his or her potential, and that requires a more complete commitment to establishing an equal opportunity society. In this book, I will demonstrate that certain Canadian beliefs and practices fall short of promoting the equal opportunity ideal, and that this is the source of our declining standard of living. I will also argue that we need to reflect on the American situation to learn more about the practical meaning of the equal opportunity ideal, all the while keeping in mind that this ideal was not given to us by America, but rather, by reason itself.

Myth Two

CANADA IS A PRODUCTIVE & PROSPEROUS COUNTRY

What Do the Numbers Say?

Some of our political leaders say that we shouldn't worry about the fact that Canada's standard of living is 20% lower than America's because, after all, compared to the rest of the developed world, Canada's performance is the envy of all. To assess that claim, we can examine comparative economic reports that are provided by the Organization for Economic Development and Co-operation (OECD) as part of its mandate of promoting democratic government and free markets among its 30 member states. When we look at the results for Canada, we find that it's highly ranked on the basis of Gross Domestic Product (GDP) per capita and the rate of economic growth. Unfortunately, we also see that over time Canada has been losing ground. To understand how OECD economists produced these findings, we need to review briefly the basic principles that guide their studies.

First, let's recall that the GDP is defined as the measure of all goods and services (the actual wealth) produced by a nation in a given year. The GDP *per capita* is calculated by dividing a nation's GDP by its population. In order to compare the relative value of GDP per capita among member states, the OECD takes the U.S. dollar as its standard.

There are two ways to rank countries on this basis. The first is to calculate the GDP per capita for each country other than the United States, and then convert those figures to the U.S. dollar based on current exchange rates. The second method, which is the one actually used by the OECD, is based on the concept of purchasing power parity. This approach is a little more sophisticated. The OECD takes a bundle of consumer goods in America, and determines how many U.S. dollars would be needed to purchase them. Then it determines how many units of foreign currency would be needed to purchase the same goods in each member state. The final step involves ranking the states based on the ratio of prices for the bundle of goods. Here's a brief example, taken from the World Bank website, which explains how this ratio is determined:

> A simple and humorous example of a measure of absolute PPP [purchasing power parity] is the Big Mac index popularized by the *Economist*, which looks at the prices of a Big Mac burger in McDonald's restaurants in different countries. If a Big Mac costs USD$4 in the US and GBP£3 in Britain, the PPP exchange rate would be £3 for $4.[1]

Establishing the ratio of prices simply involves measuring the value of the English Big Mac in American dollars. That's done by dividing the U.S. price ($4) by the British price (£3), which gives a result of US$1.33. If the Big Mac was taken as the sole standard of measurement, then this comparison indicates that one British pound buys US$1.33 of goods in the United States. In practice, of course, comparisons are made among a bundle of consumer goods and the average result of the comparisons would become the true PPP exchange rate for the two currencies.

I will indicate any calculation made on the basis of purchasing power parity (PPP). If I do not indicate PPP when citing comparative statistics, then the comparison is based on the currency exchange rate. In my experience, the PPP rate is almost always lower than the currency exchange rate, as the McDonald's example shows. So, we can take PPP as the low-end estimate of the difference between two countries and the currency exchange as the high-end estimate.

Now that we've established the difference between the two ways of using the U.S. dollar as a standard measure, we can return to the OECD's analysis of Canadian economic performance. According to OECD studies, Canada reached its economic zenith when it placed third in GDP per capita among member states in the years just after the Second World War. Unfortunately, over the past three decades, Canada has gradually slipped. As of 2000, it was eighth on the list with a GDP per capita of US$27,000 (PPP), while the United States ranked second at US$35,619. (Luxembourg was first at US$47,053.) Although Canada has made gains since 2000, by the end of 2003 it was in the sixth position at US$31,000, while the United States was second again at US$37,600. Comparisons between the OECD countries and Ontario, which produces over 40% of Canada's GDP, are more favorable. In 2000, for example, if Ontario had been placed on the OECD list, it would have ranked third in average GDP per capita at US$36,808 (PPP).[2]

While it's encouraging that Canada is moving up on the GDP scale, and Ontario sits higher, the statistics on historical growth rates are less cheerful. From 1950 to 2001, Canada had the third lowest real growth rate among all OECD countries.[3] And even though during the 1990s Canada had an annual growth rate that was slightly higher than the OECD average, Canada ranked 15th among the 22 member states on this measure.[4]

By comparing Canada and the United States in the post-war period, we can see how we reached our current position. For almost 20 years, from 1946 to 1973, when measured on the basis of real GDP per capita, Canada's economy grew 16% faster than America's.

However, the United States went on a tear over the next 20 years. Its economy grew 36% faster than Canada's during the 1980s, and 325% faster during the first-half of the 1990s. Canada finally reversed the trend between 1995 and 2001, when it regained supremacy and grew 20% faster.[5]

We can add to this picture by comparing the Canadian and American real GDP per capita at various key points. In 1946, the Canadian real GDP per capita was 72% as compared to the United States' on the basis of purchasing power parity. In 1975, it reached 91%, but then began to decline in the 1980s, until it reached 81% in 1992, where it has remained, give or take a few percentage points. The good news is that Canada has narrowed the real GDP gap by around 10 percentage points since 1946. The bad news is that we were very close to catching up in the late 1970s and early 1980s; then we lost significant ground.[6]

Even though Ontario's situation is generally brighter, recent studies demonstrate that Ontario still has a long way to go. Here I draw on information provided by the *Ontario Task Force on Competitiveness, Productivity and Economic Progress*, which was established by the Ontario government in the year 2000 under the direction of Roger Martin, Dean of the University of Toronto's Rotman School of Business. The work of the task force is extremely important for Ontario, and the country as a whole, because it represents the very first publicly supported, non-partisan attempt to determine how to make a Canadian province more competitive in the global marketplace. The lessons we learn from this study may very well influence decision-makers in the public and private sectors in Canada for years to come. With seven major studies and three annual reports in circulation, the task force has already provided us with some immensely helpful information that elucidates the causes of our declining standard of living.

The task force compares economic data in Ontario and its "peer group," which is comprised of North American jurisdictions that rival

Ontario in size, population and level of economic activity: New York, New Jersey, Massachusetts, California, Illinois, Texas, Virginia, Georgia, North Carolina, Pennsylvania, Ohio, Michigan, Florida, Indiana and Quebec. Using this method, the task force has already confirmed the bad news that we've heard from the TD Bank, the OECD and independent economists. In its 2002 annual report, the task force concluded that Ontario ranked 13th in relation to its 16 peers in GDP per capita, and 30th as compared to all 50 American states. It also found that the gap between Ontario and the top three peer states was significant. While Ontario's GDP per capita was US$30,420 (PPP), New York came in at $42,115 (PPP), New Jersey at $43,151 (PPP) and Massachusetts at $44,878 (PPP).[7]

The foregoing leaves us with several different takes on the Canadian situation. If we rely on the OECD studies, which employ the method of purchasing power parity, Canada's standard of living is 15% lower than America's. If we rely on the TD Bank studies, in which the bank employs its own unique PPP analysis, the gap appears to be 20%. When we refer to the Ontario Task Force, and compare Ontario's position to its top rivals, the gap is over 45% for Ontario, and considerably higher than 45% for most of the other provinces. However we look at it, Canada and the United States are separated by a very real prosperity gap. That leaves us with the problem of determining why the gap exists, and how it can be bridged.

Two Causes—One Solution

According to leading economists, as well as the Ontario Task Force, Canada cannot improve its standard of living relative to the United States in conventional ways. We cannot increase GDP by increasing the participation of people in the workforce because the number of working-age people is declining. Nor can we do it by increasing the number of hours worked, because we're already working long hours and are very close to leading American states in this regard. We could increase wealth by lowering our unemployment rate. But that begs the question: What kind of policies do we need to make that happen?

During the past 25 years, we were able to increase productivity, in large measure, simply by getting more people into the workforce. That was possible because members of the baby boom generation were flooding the job market. However, Canada's demographic profile militates against making further gains on this basis. By the year 2018, the working-age population will begin to shrink dramatically due to the mass retirement of baby boomers, with the result that fewer workers will be producing for an expanding, dependent population. This problem becomes more pressing when we consider that the United States will not experience the same shrinkage in its workforce because it has a younger working-age population. All things being equal, these demographic facts dictate that Canada's standard of living will continue to decline relative to that of the United States.[8]

Since we can't increase the number of people in the workforce, or dramatically increase the hours they work, we're left with two ways of improving our standard of living. The first is to find ways of producing goods and services more efficiently.[9] The second is to create new products that increase our wealth by generating new forms of demand in world markets.

The need for more efficient production is supported by statistics that demonstrate that America's higher standard of living is directly related to its superior *productivity*. In 1946, when the prosperity gap was almost 30%, America was 40% more productive than Canada; in 1977, when the prosperity gap was around 10%, the United States was 10% more productive; and in 2002, when the prosperity gap was at least 15%, and perhaps as high as 20%, the United States was 20% more productive. Ontario's position compared to its peer group underscores the problem. In 1997, the last year for which figures are available, Ontario ranked 13th on the list of 16 cohorts and was 25% less productive than Massachusetts, 31% less productive than New Jersey and 40% less productive than New York.[10]

The need for more creative production—our second solution—is reflected in statistics regarding patent registration. In 1998, for instance, the patent registration rate in Canada was 31 per million persons, whereas the U.S. rate was 289 per million. When you think about it, this is a staggering difference—proportionately, Americans register almost *10 times* as many inventions as Canadians. Ultimately this difference translates into a mammoth American advantage in creating new forms of wealth.[11]

However, Canada's low rate of invention is not a problem that exists only in comparison to the United States. According to the World Economic Forum, which ranks 58 countries based on economic analyses and surveys of over 4,800 business leaders from around the world, Canada fares poorly in measures related to creative production. For example, in 2004, Canada ranked 28th in the world in the "propensity to compete on the basis of unique products rather than low cost labor or raw materials," and 25th in the creation of new brands, which correlates with the tendency of a country to compete on the basis of unique products.[12]

The Rate of Innovation Determines Future Prosperity

Dr. Horace ("Woody") Brock, President of Strategic Economic Decisions, has produced a theory that contributes to our understanding of how innovation fueled the American economic boom during the last two decades of the 20th century. During this period, compared to any other nation in the world, and even the European Community, the U.S. had the greatest rate of productivity growth, the fastest growth of investment spending as a share of GDP, the largest net growth in employment, the greatest improvement in fiscal balance, and the highest rise in corporate profits. Relative to itself, it also experienced an unprecedented rise in national net worth. Dr. Brock's thesis is that America's superior economic performance during the 1990s can be attributed to its superior levels of innovation; and this fact continues to augur well for American prosperity in spite of the dot.com collapse and the large national debt that has been incurred by recent tax cuts and the war on terror.

The key to understanding America's prosperity in the late 20th century is not simply to focus on the rate of innovation as reflected in the patent figures cited above. The American advantage consists in its global share of new technologies that have been patented, funded and *commercialized* in the United States. According to Dr. Brock, from the mid-1980s to the end of the 1990s, "America created 85% of the world's share of commercialized technologies even though it produced only 25% of the world's GDP." Dr. Brock expresses this advantage in the form of a ratio, referred to as the Relative Innovation Quotient (RIQ), which relates the share of a country's innovation to its share of the world's Gross Domestic Product. On this basis, the United States led the world with a ratio 17:1. (The mathematics that produces this result is too complex to reproduce here, but I cite the result to give you some idea of the magnitude of the American advantage in innovation.) Dr. Brock stated that "no other single nation ha[d] a quotient that even equals unity, with the possible exception of Taiwan or Japan." In other words, the ratio for almost all other nations was at least .9:1 or lower. Even the European Community with its 30 member states was far behind the United States with a Relative Innovation Quotient of 10:1.

According to Dr. Brock, the truly important point about America's superior rate of innovation is that it allowed the United States to lead the world in productivity gains, which in turn accounted for America's superior rate of capital investment and its superior growth in GDP. These conditions were related synergistically. America's preeminent rate of innovation produced a superior rate of productivity, which, in turn, produced larger profits, which, in turn, gave American companies the surplus that allowed them to lead the world in making new capital investments, particularly in information and communications technology. And those investments led to further increases in productivity, which, in turn, produced greater profits. This interaction of innovation, productivity, profits and capital investment was ultimately reflected in America's superior GDP growth, that is, in superior wealth creation.

America's rate of innovation and its impact on wealth creation also explains why America led the world in job creation (innovation created more jobs than it eliminated); why household net worth increased substantially (wages, housing and equity investments all increased in value); and why the U.S. government went into a surplus position for a brief period (the creation of more jobs and wealth provided a larger base of taxation).[13]

Where Does This Leave Us?

I began this chapter by demonstrating that studies conducted by leading authorities indicate that Canada's standard of living is anywhere from 15% to 20% lower than America's. If we compare Ontario to leading American states, we find the gap widens to at least 45%. Put simply, Americans have more wealth at their disposal. This immense and growing prosperity gap has been caused by a productivity gap—a lower rate of efficiency in the production of goods and services—and a creativity gap—a failure to match America's seemingly boundless ability to create new products. (And, based on Dr. Brock's analysis, we can see that there is a correlation between the rate of innovation (creativity) and the rate of productivity, so that Canada's productivity gap can be linked to its creativity gap.) To solve these problems, we need to develop policies that will encourage Canadians to create new products and discover new ways of producing existing products.[14] While Canada's federal and provincial governments have established programs aimed at bringing about these results, our statistical analysis indicates that these programs are failing.

So, if we want to close the prosperity gap, our challenge is to develop a new innovation strategy that will improve our creativity and productivity. But this produces a conundrum. I've already argued (i) that our governing elites are mired in bad thinking; (ii) that this is manifested in beliefs and policies that undermine the equal opportunity ideal; (iii) that this, in turn, has compromised the liberal goal of liberating human potential; and (iv) that this, in turn, has prevented us from attaining a higher standard of living. Given that our elites hold beliefs that are opposed to vindicating the ideal that promotes productivity and creativity, how can we expect them to create policies that will put us on the road to closing the prosperity gap with the United States? If we can't expect a solution from above, we need one from below. *Every citizen will have to rethink how we do things in Canada, and bring that thinking to bear on the conduct of public business.* This book is one example of how we might attack and correct the deeply flawed beliefs of our elites and begin the process of rethinking how our country should be governed.

Causes of the Productivity and Creativity Gaps

We have to begin by examining the economic and political conditions that have caused the creativity and productivity gaps. I will explore these conditions based on studies conducted by independent thinkers, the Ontario Task Force and participants at the TD Economic Forum. This analysis will allow us to begin to reason our way toward policy solutions that will close the prosperity gap. At the same time, it will compel us to examine the mistaken notions that have compromised the equal opportunity ideal. Such faulty thinking will have to be challenged before decision-makers can enact innovative policies that will improve our standard of living.

Lack of Investment in Research and Development

Canada's low level of investment in research and development (R&D) is a problem that has been dogging us since the end of the Second World War. In the year 2002, Canada spent 1.85% of GDP on R&D, while the United States spent 2.82%. OECD figures underline the fact that we are underinvesting not just in comparison to the United States, but also in comparison to other Western nations. In 2000, among the 30 member states of the OECD, the United States ranked fourth in R&D investment, while Canada was 14th. Canada's abysmally low level of patent registration and low level of productivity reflect a failure to invest in R&D that would foster the development of new products and more efficient production processes.[15]

The reasons for Canada's relatively poor commitment to research and development are well known and really quite basic. They speak to the fact that the Canadian economy, with its enormous base of natural resources, has always been oriented toward exporting commodities, an activity that does not require a large investment in R&D. Also, a significant segment of the Canadian economy, particularly manufacturing, is comprised of branch plants or subsidiaries of American companies. American businesses tend to do most of their R&D work at head offices in the United States with the result that Canadian subsidiaries do not receive the mandate or the resources to create new products or production processes.[16]

For more than 15 years, both the federal and provincial governments have implemented programs designed to increase our R&D

activity. In Ontario, since 1987, the federal and provincial governments have combined funding to establish Centers of Excellence, which establish partnerships between government, business and academia to promote cutting-edge research in commercially viable technologies. The total investment in Ontario's five centers is approximately $127 million per year. More recently, the federal government has substantially increased its funding for councils that conduct scientific and technical research. And it has also undertaken to create 2,000 research chairs at universities across the country over the next few years, at a total cost of $900 million. The federal strategy is completed by the R&D tax credit, which provides companies with around $1.5 billion in tax incentives annually.[17]

While the tax credit should be the most effective aspect of the federal strategy, so far, it seems to have had little impact. Dr. Jack Mintz, economist and president of the C.D. Howe Institute, believes the reason is that any gains that accrue from the credit are offset by the relatively high tax burden on business.[18] Clearly, Canada must keep the R&D credit in place and also examine other ways of encouraging R&D. Only by doing this can we hope to invent new products and new production techniques that will raise our standard of living.

Lack of Investment in Education

For over 40 years, most Canadians have believed that our public education system at the primary and secondary levels is superior to the American public system. And, until recently, this was true, if we take money as an indicator and Ontario as the example. Until the late 1990s, Ontario was investing more than its peer states in primary and secondary education. By 1999, however, Ontario began to fall behind. Measuring the difference in Canadian dollars, Ontario was spending only 84% of the U.S. level on primary and secondary education on a per-student basis and 74% of the U.S. level on community colleges. When it comes to university education, the United States has been outspending Ontario for quite some time. And recent figures verify that this is still the case. From 1995 to 1999, the United States spent an average of CAN$31,227 per student while Ontario spent almost half as much, posting an average of CAN$18,334. This striking difference is due to the fact that American private schools have significantly higher tuition fees and much larger endowments. The endowments, which are investment funds derived principally from alumni donations, generate revenue to underwrite operating expenses, research projects and scholarships. The average American endowment at private schools is CAN$126,000 per student. At elite private universities, such as Harvard, Yale and Princeton, the endowments provide over US$1 million for every student. Ontario universities, have endowments that provide, on average, CAN$7,000 per student.[19]

Some people might object that comparing Ontario's public university system with the American private system is unfair. To get a better understanding of how well we're doing, we should be comparing our system to their public system. And there's logic in that position. No one has ever attempted to establish a well-funded private university on Canadian soil. The public-to-public comparison yields interesting results. On average, U.S. state universities spend only 10% more per student than Canadian public universities. However, state schools have an average of CAN$15,000 per student in their endowments, over twice the Canadian figure. This suggests that American public universities can provide greater funding for vital resources such as research facilities and library collections.[20]

While it's tempting to focus our attention on our position in relation to American state schools, that perspective tends to obscure the problem that we are facing from an economic standpoint. The fact is the United States has a large, lavishly funded private university system, which represents an investment in higher education that is overwhelming when compared to Ontario and Canada as a whole. That investment gives America two significant advantages. First, it allows the university system to produce thousands of more highly trained graduates every year. And second, it facilitates a larger investment in cutting-edge research that promotes the development of new products and new production processes. Thus, America's superior investment in post-secondary education translates into conditions that allow it to achieve higher levels of creativity and productivity, and in turn, a higher standard of living.

America also has an advantage in terms of the level of attainment at the university level and in subjects that are studied. At first glance, Canada and the United States seem to have similar levels of educational attainment. In 1999, the OECD reported the average Canadian and American each had approximately 13 years of education. It also found that Canada and the United States had similar levels of post-secondary education—40% for women and 36% for men in Canada; 34% for women and 35% for men in America. This finding is supported by Roger Martin, who notes that the United States has proportionately only 5% more university grads with B.A.s than we do, and only 6% more grads in science and technology. However, this is where the similarity ends. In post-graduate studies, that America outperforms us to an embarrassing extent, producing proportionately 103% more graduates with Master's degrees and 76% more graduates with Doctorates. As well, the United States produces almost twice as many business graduates and over two and half times as many MBA graduates. Martin is particularly concerned about the deficit in business education, which is not being addressed by the federal government's most recent investment in higher education. Of the

2000 new university positions that will be funded by Ottawa over the next few years under the Canadian Research Chairs program, only 10 will go to business scholars. Martin points out that if Canada were investing in business education on a par with the United States, the federal government would be funding 400 chairs in business schools. The federal underinvestment in business is also reflected in the Initiative on the New Economy, which provides funding for studies on the impact of the new economy; the initiative has a $200 million budget but allocates only $25 million for business programs.[21]

The fear expressed by some critics is that Canada's lower level of achievement in post-graduate training and our chronic underachievement in business education may be contributing significantly to the prosperity gap. Since innovative research tends to be conducted by individuals with post-graduate degrees, America's training advantage produces a greater capacity to produce discoveries that lead to the creation of new products and more efficient production techniques. The same can be said for America's superior investment in business education. A larger investment in business research and a larger cadre of business graduates translates into a greater ability to find ways of commercializing the discoveries that result from innovative research.

Lack of Investment in Information and Communications Technology (ICT)

Much of the increase in the productivity gap that occurred during the latter half of the 1990s can be attributed to the fact that the United States made substantial productivity gains in the ICT sector. Those gains occurred because Americans made a much larger investment in the ICT sector during the first half of the 1990s, and that investment had a disproportionate impact on general productivity since the ICT sector represents a larger share of the total economy as compared to Canada. The impact of ICT investment on overall productivity was further enhanced by the fact that sectors heavily reliant upon ICT, such as retail, financial services and professional services, also invested heavily in ICT applications during the early 1990s. It's possible that Canada will close the ICT productivity gap in this decade because we invested heavily in the ICT sector and in ICT applications during the latter half of the 1990s. However, the jury is still out on this one. Clearly, though, since ICT investment has produced a sector advantage and a general economic advantage for a wide range of businesses in other sectors in the United States, Canada must continue to invest in ICT if it hopes to narrow the ICT productivity gap as well as the national productivity gap.[22]

Lack of Investment in Machinery and Equipment

Not only are we not investing enough in R&D and ICT, we're also not investing enough in machinery and equipment. This conclusion is fully supported by the work of the Ontario Task Force. (Ontario is the obvious standard because, among all the provinces, it has the largest manufacturing base.) Since 1981 Ontario has trailed the United States in capital investment by about 10%, and since the early 1990s, the gap has increased, as Americans continue to invest more than we do to make their operations more competitive and efficient. The task force believes Ontario's declining investment has been caused by the depreciation of the Canadian dollar, which increased the cost of purchasing foreign-made equipment and encouraged businesses to compete on the basis of lower labor costs. The incentive to invest was also squelched by the burden of capital taxes, which are applied to equipment and machinery as part of an overall levy on coporate equity and certain aspects of corporate debt. While Canadians can't do much at the moment about the dollar, they can and should consider abolishing the capital taxes to encourage the capital investment that is needed to promote Canadian productivity.[23]

Governments Have Favored Consumption over Investment

According to the Ontario Task Force, Ontario has failed to exploit possible productivity gains because it has underinvested in the infrastructure, particularly in urban areas. Infrastructure investment is a key driver of productivity because it facilitates economic transactions (for instance, well-maintained roads promote the efficient transport of goods), and it attracts talented workers (well-developed urban areas are magnets for creative people). This problem is reflected in figures comparing government spending on investment and services over the last decade. In 1992, Ontario spent 53 cents on investment for every tax dollar spent on services, while its peer states spent 51 cents. By 2000, the Ontario figure dropped to 47 cents while the peer states' figures rose to 52 cents. In terms of total expenditures, Ontario invested $6.1 billion more than the average peer states in 1992; however, by 2000, the peer states on average spent $3.8 billion more than Ontario.*

While the U.S. peer states are spending more on investment, they seem to be spending less on essential services. Between 1992 and 2000, Ontario's spending on services fell drastically from 50% of GDP to 37%; but, it still managed to spend more than the peer states, which dropped from 38% to 33% during the same period. These figures turn out to be deceiving, though. Since the peer states' superior productivity gave them a larger GDP than Ontario, they could tax less and still spend more on a per capita basis. So, superior productivity gives the peer states a triple bonus: it allows them to spend more on infrastructure and more on essential services, while maintaining lower tax rates. And by spending more on infrastructure, they gain a further long-term

*Dollar amounts in Canadian currency.

competitive advantage over Ontario. Thus, we're left with a dilemma. If we increase government spending on infrastructure to increase productivity, we will also compromise the provision of essential services, such as health care. On the other hand, if we don't increase government spending on infrastructure, we might forgo future gains in productivity that will allow us to provide more essential services at lower tax rates.[24]

Lack of Business Clusters

The concept of a business cluster was developed by Harvard business professor, Michael Porter, and is used by the Ontario Task Force to analyze the competitive potential of various industries such as pharmaceuticals, biotechnology and entertainment. In Porter's work, a business cluster exists when a specific economic sector enjoys synergistic conditions that allow it to develop world-class products that are traded in international markets. When these conditions—four in total—come into being, they reinforce each other to create a whole that is greater than the sum of its parts.

The first condition exists when there are sophisticated and demanding customers in the home market; serving such customers forces the companies in a particular sector to innovate constantly to remain competitive. The second exists when companies within a sector have rivals that compete against one another for market share; this forces all companies to constantly upgrade their products. The third exists when a sector enjoys "input conditions" that support the upgrading process; they include such things as natural resources, a highly skilled workforce and university research facilities. The fourth condition exists when upgrading of sector products is supported by companies that supply high-quality components. When these four factors interact, they produce a chain reaction that creates the economic nova that Porter refers to as a business cluster.

Porter stresses that the cluster concept does not depend for its success on the concept of comparative advantage, which holds that certain industries are suited to particular geographic locations due to the existence of favorable input conditions, such as natural resources. Japan's conquest of the electronics market proves the point. Now that intellectual innovation has become the primary driver of economic success, Porter believes that the old concept of *comparative advantage* should be replaced by the concept of *competitive advantage*, which is based on the notion that the "most important sources of prosperity are created, not inherited." This notion is married to the business cluster concept to create a new understanding of how businesses can succeed in the global marketplace. Porter's conclusion is that the cluster concept can be used to explain why some business sectors are super-innovative and super-competitive, and it can serve as a model of the development for industries anywhere in the world. As Porter advocates like to say, success is no longer about "where you compete" but "how you compete."[25]

Porter's cluster concept has been supported by a major study referred to as the U.S. Cluster Mapping Project, which has established that "cluster industries [in the United States] have distinctly higher levels of innovation (patents), productivity and wages." Firms in clusters account for only 33% of total employment in the American regions that were studied, but they commanded 44% of regional business income and were over 80% more productive than firms that primarily served local markets. Using the method of the U.S. project, the Ontario Task Force has concluded that Ontario has clusters in the fields of entertainment, pharmaceuticals, biotechnology, financial services and automotive manufacturing. However, even though Ontario has a high proportion of employment in business clusters, the task force cannot explain why Ontario ranks poorly in productivity compared to most of its peer states. The task force hopes to explain that anomaly in future reports.[26] Nonetheless, for our purposes, we need only remember that Porter and his followers believe that the key to improving rates of creativity and productivity in Ontario, and Canada as a whole, is to create economic and political conditions that are friendly to the development of business clusters.[27]

Taxes Are Too High

It's hardly a secret that tax rates in Canada are higher on average than in the United States—in 2002, tax revenue in Canada was 29% of GDP as compared to 19% in the United States. The disparity is most easily seen in relation to personal rates. In Vancouver, for example, the top marginal rate of 44% kicks in at $116,000, while in Seattle the top rate of 35% kicks in at $326,000.[28] In studies conducted for the Ontario Task Force, economist Jack Mintz examines the impact of Canada's higher tax burden on labor and business, and concludes that Canada's tax rates place us at a competitive disadvantage vis à vis the United States.

On the labor side, Mintz calculates the average level of all taxes paid by employees and by employers on behalf of employees, and then subtracts the average level of government subsidies received for health care, education and social security to determine the "net" average tax burden on labor. Based on figures for the year 2000, this results in a finding that the average tax burden on labor in Canada was 55% as compared to 43% in the United States. On the business side, Mintz adds the average level of corporate income taxes, capital taxes, sales taxes and excise taxes, and then subtracts the average level of public subsidies, which include government grants and tax credits for investments in infrastructure and research and development, to come up with the "net" average tax burden on capital. This yields a finding that the average tax rate on capital in Canada is 24%, while it's only

15% in the United States. This difference is due, in part, to the fact that most American jurisdictions do not levy a capital tax, which is perhaps the most counter-productive tax in our system. Since it is applied to all business capital, it acts as a brake on investment that would make businesses more efficient, innovative and competitive.

Although in recent years Ontario has substantially reduced its tax rates, with some advantages accruing to labor, the tax burden on capital is still much higher than its peers. As a result, according to Mintz, if you take the average of all the taxes on business and labor in Ontario in 2002, and then compare it to the average in the peer states, Ontario's total disadvantage was over 9% on all costs.[29]

The finding that Ontario business taxes are not competitive is at first counter-intuitive since the top corporate rate in Ontario is 37%, which is lower than the average U.S. rate of 39%. However, Mintz concludes that the Ontario rate is effectively higher due to various advantages that accrue to business under the American tax system such as the absence of capital taxes, lower sales taxes, a more generous deduction for capital depreciation, a bonus deduction for new capital investment and greater public support for research, particularly in the transportation and communications sectors.[30]

Based on these findings, Mintz concludes in the August 2002 report of the Ontario Task Force that Canada's tax structure weighs down the economy and makes us less competitive than most American jurisdictions. The general situation is exacerbated by the fact that the Canadian tax burden is much greater in certain key sectors, such as communications. Mintz also believes that Canada's tax burden tends to discourage businesses from investing in research and development, in spite of the fact that Canada has a generous tax regime that favors R&D. As a result, our competitive standing suffers.[31]

Given Canada's relatively high tax burden, as we might imagine, several leading experts in the productivity debate have advocated significant tax cuts, and correspondingly, a reduction in the size of government. Certainly major tax cuts would have to be regarded as one of the major planks in a policy platform that aims at improving our productivity. Tax cuts for corporations would provide additional revenue that could be invested in new equipment and machinery that would facilitate productivity gains. Tax cuts for individuals would increase the pool of savings and thereby add to the money available in the banking system for loans to businesses that need to make capital investments to improve efficiency. In a more favorable tax environment, companies might also be encouraged to increase their investment in research and development, which, of course, would increase our national wealth by promoting the creation of new products.[32]

We Need to Aim Higher

According to Roger Martin, Canadians don't have an innovation supply problem: we have large numbers of scientists and technical personnel, a solid infrastructure of laboratories and research centers, and the R&D tax credit to support cutting-edge research. We do, however, have a demand problem, which has greatly contributed to our low level of innovation. Martin argues that many Canadian CEOs simply do not demand innovation from their employees. Because many Canadian companies aspire to compete within the Canadian market, rather than global markets, they do not face the external competitive pressure to maximize their investment in R&D. As Martin puts it, these companies serve the "most easily satisfied customers" and "tend to focus on replications of successful strategies observed in other markets, which require little R&D or investment in branding." They also face lower productivity levels due to the inherent inefficiencies in running smaller plants. While these firms could invest in innovation, it makes little sense to do so when they're not facing the pressure of world competition and the costs of innovation are relatively high, since they're spread over a limited market.

Companies that aspire to compete in global markets must invest in innovation because they face more demanding and sophisticated customers. If more Canadian companies took on the world, Martin argues, we could reap the productivity and creativity gains that result from innovation, as well as the productivity gains that result from economies of scale. However, how we encourage more Canadian companies to compete in global markets remains a problem. The hands of those running Canadian subsidiaries may be tied by decisions made in the United States. Nonetheless, in a free trade environment, Canadian-owned companies are facing world competition and will have to respond to it. Only time will tell whether free trade will force some of our companies to embrace a new outlook that improves our standard of living.[33]

Underemployment of Immigrants

Canada's immigrant population has the potential to improve the skill level of the workforce, and thereby boost our productivity. According to the Ontario Task Force, the skill level of new Canadians is much higher than that found in the U.S. immigrant population. The task force reports that over 60% of recent immigrants were trained in their country of origin in a profession or in a high-skill trade. This is reflected in the fact that over 40% of recent immigrants hold a university degree as compared to 20% of native-born Canadians. However, in spite of high levels of training, about half of educated immigrants are not working in their chosen vocation. This problem, needless to say, depresses immigrant earnings. The 2001 census reveals that immigrants were making 40% less than native-born workers. Immigrants who had been in Canada for 10 years reported earnings that were 16% less than the average for native-born workers.

The Ontario Task Force argues for establishing "bridging initia-tives" to ensure that Canadians are quickly streamed into the workforce at the appropriate level because "numerous studies have shown that the first job immigrants hold after immigrating can trap them in positions of underemployment." And, once that happens, the equal opportunity ideal is also affected, since we fail to take ad-vantage of the full productive potential of our fellow citizens. Sadly, the failure of Canadian employers, both public and private, to draw on the full potential of our workforce is a general problem and not limited to the case of recent immigrants. And that problem is con-tributing to our continuing inability to bridge the creativity and productivity gaps.[34]

Exports Are Too Low

During the past decade, trade with the United States has grown so dramatically that, by the year 2000, almost 83% of our exports went to America, while it provided us with 72% of our imports. These general figures, however, tend to obscure the regional patterns in the trading relationship. When you break down the figures province-by-province, you quickly realize that Ontario is largely responsible for carrying the relationship. In 2000, Ontario's exports comprised 57% of total exports to the United States. The contribution of the other provinces to trade paled in comparison. The next closest province was Quebec at 18%; the Prairie provinces weighed in at 14%, British Columbia at 7% and the Atlantic provinces at 4%.[35]

These figures confirm that Ontario is the only truly open econo-my among all the provinces. This perhaps explains why some provinces tend to prefer protectionist policies and have less favor-able attitudes toward the United States. Whatever the case, certainly these figures demonstrate that, with the exception of

Ontario, the other provinces have yet to fully exploit the opportunities presented by free trade. Thus, one clear way to improve our standard of living is for the provinces to find ways of increasing their trade with the United States. That, however, cannot be achieved until the business sectors in the provinces become more competitive by increasing their rates of productivity and creativity. Those goals point us in the direction of solving the other problems canvassed in this chapter.

Ten Solutions

So far, we have pinpointed 10 problems that contribute to Canada's declining standard of living and at least 10 solutions that would reverse the trend. The solutions are:

1. Increasing investment in R&D
2. Increasing investment in university education, and concomitantly, increasing enrollment in business programs and post-graduate programs
3. Increasing investment in ICT
4. Increasing investment in machinery and equipment
5. Shifting government expenditures toward investment and away from consumption
6. Promoting the development of business clusters
7. Reducing taxes, reforming the tax structure and reducing the size of government
8. Encouraging companies to compete in global markets
9. Accelerating the integration of highly trained immigrants into the skilled workforce
10. Increasing cross-border trade.

A very clear picture emerges from these 10 solutions.[36] The reason that Americans have a higher standard of living than we do is that they have invested more in future prosperity in both the public and private sectors over the last two decades. American governments have invested more per capita in post-secondary education, research and development, and infrastructure. While investing more in these important areas, American governments have also maintained lower corporate and personal tax rates as compared to Canada. As a result, they cleared the way for the private sector to make major investments in the conditions that promote prosperity, a fact that largely accounts for America's superior standard of living. American businesses have invested substantially more in research and development, machinery and equipment, and ICT. As well, American citizens have invested much greater sums proportionally in the private and public university systems

America's prosperity advantage, which has resulted from its investment advantage, is now creating a serious problem for Canada. The United States can leverage its superior prosperity to continue to invest more in the conditions that promote productivity and creativity. As a result, the United States may very well be on the road to achieving an advantage in living standards that Canada will never match. And, if that happens, the game will be over, since the ambitious and talented people we need to drive our economy forward will be emigrating to the United States in ever greater numbers. And the investors we need to create new opportunities will be looking to put their money in the United States, where it will get a higher return. These problems will become cataclysmic when the free trade regime is expanded to facilitate greater mobility of capital and labor.

To avoid economic capitulation, Canadians must begin to invest now in the conditions that promote future prosperity. However, that will require us to shift priorities and fundamentally change our patterns of spending, privately and publicly. Currently, the public is clamoring for governments to increase spending on health care, education and urban infrastructure. To achieve those goals, both the federal and provincial governments will have to raise taxes or maintain taxes at their current rates and shift spending away from other important areas, such as the environment or defence.

If governments were the primary drivers of economic growth, then raising taxes might contribute in some way to future prosperity. But, as we've seen above, that position is not supported by the American example. America's prosperity advantage has been created with a low tax regime that encourages private-sector investment in research and development, machinery and equipment, and ICT. The American example proves that Canadians must consider lowering taxes to create a macro environment that is hospitable to private sector investment in these areas. A more competitive tax regime is also essential to encouraging Canadian and American businesses to expand their operations in Canada. In a free trade environment, where the cost of doing business is a primary determinant of future investment, Canada must have competitive tax rates if it hopes to attract foreign and domestic capital. In support of this point of view, I cite Peter Nicholson, special advisor to Prime Minister Martin, who has argued that any increase in the size of government (hence the cost of government) is likely to result in a lower standard of living.[37] This is where we must confront current expectations and attitudes. I assume that Canadians would prefer to have a higher standard of living and a society that allows everyone to maximize his or her personal potential at work and in other aspects of life. Presently, many Canadians believe that these goals can best be achieved by increasing government spending on health care, education and our cities. But the facts as disclosed by the Ontario Task Force, the participants at the TD Economic Forum and leading economists demonstrate that spending more in all these areas will drive taxes up and discourage businesses from expanding operations here and investing in the conditions that promote prosperity.

Canadians will have to make some hard choices about how to allocate existing revenue between competing areas of concern. More generally, they will have to make a tough choice between a far-sighted prosperity agenda that would lower taxes to encourage private-sector investment and the conditions that promote productivity and creativity, and a short-sighted needs agenda that would produce higher taxes or higher public debt to satisfy the current demand for government services.

Assuming Canadians want a higher standard of living that will satisfy future needs more effectively, I would argue that there is no choice. Only the prosperity agenda will do the job. However, in the near term that means that citizens will have to accept greater responsibility for taking care of their own needs. They will have to pay more for their own health care needs, whether in a public system or a mixed private/public system; they'll have to contribute more to their own education; and, they may have to face tolls and user fees to bring about improvements in roads and transit.

Some might object that this is a prosperity agenda for those who don't currently need a high level of health care, who don't require further education or who don't live in large urban areas, and a poverty agenda for those who do. In other words, the prosperity agenda would be an unjust scheme that would force the costs of these goods and services onto the aged, the young and the working poor—those who can least afford to bear them. Furthermore, they might argue that the prosperity agenda makes no sense when measured purely in pure dollars and cents. The overall cost to society is the same whether these essential goods and services are paid for totally by the state or jointly by the state and the private individuals who need them. The first objection—that the prosperity agenda is unjust—is easily dealt with. It's a well-established principle in all liberal democratic societies that the cost of essential goods and services for the disadvantaged should be borne wholly or partially by the state. The prosperity agenda would remain consistent with that principle by providing assistance in the form of subsidies to those who are truly in need.

The second objection—that the prosperity agenda is a shell game—is based on the belief that the taxes that support essential goods and services do not necessarily discourage private-sector investment; that belief is based on the assumption that public goods and services encourage private investment because businesses are relieved of the burden of providing them as employment benefits. While there is certainly some truth in this assumption, the very existence of the prosperity gap suggests that companies have already made the decision that the current cost of doing business, as measured in the extra tax burden needed to provide these goods and services, has discouraged them from investing more in the areas that promote productivity and creativity. Given that this is the case, Canadians have to face the possibility that they will have to pay more out-of-pocket dollars for health care and post-secondary education to maintain tax rates that encourage companies to make investments in capital and R&D, both of which are essential to closing the prosperity gap with the United States.

Keep in mind that a prosperity agenda does not aim at shifting some of the costs of these goods and services to private individuals without any future reward. Based on the Ontario Task Force analysis of leading American states, we know that lower taxes can produce prosperity that eventually allows governments to provide greatly increased levels of goods and services. That's the situation the prosperity agenda seeks to achieve. In the near term, some citizens will have to pay more for essential goods and services, but in the long term everyone will be rewarded with a surplus that will finance social programs more effectively. The question for Canadians, then, is whether they will suffer some short-term pain for long-term gain.

Some experts believe that this is a false dichotomy because we've already made the sacrifices and investments that will eventually produce a higher standard of living. Call these folks the optimists. Others are not so sure. Call them the pessimists. Among the optimists, Peter Nicholson is the most persuasive. His positive view of Canada's future is based on an economic convergence theory that holds that countries with lower levels of productivity tend to catch up over time to the productivity leaders due to the diffusion of technology and best practices. To buttress his case, Nicholson points out that Canada made considerable strides in closing a labor-productivity gap with the United States during the mid to late 1970s when, he believes, this convergence process was at work. He also claims we see the same phenomenon within Canada itself, given that the economy of the Atlantic provinces has, on average, grown faster than Canada as a whole since at least 1960. Outside Canada, Nicholson offers Japan during the 1980s as the most striking example of successful convergence.

Due to the phenomenon of convergence, fiscal policies that have significantly reduced public debt, our solid showing in international student comparisons and the opportunities for economic expansion offered by free trade, Nicholson believes Canada is on course to close the productivity gap. Some experts might quibble about how strong our fiscal policies really are. But I think most observers would agree that the federal and provincial governments made substantial progress in reducing budget deficits and debt during the 1990s, and that this has promoted a more favorable environment for economic growth.[38]

Economist Andrew Sharpe is less sanguine than Nicholson about the potential for economic convergence with the United States. Based on his analysis, which indicates that our prosperity gap with the United States is 15%, Sharpe argues that Canada would have to grow 1% faster than the United States for the next 15 years to catch up. This, however, is unlikely to happen because, as Sharpe argues, Canada has never grown at that rate for 15 straight years at any time during the post-war period.[39] Sharpe's conclusion is even more dispiriting when we consider that the Baillie challenge, which is based on a belief that the prosperity gap is 20%, would require Canada to grow 1.6 percentage points faster than the United States for 15 consecutive years.

Nonetheless, Sharpe's figures on the productivity gap give Canadians a glimmer of hope. To close the productivity gap with the United States, which is the key to closing the prosperity gap, Sharpe argues that Canada's productivity would have to exceed America's by 1.2% each year for the next 15 years. (This finding is based on the fact that Canada's economy was 17.9% less productive than America's in 2001.) Fortunately, he concludes, Canada's productivity has grown that quickly for one 15-year period since the end of the Second World War.[40]

Even though, on balance, the numbers suggest that Canada would have trouble closing the prosperity gap with the United States, other Western countries have achieved sustained growth that has allowed them to substantially reduce their own gaps with the United States. Ireland is the foremost example. Over a 12-year period, Ireland reduced the gap by 32 percentage points, moving from a GDP that was 50% of the U.S. level in 1989 to a GDP that was 82% in 2001. The Irish case also suggests that it's possible to achieve productivity increases that exceed those in the United States by more than 1.2% per year for 15 straight years. The question is whether Ireland is relevant, given that its economy is only half the size of Canada's.[41]

Even if you agree that less productive nations tend to converge with the most productive nations over time, that's a tendency, not a certainty. Neither Ireland nor Japan has closed its own productivity or prosperity gaps with the United States. And Canada, which, presumably, has tended to converge in the past, has never managed to equal U.S. prosperity levels, in spite of achieving superior productivity and growth levels for sustained periods since 1945. Thus, we cannot count on convergence to completely eliminate the prosperity gap that separates Canada and the

United States. Clearly, then, any hope we have of closing the gap, and eventually exceeding American economic performance, depends on pursuing a prosperity agenda that embodies the 10 solutions mentioned above. But that would require *political will*—political leaders who would be willing to risk making fundamental changes in government policy, business leaders who would be willing to risk making fundamental changes in the way businesses are managed and a people that would be willing to embrace risk and all the changes—both bad and good—that come with it. But does the political will for change exist?

The Tolerance of Decline

Many of the 10 solutions—such as increasing investment in university education, increasing investment in R&D, increasing investment in business capital, significantly reducing the size of government or enacting major tax reform—have been on the table for years, but no government has pursued them with real vigor. It's true that the federal Liberals brought in a very generous R&D tax credit, but, so far, that has not resulted in substantial increases in R&D activity. It's also true that the federal Liberals have addressed the underinvestment in our universities by establishing 2,000 new research chairs. However, that must be seen against the background of chronic provincial underinvestment, as well as the vast increases in public and private investment in universities that occurred in the United States during the 1990s. At the end of the day, we must ask whether Canadians really care that their standard of living is falling, and if they do, whether they have the courage to explore the potential solutions to the problem. *In other words, does Canada's political culture—the fundamental beliefs that determine our choice of laws and policies—favor the reforms that are needed to achieve a higher level of prosperity?* So far, that question has not been properly addressed by the participants in the prosperity debate. The TD Bank skipped over the issue by asserting that it can be reduced to a lack of vision on the part of our political leaders. In the bank's view, Canadians would embrace reform only if someone would show them the way. This position, however, begs the question. Why have our leaders shown so little interest in meaningful reform? Isn't the fact that we have leaders who don't want to lead and people who don't demand to be led indicate that we all have political attitudes that need to be examined and challenged? How else can we explain this impasse?

To begin a serious examination of the deficiencies in our political culture, we need only ask why, for decades, we have tolerated the conditions that have taken us down the road of economic decline. Why have we put up with high taxes for so long? Why have we become inured to big government? Why have our businesses and governments failed to invest adequately in R&D? Why have governments and alumni allowed our university system to languish? Why do we fail to give full recognition to the value of business education and post-graduate training? Why have our businesses been slow to invest in information and communications technology? Why have governments enacted tax regimes that discourage investment in business capital? Why have governments failed to make necessary investments in urban infrastructure? Why have many of our companies limited themselves to competing in the national market? Why haven't we taken steps to accelerate the accreditation process for new Canadians with professional expertise? Why have some provinces failed to fully embrace free trade? We must answer these questions in order to fully understand the prevailing beliefs that have led to our current economic impasse. And then we must challenge those beliefs because they are preventing us from enacting the reforms on which our economic future and the very justice of our nation depend.

Myth Three

MULTICULTURALISM PROMOTES PEACE & PROSPERITY

Caveat Culture

This is a principled critique of multiculturalism. Some readers might presuppose that anyone who criticizes multiculturalism must be biased against minority groups and that any principles cited are there simply to rationalize that fact. Equally, readers might assume that a critic of multiculturalism is an extreme social conservative, who opposes an open immigration policy because he or she believes the success of North American politics is based on maintaining the integrity of its "white, Anglo-Saxon" heritage. For the record, I do not harbor any bias toward minorities; in fact, from 2000 to 2004, I acted on a pro bono basis for Umugenzi for Refugees, a Toronto-based non-profit organization that provided assistance to refugees from Africa and the Middle East for over a decade before it wound up its operations earlier this year. Umugenzi offered counseling, access to social services and volunteer job placements, which gave newcomers the Canadian work experience they needed to gain access to paid employment. I've also spent most of my adult years living in the center of large, cosmopolitan cities—New York, Paris, Chicago and Toronto. My preference for these cities has been based on my love of diversity—in tastes, backgrounds, culture, entertainment and, most importantly, ideas. I hope that my delight in living with diversity and my work in politics with groups like Umugenzi indicate that I am neither a bigot nor a social conservative who prefers social homogeneity.

In Chapter 1, I identified myself as a small "l" liberal democrat, who is interested in actualizing the principle of equal opportunity, which holds that educational and economic opportunities should be distributed on the basis of merit, not irrelevant criteria such as race, religion, culture, ethnicity or gender. A truly liberal society can and should be multicultural, in the sense of being blind to these distinctions when measuring the merits of individuals.

A liberal society also can and should be multicultural in the sense that it guarantees basic individual rights—such as freedom of speech and equality before the law—to everyone regardless of background or affiliation, because those rights are owed to all individuals by virtue of their status as free human beings. Among those rights is the freedom to live out cultural traditions and beliefs in the home, a temple or church, or even the dance hall at the local community center. That freedom is guaranteed to everyone equally, through fundamental rights such as freedom of religion, freedom of association and the freedom to pursue happiness. Properly understood, liberal democratic societies are designed to be multicultural because they guarantee fundamental rights without regard to culture, and, at the same time, they guarantee everyone the right to freely engage in cultural pursuits.

I favor a pluralistic, diverse society, which has an open, non-discriminatory immigration policy, and which, above all, is devoted to the guarantee of individual rights and the enjoyment of liberty.

You might say, "That's fine. I want that too. But isn't that what we already have? Doesn't our policy of multiculturalism promote that kind of society?"

To both questions, my answer is no.

By participating in federal and provincial election campaigns over the last two decades, I've learned that multiculturalism isn't what it seems to be. It fails to achieve many of its stated goals such as promoting mutual respect and understanding. It also undermines key liberal democratic principles because it fails to support the equal enjoyment of fundamental rights by every individual. In fact, the policy is inherently discriminatory. By government fiat, some groups receive funding to support cultural pursuits, while other do not; some groups receive preferences in employment opportunities, while others are passed over; and some groups are publicly recognized by government in various ways, while others are ignored. I'm all for multiculturalism. But not this kind. To explain how I reached this conclusion, I have to take you back 20 years, when I participated in my first federal election campaign and my theoretical education in liberal ideas collided head-on with the realities of practical politics.

The Summer of 1984

During the summer of 1984, I was working seven days a week for a Liberal candidate who was running for a seat in downtown Toronto in the federal election, which was to be held on September 4. My job was to provide independent policy advice on everything from street crime to Charter cases, while manning the phones, handing out pamphlets at supermarkets, prepping the candidate for debates, attending meet-and-greets, canvassing for votes door to door, handing out more pamphlets at supermarkets and sometimes making sure the door to the campaign office was locked at night. The riding was and still is more ethnically diverse than most other ridings in Toronto and, indeed, the country. To work in this riding was to become part of Canada's new multicultural mosaic. At first, this was simply a fact of the campaign for me. I didn't have a strong opinion on whether the prevailing vision of Canada as a nation of nations was workable or wise; however, a few weeks into the campaign, a dispute in the campaign office made me realize that multiculturalism was neither.

In the middle of a hot July afternoon, I entered the office hoping for some respite from our little air conditioner, but instead found myself in the middle of a heated exchange. Three men of color were complaining bitterly about something. I approached, but then held my distance; I could see that they were in no mood to include me in their shouting match. After listening for a few minutes, I came to understand what they were so angry about. A minor pamphlet, which had just been printed, had failed to mention any multicultural issues. I was stunned. Other pieces of campaign literature—glossier and larger than this one—had mentioned multiculturalism; we had Canadians from many cultures working on the campaign; and the campaign office was located in the most diverse part of the riding, making it readily accessible to minority communities. Under these conditions, I couldn't fathom why these men were so angry about the fact that a campaign worker had failed to mention multiculturalism in one pamphlet. Even more troubling was that I had no hope of engaging these individuals in a dialogue in order to address their concerns. Their perception of harm was so extreme that they were beyond talking it out.

That moment became an epiphany. I knew the party line. Multiculturalism was supposed to promote tolerance and understanding between racial and ethnic groups. Instead, I discovered that a simple omission of its mention could quickly produce anger, intolerance and misunderstanding, which could not be resolved by discussion. And this occurred among men of reason. One was a tenured professor at York University, the other a graduate student in economics at an American university and the third a recent graduate of the University of Toronto Law School.

As the campaign progressed, I continued to encounter the reality of multicultural politics on the ground. Prime Minister Turner held a rally to support multiculturalism at Harbourfront in Toronto on a sunny afternoon in August. Thousands of supporters of multiculturalism from around Metro were treated to displays of sequined and veiled dancers, while waiting for Mr. Turner to arrive. However, the pre-game show didn't do much to excite the crowd. Most looked away, indifferent, while chatting and sipping Classic Coke. Someone turned to me and said, "Ethnic dancing is great. I love being reduced to a cultural stereotype." When Mr. Turner finally took the podium, he had the good sense to avoid the standard multicultural pieties. He spoke about the deficit. The audience was grateful and set aside their Cokes for a moment. When a woman from Turner's old law firm rose to praise his commitment to social justice, the crowd resumed its chatting and drinking. I realized that many of the invitees had concluded that the festival was either boring or patronizing. After a summer of multicultural moments like these, I became deeply concerned that the policy was not doing much to create bridges between minorities and majorities.

That concern was deepened by encounters I had with minority leaders following the election. As I was mulling over my election experiences one day, I decided to call up a lawyer—a new Canadian who had been deeply involved in the campaign—to ask about her views on multiculturalism. Although some team members had viewed her participation as a sign of the campaign's minority appeal, she had a very different view of the matter. She told me: "Multiculturalism doesn't make you feel very good. You're labeled as a 'multicultural person.' You're not supposed to be well educated. Everyone has to help you because you're not good enough."

For this very capable woman, the policy had been damaging to her perception of herself as a competent professional and full-fledged citizen. She objected to the notion that she was a member a disadvantaged minority, a ward of the state and, only secondly and partially, a Canadian.

Deeper Realities

A few weeks later, I was invited to a small social gathering that was not related to the campaign. And, to my surprise, I found myself sitting in a cosy living room across from one of the angry protesters I'd encountered in our campaign office—the tenured professor. He turned out to be polite and urbane, and we had a pleasant converstation. We got along so well that I was able to raise some questions about the multicultural movement. I asked him whether he thought that discrimination against new Canadians was a serious problem. With a glint in his eye, he smiled and said no. Where was all his anger now? In addition to being well educated and cosmopolitan, I realized this man was politically astute. The meaning of the pamphlet incident was now abundantly clear. His anger had been real, but he had willfully indulged it and had encouraged his companions to do the same. He knew that multiculturalism allowed him to take the smallest grievance and turn it into an imbroglio to advance himself and his friends.

As the evidence mounted, I was forced to conclude that multiculturalism was not achieving many of its lofty goals. Instead of promoting tolerance and civility, it sometimes produced disputes; instead of creating respect for different cultural traditions, it engendered disrespect; instead of promoting equality, it made some people feel inferior; instead of empowering minority communities, it could be used by the sly to promote selfish agendas.

These results were troubling, and they promised to get worse because multiculturalism was becoming something more than a vote-getting strategy. It soon became a new interpretation of our past, a vision of our future and a formula for the redistribution of income and opportunities. Apparently benign symbols were transformed into powerful notions that had an immense influence on public policy. Among the many bad ideas that our political leaders have foisted on the country over the past 30 years, multiculturalism is one of the worst. It's a case study in how one small, mistaken notion can spread like a virus throughout the entire body politic, affecting how it sees, acts and feels.

In English Canada, there are no party lines in this matter. Politicians of all parties and ranks utter clichés about our multicultural heritage. While many French Canadians and Native Canadians saw what was coming and raised objections about losing their historical status as founding peoples, eventually their voices were drowned out by politicians who said, in effect, that the new Canada was a mosaic that encompasses any number of different cultures.

This vision has profoundly affected our political and legal principles. It inspired a new system of public justice known as affirmative action: certain minority groups were publicly identified as "disadvantaged" and hiring quotas were legislated to help them along. The logic behind this was tortured: if Canada were a cultural mosaic, we would not be truly Canadian until every culture was equally represented in every institution. Therefore, those who failed to discriminate constantly through affirmative action were guilty of discriminating against minorities.

Few will object to this reasoning in public; almost everyone seems to believe that it is consistent with liberal democratic principles. We are told that the public encouragement of cultural differences will increase tolerance, that affirmative action will favor equality of opportunity, that the vision of unity in diversity will make our fractious nation whole.

It is hard to argue with apple pie or with the Pollyanna who baked it. Intentions that seem too good to be true are very often too false to be good. In practice, as I began to understand in the summer of 1984, multiculturalism is self-defeating, illiberal and decidedly un-Canadian.

The Origins of Multiculturalism

Strangely, multiculturalism grew out of the attempt to convince French Canadians to remain part of Canada. In 1963, in response to growing unrest in Quebec, Prime Minister Lester Pearson appointed the Royal Commission on Bilingualism and Biculturalism (the B and B Commission), which was to report on "the existing state of bilingualism and biculturalism in Canada and to recommend what steps should be taken to develop the Canadian Confederation on the basis of an equal partnership between the two founding races." With an ongoing mandate, the B and B Commission reported in 1969 that special measures were needed to deal with Quebec's discontents. These were embodied in the Official Languages Act of 1969, which, among other things, declared that French and English would be Canada's two official languages, that both languages would be used in federal institutions, and Crown corporations and that federal services would be available across the country on a bilingual basis.

This solution also embodied Prime Minister Pierre Trudeau's vision that a bilingual Canada would represent the interests of French Canadians in Ottawa, while protecting the English-speaking minority in Quebec and French-speaking minorities in other parts of the country. The idea that Canada is a multicultural nation—an idea at variance with the Commission's mandate to concern itself with the "two founding races"—grew out of the fourth and final volume of the report, which was published in 1971. The Royal Commission was trying to assuage a small number of vocal minority leaders, who feared that their groups would be forgotten or mistreated in a bicultural Canada. Several measures were proposed, such as multicultural broadcasting to help minorities integrate into Canadian life while preserving their cultural identities: "Canadian society, open and modern, should be able to integrate heterogeneous elements into a harmonious system, to achieve unity in diversity."[1]

In the fall of 1971, Prime Minister Trudeau gave the report his blessing in Parliament: "To say that we have two official languages is not to say that we have two official cultures, and no particular culture is more official than another. A policy of multiculturalism must be a policy for all Canadians."[2]

At the time, he said that "the preservation of ethnic identity is a voluntary matter."[3] Because of the changing needs and attitudes of the ruling party, however, it soon became a state matter. In the mid-1970s, when the Liberals' once broad electoral base had been whittled down, the party decided to rely increasingly on the support of labor, women, the poor and recent immigrants. And so the government decided to secure its minority constituencies with special favors. Soon, the idea of special treatment was enthusiastically embraced by certain Liberals, who believed that visible or non-white minorities needed help "to overcome the effects of past discrimination suffered at the hands of whites." Other Liberals wanted to foster the cultural diversity that they (quite wrongly) supposed distinguishes Canada from the United States. This was a heady brew, combining the imperatives of the pork barrel with liberal guilt and anxiety about national identity.

Like many other Liberal ideas, multiculturalism was quickly endorsed by Mulroney's Conservatives after they won the federal election in 1984. For many, including the prime minister, this was political cunning. By associating themselves with minority interests, the Tories hoped to dress themselves up as truly "Progressive" Conservatives, with the hope of attracting votes from the old Liberal coalition to a new Conservative one based on "national consensus"—Quebec, the West, Ontario, women, minorities, *anyone*.

Soon, multiculturalism blossomed into its own ministry, and later, under the Conservatives, into the most prominent responsibility of the Secretary of State, David Crombie. Then the Tories took the next logical step and decided to make multiculturalism a permanent feature of Canadian government; they proposed the *Canadian Multiculturalism Act*, which was adopted by Parliament in 1988. It declared that it is "the policy of the Government of Canada to ... recognize and promote the understanding that multiculturalism is a fundamental characteristic of the Canadian heritage and identity and that it provides an invaluable resource in shaping Canada's future." Needless to say, since regaining power in 1993, the Liberals have used this legislation to ensure that multiculturalism continues to play an important role in the expression of national identity and the development of public policy.

Our Canadian Heritage?

But, is it true, as the Act states, that "multiculturalism is a fundamental characteristic of Canadian *heritage*," one that stretches back to our foundations? Although that claim has been embraced by the multicultural lobby to justify hand-outs and by federal politicians to bring in votes, the claim itself is false. No important multicultural movement existed before the 1960s. The history of Canada's settlement bears that out.

The first considerable wave of settlers after the explorers and traders, mostly French and British, were the United Empire Loyalists, numbering somewhere between 40,000 and 50,000, who fled the American colonies at the time of the Revolution. These were Americans whose ancestry was, for the most part, British, Scottish and Irish. The Loyalists were soon outnumbered by other American settlers who entered Canada (in search of land) at the end of 18th century and the beginning of the 19th century. (By 1812, almost four-fifths of Upper Canada's 100,000 inhabitants were American-born, and of those only one-fifth were Loyalists or their descendants.) More than a million working-class British and Irish entered the country between 1812 and 1851. At the time of Confederation, Canada was a mixture of French, Loyalists, Americans, recent British and Irish immigrants and Aboriginal peoples.[4]

Did an increase in immigration soon after Confederation create a cultural mosaic? The first wave of European immigration (excluding the British and French) began in the late 19th century and continued into the 20th century. It included Germans, Ukrainians, Poles, Dutch, Danes, Hungarians, Russians, Italians and Jews. In 1881, these groups together made up 8% of the population. There was virtually no immigration from other sources: the Chinese and Japanese together comprised one-tenth of 1% of the population, and blacks, who left the United States after the Civil War, accounted for less than one-half of 1% of all Canadians. (After 1881, the percentage of blacks would decline steadily until the late 1960s.) By 1901, the situation had not changed—the combined presence of all these immigrant groups was still less than 10% of the whole. By 1921, the total non-French and non-British immigrant population, including immigrants and the descendants of immigrants, rose to 15%, but Europeans continued to predominate. "Visible minorities" made up just over 2% of the population, and most of these were Canada's Aboriginal peoples. These figures remained more or less constant right up to the 1960s. While Europeans represented the bulk of Canada's immigrant population at the beginning of this century, their share of the whole population did not rise above 18% until after the Second World War. And the great majority had been thoroughly assimilated into the prevailing ethos in English or French societies.[5]

While historical figures fail to support the notion that Canada has a multicultural heritage, recent figures fail to support the claim that Canada has become a thoroughly multicultural society. Those who trace their ethnic origins to categories other than Aboriginal, Canadian, American, English and French comprise about 40% of the population, and they represent over 190 different national or ethnic origins, ranging from Jewish to Guyanese. Although the 2001 Census demonstrated that Canada's immigrant profile is in flux, it does not signal a radical shift. The total "visible minority" population has risen to 13.4% from 11.2% in 1996, with most of the increase taking place in Toronto and Vancouver, where visible minorities make up over 35% of the population. While these figures indicate that Canada is a nascent multicultural society, they are certainly not large enough to support a shift to a multicultural vision as the defining characteristic of the country.[6]

Perhaps the most common complaint about multiculturalism is the one dictated by common sense, which is that it invites new Canadians to identify with their native countries rather than Canada itself; hence, the identification of new Canadians as hyphenated Canadians. This has the corrosive effect of undermining patriotism and our conception of national citizenship. This complaint was placed front and center in the early 1990s by the Citizens' Forum on Canada's Future, a series of town hall meetings held across the country, at which Canadians were consulted on issues of national concern. Commissioned by the federal government and chaired by the flamboyant journalist, Keith Spicer, the forum devoted part of its mandate to matters relating to cultural diversity. When dealing with cultural issues, the report stated: "The essential complaint is that, in the words of a group discussion from Oakville, Ontario: 'Multiculturalism is by itself divisive ... we spend too much time being different and not enough being Canadian.' "[7]

Here, common sense makes perfect sense. Historically, Canada has been riven by geography, language and regional disparities in wealth—and obviously these are still with us. The enduring theme of Canadian history, as we'll see in Chapter 7, is the attempt to use the state to build a national community against the odds. This effort begins with a series of public works projects in Upper and Lower Canada in the 1800s, peaks in post-Confederation Canada in projects such as the construction of the National Railway, the creation of the CBC, the institution of national health care and the entrenchment of a Charter of Rights in the repatriated Constitution and continues to the present day in equalization programs that transfer wealth from the more prosperous to the less prosperous provinces. Multiculturalism is an affront to our tradition of nation-building in so far as it invites Canadians to split their allegiances between Canada and their ancestral nations. So, not only is our multi-cultural "heritage" refuted by demographics, it also conflicts with one of the most important themes in our national history.

Even after we have disposed of the argument from numbers and history, we are still left with the claim that Canada has a unique tradition of tolerating cultural differences, whenever and wherever they show up. This is put forward as the key difference between our liberalism and the kind you find south of the border. While the United States is damned as a "melting pot" in which cultural identities have been emulsified, Canada is praised for letting everyone transplant his or her roots.

This contrast is very much overstated as anyone, who has visited New York, Chicago, San Francisco or Los Angeles knows. Far from suppressing cultural diversity, American politicians are as eager as their Canadian counterparts to cater to it. Even without public money, cultural festivals are a regular part of American urban life. In some parts of the United States, Hispanic immigrants have resisted assimilation so successfully that some legislators have advocated a constitutional amendment to make English the nation's official language.

Americans have always treated culture and religion as private matters. Everyone is free to pursue a way of life, so long as it does not lead to trouble with the neighbors, with the law or with the steady progress of material accumulation. This isn't simply the American solution; it's the small "l" liberal democratic solution. Immigrants to the United States have been willing to assimilate under these conditions for some time now, and, indeed, much of the world is trying to assimilate to this way of life, recent events in the Middle East notwithstanding. The common pursuit of material gain leaves most Americans and Canadians, and modern people generally, with little time or energy for culture; trying to get ahead is sufficiently engrossing. Do Canada and the

United States differ in this respect? There are major differences, of course: in style; in respect for authority; in the two systems of government; in the tolerance of public intervention; in the French language. There are many thousand little variations, some regional, some national. But in the overwhelming desire for comfort and security and material improvement, what is the difference?

Cultural traditions continue to flourish in Canada and the United States because cultural freedom exists; it is guaranteed by freedom of expression, religion, assembly and association. But very few communities have managed to cultivate a profound and unique culture, in the manner of the Mennonites or Shakers. In French Canada, it's true, religion and culture were paramount for many years. The Quebecois successfully resisted liberalism until the early 1960s. However, when they took control of the levers of their own economy during the Quiet Revolution, they silently embraced a secular outlook. They still fight for the preservation of the French language (an effort I endorse as a bilingual Canadian), but the fight is carried on within limits imposed by concerns about growth rates and unemployment figures.

No matter how much money is spent on it, multiculturalism will not produce profound cultural differences because the liberal way of life is so attractive. Still, multiculturalism will do some damage; it can "politicize" cultural differences and lay the groundwork for nasty divisions and squabbles. The genius of North American politics has always been to remove the causes of internecine strife by making culture a matter of private choice, but now we are promoting them. After so many years of relative domestic harmony, we have forgotten that flaunting cultural differences can lead to things much less innocent than belly dancing. No one has yet fully considered that multiculturalism may have contributed to the proliferation of schoolyard gangs and the marked increase in youth violence in Toronto, and elsewhere, by galvanizing group identities.

A Regime of Group Rights

While the danger to civil peace posed by cultural politics is real, my greatest concern about the policy of multiculturalism is that it has fostered the creation of a regime of group rights that undermines the equal opportunity ideal. This second phase in the unfolding of the policy occurred in the early 1980s when the clamor for "minority rights" was sufficiently loud to induce Trudeau's last government to commission two more reports *Equality Now* and Justice Rosalie Abella's Royal Commission study, *Equality in Employment*. Their purpose was to find some justification for the claim that racial minorities need special help to make up for past discrimination. Both reports recommended extensive remedial programs.

In part, the reports dealt with uncontroversial demands for an improvement of Canada's adjustment programs for immigrants. These have been around since the early 1950s; they provide language skills, job training and lessons on race relations. No one should object to improving such skills. They are conventional welfare state measures that promote equality of opportunity; they also give immigrants essential information to help them navigate Canadian society. Both reports proposed to extend these programs to include all immigrants, in particular, women and the elderly.

At the same time, they denounced current measures for failing to achieve "real" equality of opportunity—meaning, equality of result. Just when the last discriminatory barriers had been lifted (by adjustment programs and human rights guarantees), these reports argued that reality was the opposite of the obvious. According to them, racism was rampant and was preventing visible minorities from getting ahead.

The *Abella Report* is not remarkable in so far as it alleges that racial discrimination is an intractable problem. Just step into a law library and take out the binder of cases decided before a provincial human rights commission, and you'll find that discrimination is alive and well in Canada. I would not for a moment deny that individuals have been discriminated against based on race, gender, sexual orientation, culture and religion in our country. Nor would I deny the need for continuing vigilance, both publicly and privately, to ensure that discrimination can be prevented; and when it can't, that it will be exposed and remedied. (That was my position in 1984, when the *Abella Report* was published, and it remains my position today.) However, the *Abella Report* made stunning claims that went far beyond recognizing that discrimination is a problem, and that government has a role to play in policing it. The view it presented was extreme. And that view deserves close attention because it became the basis for a new multicultural vision of justice that still resonates with courts and tribunals across the country.

According to the report, "white males" controlled the distribution of opportunities in Canada and intentionally excluded minorities from the best jobs. Furthermore, these "white males" had rigged employment criteria to favor their advancement. These two methods of discrimination merged to create a powerful force called "systemic discrimination," which prevented non-whites from enjoying successful careers. The report concluded that this system could be eradicated only if employers in the public and private sectors set hiring quotas for visible minorities.[8]

The extreme nature of the claim is obvious. The claim was not that a region, certain industries, or a few government departments had developed systems that discriminated against minorities. The claim was that the entire Canadian employment system had been corrupted by discrimination perpetrated by white males. Although the report was supposed to supply decisive proof that systemic discrimination was real, it failed to marshal empirical evidence to make its case.

Buried in the middle of the report was an admission that commission researchers could not find statistics on income, hiring and promotion to support the concept in relation to minority groups. (Human rights commissions had frowned upon the practice of gathering statistics based on race.) Furthermore, while many of the minority leaders who testified before the commission complained of racism, the report states that others did not. The report also failed to explain coherently how the vast conspiracy it alleged actually worked in practice. The sort of provable, specific cases that might impress a sober-minded person are nowhere to be found in the report.[9]

That, however, didn't stop the Conservatives from responding to the report with a scheme of massive remedial action. They established various multicultural quotas, for government advertising and communications, boards and commissions, employment training programs and the entire federal civil service. As well, federal contractors and sub-contractors, and all federally regulated companies (including the chartered banks), were required to report on the status of their minority workforces. This measure pressured companies to create their own internal quota bureaucracies, to quantify progress at the end of the year.

As a result of these initiatives, many supporters of the *Abella Report* became representatives of pressure groups (some bankrolled by the government) or found work in government bureaucracies (provincial as well as federal). Their cadres made the case for "systemic discrimination," with a vested interest to preserve funding and keep their jobs. They made the most extreme case possible because overstatement works. Soon it became difficult for anyone either inside or outside the government to call embellished claims into question, and so systemic discrimination became a permanent problem on the national agenda.

Once formal and informal quota systems, and their in-house supporters were in place, the equal opportunity principle came under severe attack. "White males" who qualified for jobs on merit were turned away so that quotas could be filled by minority applicants who were sometimes less qualified. And the practice spread. As a result, reverse discrimination was institutionalized in the federal public sector, and in provincial and municipal bureaucracies throughout the country. Companies competing for business with governments were also forced to comply. And human rights tribunals sometimes forced private employers to establish quotas to avoid suits claiming that minorities were underrepresented in the workplace. All this was justified on the Orwellian ground of achieving "employment equity."

Whether quota systems that lead to reverse discrimination can ever be justified is an issue that I will deal with in the next chapter. For the moment, all we need consider is that employment equity schemes violate the equal opportunity ideal by forsaking criteria of merit in favor of criteria based on race and gender. The implicit undermining of equal opportunity through employment equity is why Canada must recommit itself to a merit-based, equal opportunity society in order to remain competitive in the 21st century. Multiculturalism undercuts our most important national objective.

Yet, some say that we shouldn't worry; a policy of multiculturalism is exactly what we need if we want to prosper in a global economy. Government officials like to say that our diverse communities can reach out to foreign markets, utilizing their language skills and social links in their countries of origin. It's a nice idea. And I know some new Canadians who have become wealthy by leveraging their language skills and contacts in their native countries. However, since 87% of our foreign trade is with the United States, any hope that this strategy will produce a marked increase in GNP in the near future is unrealistic. Furthermore, the whole approach can be rebutted with one observation. Japan did not conquer the North American auto market because its auto executives learned English and reached out to friends and relatives over here; they did it by building a better car. And they built a better car by adopting new production techniques based on the teachings of American management guru, Dr. Edwards Deming, who created the philosophy of Total Quality Management. By drawing on Deming's radical and innovative work, which had yet to be discovered by American manufacturers, Japan was able to improve its efficiency and quality to the point that they exceeded American standards in several industries. That's how the Japanese came to dominate the North American automotive market, as well as the electronics market.

So far, we've only canvassed the first two phases in the development of multiculturalism. In the first, the federal government sought to promote civic harmony by providing public support for cultural activities and festivals, and by promoting the new vision of Canada as a multicultural mosaic. These policies have had the unforeseen effect of producing civil conflict and many other troubling problems. In the second phase, governments across the country established employment schemes designed to promote equal opportunity, which had the effect, perhaps more readily foreseen, of undermining that principle by allowing criteria based on ethnicity and gender to influence employment decisions. In the third and final phase, which is now unfolding, the academic world has taken up the cause of multiculturalism in order to liberate minorities from various forms of cultural oppression. This effort, too, has had one consequence that was not foreseen—it threatens to curtail one of the fundamental rights that support cultural freedom, namely, freedom of expression.

The Politics of Recognition

In the academic world, two Canadian scholars with impeccable credentials—Charles Taylor of McGill and Michael Ignatieff of Harvard—are on the vanguard of the multicultural movement. Both believe that liberal societies are inherently unjust when seen from the standpoint of minority groups. They argue that every cultural group has a deep-seated desire to survive, and this essential need can be satisfied only when the state recognizes the equal worth and dignity of all groups. In their view, when the state withholds this recognition, as it does in most liberal societies, minority groups are forced to assimilate to the majority culture, and this is the essence of cultural oppression.[10]

In his recent book, *The Rights Revolution*, Ignatieff presents this perspective with particular vigor. His argument begins with a critique of the liberal view of civil society as a collection of free individuals, enjoying the same fundamental rights in equal measure. This vision—one shared by people as diverse as the philosopher John Locke, the Framers of the American Constitution and Pierre Trudeau—is inadequate, according to Ignatieff, because it provides a partial and limited view of what it means to be a human being. Ultimately, it leads to assimilation to the norms of the "white, heterosexual, family-oriented, native-born" majority. So, it fails to deal with the other essential source of our humanity: the commitments that define us as members of groups, for example, gay, straight, Catholic, Buddhist, African-Canadian, Anglo-Saxon and so on. These commitments are essential because they are the primary source of individual identity. Ignatieff argues that no one really feels that he or she is an equal until the state publicly values his or her "culture, heritage and distinctive point of view" by extending rights or entitlements to his or her group. Furthermore, the real source of recognition—the approval that an individual should experience in his or her daily interactions with fellow citizens—will only be realized once the state extends approval in concrete ways.[11]

Ignatieff innovates here, but, in a way, as we shall see, that turns out to be reactionary. He founds a new right that is not found in the liberal lexicon: the right to "equal moral consideration." This novel right gives us a duty that goes beyond simply tolerating different ways of life; now we must extend special entitlements to signal that we regard those ways of life as equal to our own.[12]

Ignatieff is confident that any conflict between group rights and individual rights can be resolved when the purpose of granting group rights is to recognize the identity of minority groups. In this respect, Canada emerges as a great success and America as a failure. Yet Canada looks successful only because Ignatieff ignores the implications of Canadian policies, and America seems to be a failure only because he almost willfully misunderstands America's basic liberal principles.

In the case of Canada, for example, when examining affirmative action programs, Ignatieff fails to consider that they can lead to reverse discrimination. When dealing with the question of whether self-governing Aboriginal groups can deny women the right to vote or hold office, he urges the parties to engage in "intercultural negotiation," the equivalent of saying, "Can't we all just get along?" When discussing English Canada's rejection of Quebec's demand for a distinct society clause, he fails to mention that many people were concerned that the clause would empower Quebec to limit individual freedoms guaranteed by the Charter.[13] Throughout, Ignatieff can argue for Canada as a model because he ignores the conflicts between groups and individuals. Similarly, America's ability to reconcile individuals and groups is underrated because he does not fully articulate what the Framers had to say about the ends of liberal government.

Ignatieff is right in asserting that this model tends to mitigate differences between groups. And the founders of liberalism wanted it that way. In pre-liberal societies, people were mired in endless political disputes over whose religion or culture deserved pre-eminence. Those disputes produced nothing but war and poverty. By focusing society on the pursuit of material gain, and assigning religion and culture to the private domain where they would become matters of individual choice, liberals hoped to diminish religious and cultural ties in some measure, and above all else, keep them out of the public domain. Liberals would never have accepted the politics of recognition, fearing that they would re-invigorate group differences at the expense of peace and individual rights. And, that, of course, is exactly what those politics have done in Canada and elsewhere.

But the liberal solution also cuts in a completely different direction. For Ignatieff, liberalism forgets the importance of recognizing minority groups because his American model is an incomplete articulation of the liberal view of government. Citizens lack identity in this model only because it views them from one perspective—that of the state. From the government's standpoint, group identity is a non-issue because everyone deserves to have his or her rights protected regardless of his or her aims, beliefs or affiliations. But the point of protecting these rights, when seen from the standpoint of the citizen, is to provide an expansive private domain where the real richness of human life can be experienced, where everyone has the freedom to pursue happiness—regardless of how it is understood.

Ignatieff unfairly stacks the deck against a liberal regime of individual rights by assuming that it necessarily leads to assimilation, when in fact it is the essential pre-condition to the protection of individual and group differences, and the achievement of genuine diversity. That some groups may not thrive in the private domain is not an argument against the liberal solution. A liberal would argue that groups flourish best when they are left to flourish on their own, and the test of whether they deserve to flourish is whether they can flourish on their own. A liberal would oppose Ignatieff's view that cultural groups should receive public entitlements because we could not distinguish between groups that are held together by greed and those held together by real historical and spiritual ties.

Some might object that Canada has never been a purely liberal democratic society and that the concern about preserving liberal principles is not in tune with our political tradition. This objection is based on the notion that Canadian political culture contains an illiberal streak imparted by feudalistic beliefs that were present among the United Empire Loyalists, who emigrated to Canada after the American Revolution. Those who take this view argue that Canadian political culture has an inherent bias toward policies that favor group rights, particularly in matters relating to education and culture. Early examples are the public funding of Catholic schools and the willingness to unite two different linguistic groups in one nation. However, as I will argue in Chapter 7, the idea that Canadian political culture contains illiberal elements can be refuted by an historical analysis of our founding groups and their beliefs. So, I maintain here that we are fully justified in measuring multiculturalism in relation to basic liberal principles.

And it's from a liberal perspective that we can see what is perhaps the greatest problem with Ignatieff's multiculturalism: it fails to address how the demand for equal approval can block human development. This demand prevents us from questioning different commitments and beliefs. For example, we cannot ask whether a life devoted to cross-dressing deserves the same approval as one devoted to eradicating injustice. But can we really believe that Rue Paul is the moral equal of Martin Luther King? In a world where equal approval is required, we cannot ask that question for fear of offending Rue Paul or his fans and, indeed, every citizen who believes in the right to equal approval. What this means is that we no longer have the freedom to discuss what it means to lead a good life, an inquiry that requires us to ask whether some ways of life are better than others. Properly understood, Ignatieff's politics lead to wholesale political correctness and the end to liberal democracy's greatest claim to fame—freedom of thought.

This result is certainly troubling from a political standpoint, but it's also problematic in economic terms. In an age where we have to compete against other nations on the basis of intellectual discovery, multiculturalism presents a strange threat to economic advancement by undermining the atmosphere that promotes freedom of inquiry. Again, while some politicians would have us believe that multiculturalism promotes wealth creation by facilitating foreign trade, in fact, it has the potential to subvert the conditions that promote national prosperity.

This point brings us back to the main object of this book, which is to promote national prosperity by arguing for a more complete actualization of the equal opportunity ideal. As we've seen in the discussion of "employment equity," multiculturalism has undermined the equal opportunity ideal by creating an atmosphere where employment systems in the public sector, and in some cases, the private sector, have placed considerations relating to race and ethnicity ahead of criteria based on merit. If Canada hopes to become truly competitive, it must make sure that it's getting the most out of its people, and the only way to do that is to ensure that public and private employers focus on matching people's talents with the work that must be performed. By diminishing the focus on talent, employment equity is taking us down the road to a society that is politically correct, but that fails to maximize its individual and collective economic potential.

The politics of multiculturalism also eat away at the social conditions that promote national prosperity. The project of recommitting Canada to the equal opportunity ideal as the necessary means to achieving our economic potential will require all Canadians to focus on the task of cultivating their own talents and the talents of those around them, with a view to creating an atmosphere where decisions regarding advancement in schools, community associations and the workplace are based on merit. Yet the great Canadian problem continues to be how to manifest a national will in the face of regional and linguistic divisions, and the omnipresent influence of American society.

That problem has been exacerbated by multiculturalism, which invites us to divide ourselves in an almost infinite number of ways. Can we manifest the national will we need to build a just and prosperous society when the government asks us to define ourselves in relation to over 190 different ethnic categories at last count? This problem is made all the worse by the conflicts that necessarily arise when groups compete for public entitlements and recognition. Multiculturalism undermines the national cohesion that we need to succeed in a fiercely competitive global economy.

The Need for Understanding

The failure of multiculturalism to promote national cohesion is well illustrated in Neil Bissoondath's best-selling book, *Selling Illusions*. Bissoondath argues that multiculturalism does not achieve what should be its most important goal: to demystify the other. The views of cultural life presented by multiculturalism are uninspiring and uninteresting, in his view, because they present culture in the form of mind-numbing displays of folklore. Precisely because they are so superficial and limited, these displays tend to discourage others from seeing anything in a culture that is worthy of exploration. As a result, multiculturalism tends to encourage tolerance of the other rather than an exchange between individuals that might lead to real understanding and acceptance. Bissoondath argues that Canada is sorely in need of national cohesion, but we are unlikely to achieve it because multiculturalism discourages individuals from different backgrounds from truly engaging with each other on the street, in neighborhoods and in the workplace.[14]

Unfortunately, some of my most recent experiences with multiculturalism tend to confirm Bisoondath's views. In late 2003, I was invited to IBM's Diversity Night to hear a friend give a keynote speech. Over a thousand visibly diverse IBM employees from across the country attended this event to celebrate the company's commitment to diversity in the workplace. A white, female senior executive from IBM Canada, posted here from the United States, gave the first official speech in which she praised the founder of IBM for establishing a non-discriminatory employment policy as early as 1948. I learned later, however, that IBM management wasn't completely in the festive spirit—the participants had to foot the bill for the event themselves. Following the speech, organizers played a video that featured footage of Martin Luther King and important moments in the American civil rights struggle. The rest of the evening consisted of speeches—the best given by my friend, who began by questioning whether IBM needed a diversity night—and a series of performances by IBM employees. Ethnic costumes, dance routines and Chinese employees hiding beneath a 20-foot-long dragon were featured.

By the end of the night, I didn't feel that I knew the people in that audience any better as a result of the displays. However, the Chinese display left a strong impression because it was accompanied by drummers who were so loud that I suffered a noticeable hearing deficit after the event. It had been almost 20 years since I had attended that first multicultural festival at Harbourfront. And this one wasn't much different, except that the audience appeared to be more interested in the performances. From Neil Bissoondath's perspective, though, this event might have been regarded as a perverse twist on selling illusions. Instead of presenting folklore as real identity to "the other," multicultural Canadians were now presenting it to themselves.

The Fate of the Individual

In the fall of 2003, I was the canvass chair for a candidate in the Richmond Hill area north of Toronto during the Ontario election campaign. I spent over a month in Richmond Hill, which was and still is the fastest-growing city in the province; it's also ethnically diverse with large Asian communities and a growing Eastern European presence. I organized teams to go into neighborhoods to drop literature and ask for votes, and when I wasn't doing that, I was canvassing. Since I was working for an outstanding candidate, who had assembled a strong campaign team, I assumed this was going to be a happy experience. And it was, at first. But after a week or two of going door to door, my spirits began to flag. When I drove back to downtown Toronto at the end of each evening, I was depressed. I didn't understand why. As I reflected, I realized that Richmond Hill itself was the source of my melancholy. There were a few old neighborhoods that harkened back to the city's small-town origins. And the city still had some vestige of a downtown core that served as a point of contact for the community. But the city was largely a series of strip malls and large discount stores surrounded by discrete housing developments that were unrelated by any architectural aesthetic or any evident plan to encourage human contact. Some homes had been placed so close together that they might as well have been townhouses; but I never had the sense, when going door to door, that this had produced a feeling of togetherness. The homes were large, but poor design and slap-dash construction robbed them of any charm—they weren't inviting.

I had the feeling that Richmond Hill had somehow been developed to make sure that groups of new Canadians would never find real points of contact that would lead to individual understanding and acceptance. That feeling grew as the weeks went by and I discovered that no one came to the door at some of these homes because they were owned by non-resident Canadians. All this reminded me that a character in a Yann Martel novel had described Canada as "the big hotel."

There is much to recommend the notion that we must concern ourselves with the status of groups. After the collapse of the Soviet Union, most major political upheavals have involved clashes between ethnic or religious groups: Muslims vs. Christians (Bosnia), Russians vs. Chechnyans (Russia), Hutus vs. Tutsis (Rwanda), Arab Muslims vs. Black Christians (Sudan) and Arabs vs. Jews (Israel). In the end, though, I'm forced to wonder whether multiculturalism is really suited to the times. Given the prevailing forces in the world today, I am less concerned about the survival of group identities, and much more concerned about the survival of the individual. High technology has created a world of rapid change that has improved the lives of millions of people, but at a cost; in North America alone, new technologies have caused hundreds of thousands of people to lose their jobs due to redundancy and outsourcing. Governments like Canada, which have embraced free trade, have increased the wealth of the nation as a whole, but global competition has put untold numbers of people out of work as companies move to lower-cost jurisdictions or simply fold under market pressure. In a world where everything is increasingly measured solely in terms of group outcomes, such as shareholder return and Gross National Product (GNP), individual well-being has dropped off the screen. Focusing on the net result obscures the fact that there are winners and losers in this new game. And the losers don't always have recourse. In such a world, a sane and truly just policy of multiculturalism would focus on ensuring that highly skilled new Canadians are given the opportunity to adapt their skills to the Canadian workplace, either through apprenticeships or qualifying examinations. The less highly skilled should be given guidance and support in acquiring skills that will bring them opportunity and income. And, as I've learned in my work with Umugenzi for Refugees, special support is needed for immigrants whose lives have been shattered by war.[15]

And then there are the unaffiliated. Close to dusk, during one of my last trips to Richmond Hill, I pulled off the highway and found myself behind slow-moving cars at an intersection. As I prepared to turn left,

I saw a young woman, standing on the corner, who was no more than 17 years old. Her face was weathered; her jeans and suede jacket flattered her slender frame, but they were worn and dirty. The German shepherd at her side had a dingy coat. As I passed, she held up the bottom of a pizza box on which she had written, "Can you help a girl and her dog who are down on their luck?" I wanted to stop, but I was forced by the traffic to complete my turn and accelerate to highway speed. Even if I'd turned back, I realized there was no hope of getting to her because the highway didn't have a shoulder. (That she'd chosen this spot to make her plea was proof that she really needed help.) I was already late for dinner and kept going, but with a guilty conscience. What was a homeless teenager doing at a highway exit at nightfall on the edge of this prosperous city? I've been haunted by the image of that girl and her dog, and wonder, from time to time, what has become of them. I wish now that I'd decided to be late, parked in a mall and walked back to find out what kind of trouble they were in.

That experience turned out to be the defining moment of the campaign of 2003. It captured my feeling that we were wasting a lot of time worrying about cultural politics and group rights when we really needed to be focusing our energies on those forlorn souls who had lost their way on the road to a brighter future.

Myth Four

EMPLOYMENT EQUITY PROMOTES EQUAL OPPORTUNITY

Equal Opportunity, circa 1878

When Sir John A. Macdonald stood up in Parliament in 1878 and moved that the government adopt the National Policy, he presented a sublime vision that linked the policy to achieving economic greatness, developing the national character and securing domestic justice. He began by arguing that Canada could not become a great economic power by continuing to rely on farming as its principal source of wealth: "... no nation has arisen which had only agriculture as its industry." The National Policy, which would establish a customs tariff that would protect the Canadian economy from American competition, would solve that problem by giving new Canadian enterprises a chance to flourish, when otherwise they could be wiped out by well-established American firms that could produce goods more efficiently and cheaply. But the National Policy would not simply aim at economic well-being. It would be the necessary means of creating our national identity. "There must be a mixture of industries to bring out the national mind and the national strength and to form a national character." At the same time, the policy would bring the promise of equal opportunity that would make it desirable for talented Canadians to stay at home instead of moving to the United States in search of a better life:

We must by every reasonable means, employ our people, not in one branch of industry, not merely as farmers, as tillers of the soil, but we must bring out every kind of industry, we must develop the minds of the people and their energies. Every man is not fitted to be a farmer, to till the soil; one man has a constructive genius, another is an artist, another has an aptitude for trade, another is a skillful mechanic—all these men are to be found in a nation, and, if these men cannot find an opportunity in their own country to develop the skill and genius with which God has gifted them, they will go to a country where their abilities can be employed, as they have gone from Canada to the United States. [1]

To match America's economic performance, Sir John A. Macdonald saw very clearly that Canada needed an economic policy that recognized the intrinsic connection between justice and prosperity. Under the protection of the tariff, new Canadian industries would be born, and they would succeed because, and only because, they would provide new opportunities for Canadians to use their unique talents and profit from them.

One hundred and ten years later, when another Conservative government, led by Brian Mulroney, decided to enter into a free trade agreement with the United States, it inverted Sir John A.'s position. The government argued that free trade—not protectionism—would increase national wealth because it would give Canadian firms access to the American market and also force them to become more innovative and efficient in response to American competition. But the grand language of Sir John A. was notably absent from the government's statements and position papers. The government linked free trade to future prosperity, but was silent on whether it would build national character, develop the public mind, or promote equal opportunity.

The government's failure to make reference to the equal opportunity ideal was perhaps understandable—Canada had already forsaken it when it adopted the equality provisions of the Canadian Charter of Rights and Freedoms, which came into force in 1985. Section 15(1) of the Charter provides a basic guarantee of equal opportunity by stipulating that government cannot discriminate against anyone on the basis of criteria such as race, sex or age, which are regarded as irrelevant to the determination of the government's distribution of benefits and burdens. The provision states: "Every individual is equal before and under the law and has the right to the equal protection of the law and equal benefit of the law without discrimination, and, in particular, without discrimination based on race, national or ethnic origin, colour, religion, sex, age or mental or physical disability." But this fundamental guarantee was undermined by the inclusion of section 15(2), which allowed government programs to discriminate in favor of "disadvantaged groups" that are identified on the basis of the prohibited criteria listed under section (1). The provision states: "Subsection (1) does not preclude any law, program or activity that has as its object the amelioration of conditions of disadvantaged individuals or groups including those that are disadvantaged because of race, national or ethnic origin, colour, religion, sex, age or mental or physical disability."

As I argued in the first chapter of this book, the equal opportunity ideal is based on the principle that it's wrong to discriminate against anyone on the basis of criteria, such as those listed above, because they are irrelevant to determining whether an individual has the merit to qualify for employment or educational opportunities. Equally, these criteria are irrelevant to determining whether an individual deserves to receive a benefit from, or is to be penalized by the state. But, taking section 15(2) as its authority, federal and provincial governments are empowered to distribute privileges and benefits, as well as opportunities in public employment and in college and university admissions, to favor arbitrarily designated disadvantaged groups.

What this means is that a highly qualified person whose "group" doesn't happen to be on the government's "list" of disadvantaged groups can be denied a public-sector job in favor of a less-qualified person whose group happens to be on the list. The same holds true for federally regulated companies, such as the banks, where the government has successfully pressured employers into adopting "employment equity" plans that require employers to hire and promote individuals based on their status as members of groups favored by the government. The same also holds true in some of our public universities and colleges, where admissions criteria are lowered to ensure that admissions reflect the government's concerns about minority representation. Governments at all levels can also distribute government contracts or program money to favor disadvantaged groups at the expense of "advantaged groups." In each of these situations, government policies designed to level the playing field have created the very discrimination that they were supposed to prevent. Whichever way you look at it, the government and its minions are practicing reverse discrimination.

Built into the Charter from day one was the notion that racial and sexual discrimination were so deeply ingrained in Canadian society that the state had to remedy the situation. That notion was never put to the test by outside criticism or by any verifiable public analysis of the actual state of Canadian justice. Certain high-level legal and political advisors, who were in the business of promoting minority rights, just assumed that discrimination was so widespread that the country was justified in departing from the equal opportunity ideal.

The End of Equal Opportunity: The Abella Report

At first, the notion that discrimination was pervasive was not stated openly. But, in 1984, this view saw the light of day when the federal Liberal government commissioned Justice Rosalie Abella of the Supreme Court of Canada, then a judge at the Ontario Family Court, to single-handedly conduct a Royal Commission study on the status of equality in employment among 11 Crown corporations. The commission was authorized by the government to proceed on the basis that women and "visible minorities" were underrepresented in the workplace due to the effects of widespread discriminatory hiring practices. The Terms of Reference were based on the premise that "the measures taken by Canadian employers to increase the employability and productivity of women, native people, disabled persons and visible minorities have as yet not resulted in nearly enough change in the employment practices which have the unintended effect of screening a disproportionate number of those persons out of opportunities for hiring and promotion."

From the start, the commission was not a dispassionate inquiry into the nature and extent of discrimination in Crown corporations. Its objective was to devise group-based remedies to deal with the assumption that discrimination was a major obstacle to the advancement of women and minorities in these companies. Judge Abella (as she then was), however, didn't stop there. She refused to work in a "cultural vacuum." She personally extended her mandate by arguing that her analysis of the employment practices of these Crown corporations could serve as an analysis of the problems faced by minorities in Canadian society as a whole. Even though these corporations comprised a mere 1.8% of the total workforce in 1984, their practices were deemed to reflect the reality of the other 98.2% of the Canadian workforce.[2]

Over 20 years after it was first published, *The Royal Commission Report on Equality in Employment*, otherwise known as the *Abella Report*, deserves our attention because it became one of the most influential Royal Commission studies in Canadian history. It became a bible for human resource professionals from coast to coast, who used it to expand their duties to include "equity initiatives"; it gave rise to university and college courses that teach young people how to seek equity for themselves and others; it has been used by federal and provincial governments to justify the use of race and gender as considerations when making employment decisions; and it's been cited by the Supreme Court of Canada as authoritative proof that discrimination is indeed "systemic."

The *Abella Report* got the equity movement rolling in Canada by alleging that racism and sexism were "pervasive" and "systemic." And we've been saddled with that allegation for two decades. As a result, an immense amount of time, money and energy have been needlessly devoted to equity initiatives designed to rectify and prevent discrimination in the public—and private—sectors. But, as we shall see, the *Abella Report* never proved that discrimination was widespread in the 11 Crown corporations it studied, much less in Canadian society as whole. Furthermore, its preference for what Judge Abella called "employment equity" measures was clearly designed to gloss over the fact that employment equity was just another name for "affirmative action," the practice of reserving benefits and employment opportunities based on race and gender. When we look at what the Royal Commission actually said, we find that the charge of massive discrimination was made recklessly without adequate evidence and the remedy of employment equity was created without considering that the assignment of group preferences would give rise to the practice of reverse discrimination, which would utterly destroy our founding commitment to an equal opportunity society.

Judge Abella began her report by asserting—but not proving—that Canadian human rights tribunals and courts had turned out to be ineffective in dealing with the problem of discrimination. The case-by-case style of adjudication was deemed to be inadequate to deal with the fact that discrimination was a problem that permeated the entire employment system: hence the term "systemic discrimination." The report stated that human rights commissions are "in the position of stamping out brush fires when the urgency is in the incendiary potential of the entire forest." The forest was deemed to be full of white males who had intentionally or unintentionally rigged employment criteria to favor their own kind in hiring and promotion. These systemic biases justified the commission's concern with the putative underrepresentation of women and minorities in the workforce. Since Judge Abella had already decided that the system was corrupt, she could safely assume that "adverse impact"—low participation rates for women or minorities in any job category—could be attributed to systemic discrimination.[3]

The assumption that adverse impact could automatically signal the presence of discrimination was, needless to say, problematic. This one-dimensional approach failed to consider that the underrepresentation of a group in a particular field might be due to any number of factors that have nothing do with discrimination practiced by a particular employer or industry. For instance, as the American economist Thomas Sowell demonstrated in the early 1970s, the underrepresentation of Hispanics in management positions in the United States could be explained simply in relation to demographics. The median age of Hispanics in 1970 was 18, while the national average was 28. As management positions are generally awarded to older workers with considerable work experience, one could not expect Hispanics to have as many candidates available for management positions as groups that had graying populations, such as Irish-Americans, who had a median age of 37. Variations in participation rates could also be explained by preferences among the members of a group concerning desirable types of education or training. Rates could also fluctuate simply based on variations in the presence of minority groups in local populations.[4] Factors such as these were never considered by Judge Abella. And, in fact, the whole idea of underrepresentation was never completely defined. Was it tied to the percentage of a particular minority within the whole Canadian population or within the local labor force? Was it judged in relation to the percentage of qualified individuals nationally or locally?

Where's the Beef?

The Royal Commission did not use statistics to refine the notion of adverse impact because it didn't have access to any data concerning the representation of minorities in the workforce. Objective information had yet to be gathered by public agencies, in part, because it was considered to be contrary to existing human rights guarantees to gather employment statistics based on race or ethnicity. Buried in the middle of the report is the admission: "There is in Canada at present an insufficient data base to determine with accuracy the number of available qualified woman and minorities in the relevant labor market."[5]

Although the Royal Commission was charged with analyzing the employment practices of 11 Crown corporations, it devoted only 27 pages of the 393-page report to the analysis because the corporations had no information concerning the participation rates of minorities. And the commission soon discovered that the few available statistics on minority employment tended to rebut the commission's thesis that society's rewards were concentrated in the hands of a white (presumably Anglo-Saxon) elite. In 1981, with one exception, all single-origin immigrant groups had lower unemployment rates than the national average of 7.5%. Examples include Indo-Pakistanis 4.5%, Japanese 3.1%,

Korean 4.9% and Blacks 7.3%. The Japanese shared with Anglo-Saxons the distinction of having the highest percentage of men earning more than $30,000 per year. While 12.6% of Anglo-Saxon males occupied managerial positions, similar participation rates were recorded for the Japanese (13.4%), and Indo-Pakistanis (11.4%).[6]

The federal Liberal government had given the Royal Commission the mandate to recommend ways of dealing with the underrepresentation of women and minorities in the workplace when it knew, and Judge Abella knew, that there was no empirical evidence to prove that discrimination was a "systemic" problem. As a result, the Royal Commission embraced a perverse logic. It recommended that all minorities deserved to be given preferences in hiring and employment until Statistics Canada gathered data that would allow the government to determine "which visible minorities appear *not* to be in need of employment equity programs."[7]

The New Dogma

All this gave rise to a new dogmatic principle, which became the clarion call for the new equity movement: "Systemic discrimination requires systemic remedies." Of course, the systemic remedy was the use of "employment equity" programs that would allow the federal government to force companies to set quantifiable goals and timetables for increasing the number of jobs and promotions awarded to women and minorities. Judge Abella went to great lengths to distinguish employment equity from the American remedy of affirmative action, which was associated with government-imposed or court-ordered employment quotas. The report indicated that there had been a lot of controversy at the commission hearings concerning the possible use of affirmative action remedies, presumably because some people objected to racial preferences that would result in reverse

discrimination and the destruction of the merit principle. In the interests of avoiding "intellectual resistance and confusion" (i.e., real debate
concerning the problem of reverse discrimination), Judge Abella decided to call her plan "employment equity." After all, who can be
against equity in employment? Unlike affirmative action, her plan
would not require the use of government quotas and would, therefore,
appear to avoid the problem of reverse discrimination.[8]

But the report was hardly convincing on this point. By forcing companies to set their own "annual internal objectives," government would
in fact be forcing companies to set their own quotas to avoid fines and
penalties. At the very least, companies would be encouraged to set "soft
quotas" by elevating an undefined number of candidates based on
group preferences to demonstrate progress and satisfy the authorities.

However, once a company promotes candidates on the basis of race
or gender, it also demotes others on the basis of race or gender—and
that's the essence of reverse discrimination. Running away from this
objection, Judge Abella argued that the oppression of one group by
another would bring us closer to a true state of equality: "The effect
may be to end the hegemony of one group over another over the economic spoils, but the end of exclusivity is not reverse discrimination;
it is the beginning of equality."[9]

While the Royal Commission finessed the issue of reverse discrimination, it underplayed the negative psychological impact of
employment equity. Judge Abella advanced the view that women
and minorities have often failed to achieve their potential due to low
self-esteem caused by societal assumptions that they can't do the job.
Those assumptions are based on stereotypes that grow stronger the
longer disadvantaged candidates are denied employment opportunities. So, by the commission's logic, unless special places were
reserved for members of disadvantaged groups, the stereotypes
would never be eliminated and the disadvantaged would continue to

underestimate their capabilities and employers would continue to withhold opportunities.

What Judge Abella failed to consider is that affirmative action programs actually perpetuate stereotypes and do further damage to the self-esteem of minorities. Once everyone knows that a school or an employer is reserving places for candidates, then the assumption that minorities cannot do the job is reinforced, not eradicated. Justice Powell of United States Supreme Court made this point in the famous *Bakke* case, in which quotas at the medical school at the University of California at Davis were struck down as a violation of the Constitution's equal protection clause. He stated that: "preferential programs may only reinforce common stereotypes holding that certain groups are unable to achieve success without special protection based on a factor having no relationship to individual worth."[10] Surely the Royal Commission must have been presented with this objection during its cross-Canada hearings. One suspects that Judge Abella was alluding to the objection when she wrote that "[s]ome individuals found the groupings insulting." Clearly, she discovered that some people were concerned that they might become token representatives in such a system: "They resisted vigorously the notion that they are a fringe rather than an integral part of the community."[11]

Although high-minded liberals might have trouble believing it, some members of so-called disadvantaged groups don't want to be patronized with hand-outs and quotas. Like the rest of us, they want the chance to prove that they can make the grade based on their own initiative, hard work and skills. In the late 1970s, when affirmative action had become widespread in the United States, Gallup conducted a poll that revealed that 64% of African-Americans and 80% of women rejected preferential treatment in employment and college admissions. In 2003 Gallup found that a majority of African-Americans favored affirmative action, but 46% were opposed when it conflicts with merit principle.[12]

Fallout from the Abella Report

After the report was published, Judge Abella gave a talk at the University of Toronto Law School to a packed house of law students eager to get on the equity bandwagon. I attended as an alumnus and turned out to be the only dissenting voice in the lecture hall. During the question and answer period, I raised the possibility that the use of quantifiable goals would force employers to set group preferences that would result in reverse discrimination. Judge Abella emphatically denied that the government would set quotas under the proposed plan. I later wrote to the judge to make my case more cogently, and in her reply she stated that she found my criticism "thoughtful and valuable," but she again denied that employment equity plans would deny opportunities to qualified people.

After my encounters with Judge Abella, I began to realize that the equity movement was going to hit the country like a tidal wave. I was concerned that courts and human rights tribunals might take the report's definition of systemic discrimination—the underrepresentation of minorities judged by some arbitrary standard—as sufficient to find that a public or private employer had engaged in discriminatory conduct, and that mandatory employment equity remedies would follow. My fears were almost realized in 1987when the Supreme Court of Canada agreed to hear a case that dealt with an affirmative action plan where the Canadian Human Rights Commission had ordered the Canadian National Railway (CNR) to improve the representation of women in its blue-collar workforce [13]

Based, in part, on the finding that 6.7% of blue-collar jobs were held by women at the CNR (St. Lawrence Region), as compared to 13% of the blue-collar workforce nationally, the commission found that CNR had been discriminating systemically. Consequently, it ordered the railway to reserve one in four blue-collar jobs for women until they represented 13% of the company's local workforce. CNR appealed the case to the Federal Court on the basis that the commission did not have sufficient evidence to support the finding of systemic discrimination and the imposition of the quota scheme. The Federal Court overturned the Commission's decision and a union representing female employees at CNR brought the case before the Supreme Court, which reversed the Federal Court ruling and upheld the commission's original decision.

At first glance, the *CNR* decision appears to provide direct support for the notion that the underrepresentation of a minority group—"adverse impact"—would be sufficient to prove the existence of systemic discrimination and the need for a remedy in the form of a quota scheme. But a closer reading reveals that the court did not, in the end, endorse such an extreme point of view. The court noted that the Human Rights Commission had based its finding of systemic discrimination on the fact of adverse impact and the existence of deliberate discrimination. The proof of deliberate discrimination was revealed in several wrongful employment practices: CNR had encouraged women who applied for blue-collar jobs to apply instead for secretarial positions, had failed to inform some women about the qualifications they needed to fill blue-collar openings, and had required applicants to have experience in soldering—a criterion unrelated to job performance.[14] Since the evidence relating to deliberate discrimination played a crucial role in the Supreme Court's decision to uphold the quota scheme, the case left open the question of how the court would decide a case if adverse impact were the only evidence of discrimination tendered by a complainant. And that question still has not been answered. Sooner or later, however, a public interest group is going to bring a complaint before a human rights tribunal in which it alleges that a private employer is guilty of systemic discrimination because its workforce does not adequately reflect the mosaic of the local community. Then we'll see whether the adverse impact test prevails.[15]

While courts and tribunals have shown some restraint so far in determining when employment equity plans may be used, the federal government has not. The latest version of the federal *Employment Equity Act* (1995) requires the entire civil service, crown corporations and federally regulated companies to develop employment equity plans that set numerical targets for improving the representation of women and visible minorities. The Canadian Human Rights Commission audits these reports and can use "persuasion and negotiation" to encourage employers to speed up recruitment and promotion practices. If an employer doesn't comply, the commission can expose its discriminatory practices in the press or bring it before the Human Rights Tribunal and seek an order enforcing the terms of the plan.[16] Thus, the federal government has claimed the right to compel any organization under its jurisdiction to establish job quotas for designated disadvantaged groups whenever they are perceived to be underrepresented.

Provincial governments across the country follow similar practices, depending on which party is in power. For example, in Ontario in 1993, the NDP passed the *Employment Equity Act*, which required all public and private employers with more than 50 employees to establish employment equity plans for the Royal Commission's four designated groups—women, the disabled, visible minorities and aboriginal Canadians. Employers would be required to ensure that every disadvantaged group was represented in every job category in proportion with its percentage representation in the local community. When the Conservatives under Mike Harris came to power in 1995, they moved quickly to abolish the Act. I suspect that McGuinty's Liberal government has revived the practice of giving preferential treatment to members of the four designated groups when making decisions regarding hiring and promotion in the civil service, but it has yet to make employment equity a public issue.

The Flawed Case for Reverse Discrimination

The advocates of employment equity ask us not to worry about the problem of reverse discrimination because the principle of merit is not a just principle. They argue that a well-qualified white male candidate deserves to be denied a job in favor of a less-qualified minority candidate. It is assumed that he, like all other white males, has discriminated against minorities and ought to be punished for it. It is also assumed that the white male's, present advantages, which account for his merit, were acquired by means of discrimination—access to better schools, for example. The flipside of this argument requires us to assume that all minorities are victims of discrimination. We must assume that a member of a minority group who does not qualify for a job would have qualified for it if he or she had not been deprived of advantages by means of discrimination. By rewarding a less qualified member of a minority group with a job, we are simply compensating him or her for the harms he or she suffered in the past and the resulting disadvantages he or she suffers in the present.

But these arguments cannot be supported in the face of the world as it really is. On the one hand, we can never assume that a white male who qualifies for a job has risen in society by stepping on the backs of poor minorities. Perhaps this individual is a newly arrived immigrant, or a well-intentioned second-generation Canadian whose parents supported the civil rights movement; or perhaps he is poor and disadvantaged. In any of these cases, the white individual should not be denied an opportunity as though guilty of racism. Equally, we cannot assume that a person from a particular minority who does not qualify for a job is a victim of discrimination. The dispensations of the welfare state in the 1960s and 1970s allowed members of minority groups to climb safely into the middle class—many are now advantaged people. And yet they will still profit from preferential treatment.

Even if we were to accept that some groups became advantaged, and others disadvantaged, due to historical injustice, as would have to be conceded in the United States, the advocates of quotas would still have trouble making their case to justify reverse discrimination. Liberal justice begins with an idea of the individual; it holds that an individual cannot be penalized by the state unless he or she is proved to be guilty of a legal wrong. This means that every time a government department, for example, decides to deny a qualified white male candidate a position in favor of a less qualified minority candidate, it would have to undertake a searching inquiry to determine whether the white individual's advantages (his abilities and skills) can be traced to acts of discrimination he had committed or that previous generations in his family had committed. Can we really believe that this inquiry could ever realistically be undertaken? Will a court ever be able to prove that someone's great-grandfather committed acts of discrimination that have resulted in genetic or financial or educational advantages for an individual three generations later? The inquiry would either be too superficial to be legitimate or too expensive to be practical.

But there's another side to the equation. The same kind of analysis would have to be pursued in relation to the disadvantaged candidate to prove that his or her lesser qualifications were the result of historical discrimination. And then, if we really wanted to remain true to liberal principles, we would have to show that the historical wrongs committed by the family members of the white candidate had a direct impact on the family members of the minority candidate. Thus, not only is the historical theory indefensible as a basis for justifying reverse discrimination, it is simply unworkable. And any attempt to make it work would launch the courts on costly and tyrannical inquiries.

The result of employment equity is to put the advantaged in the camp of the disadvantaged, and to place the disadvantaged in the camp of the advantaged. This is what makes employment equity a truly illiberal measure. Liberal societies were founded in order to liberate individuals from a feudal society where outcomes were unjustly determined by group status. Though born with talent, a serf would be deprived of the opportunity to prove his or her worth and profit from his or her ability. Once a serf, always a serf. Though born with no talent or drive, a noble would always be a noble. Liberals successfully argued for the consideration of individuals *as individuals*, as opposed to members of groups, with a view to giving every person the freedom to define his or her own worth and the freedom to pursue happiness. The guarantee of equal protection of the law was seen as an essential means to achieving that end; no one would really enjoy the freedom to define his or her own worth if governments continued to distribute power and privileges on the basis of group criteria, such as race, gender, social status and religion, which were irrelevant to the determination of individual merit.

Employment equity makes a radical break with the liberal tradition by re-categorizing individuals as members of the groups—the advantaged and the disadvantaged—with the result that the injustices of pre-liberal societies return to haunt us. Individuals receive a reward when they do not deserve it, and are deprived of it when they do deserve it. By means of quotas, employment equity allows the government to tell us which members of which groups should prove their worth and in what numbers. In effect, this is a return to feudalism.

Insofar as some people, no matter what their origin, are lacking the minimal social and economic conditions to enter the race and compete for opportunities, liberal societies should come to their aid. A greater transfer of wealth from the rich to the poor is consistent with equal opportunity because it doesn't require us to depart from the consideration of individuals on their merits. Providing better schooling in poor neighborhoods and increasing the quality of workfare training are examples of measures that can help people in need in their efforts to compete for opportunities. Many of the measures that Judge Abella mentioned in her report fall into this category, such as better general and technical language training, bias-free systems for determining the validity of foreign credentials, fewer restrictive requirements for loans to new Canadians who are trying to start businesses and child care for new Canadians who are taking language training or looking for work.[17] All these measures are legitimate in a liberal state because they fall short of redistributing opportunities on the basis of race or sex; instead, they foster the economic and social pre-conditions that allow disadvantaged individuals, regardless of their race or gender, to compete for opportunities on the basis of merit.

A Free and Democratic Society?

We've already seen that section 15(2) of the Charter creates an exception to the equal protection of the law guaranteed under section 15(1) by allowing governments to discriminate in favor of members of "disadvantaged" groups on the basis of race, sex or ethnicity in the distribution of benefits and opportunities. Courts and human rights tribunals have married this exception to Judge Abella's report and ruled in favor of employment equity plans. However, they've done so without facing the real problem: these programs necessarily lead to reverse discrimination.

And yet they might have dealt with this problem. In one of the Supreme Court's early and most influential decisions, *Regina v. Oakes*, Justice Dickson stated, "the very purpose for which the Charter was originally entrenched in the Constitution [is that] Canadian society is to be free and democratic."[18] When dealing with employment equity plans under section 15(2), the court might have asked whether a truly free and democratic society, that is to say, a liberal democratic society, could tolerate the injustice of reverse discrimination.

Given that the very purpose of liberal justice, as we've seen, is to do away with unjust group privileges in order to allow everyone to compete for opportunities on the basis of individual merit, the courts might have cast a skeptical eye on section 15(2). They might have said that employment equity programs could be justified under section 15(2) only in limited circumstances. For example, group preferences in hiring might have been limited to situations where a court or tribunal had found that a particular employer had committed discriminatory acts against a specific group of qualified minority candidates. Firing the members of the under qualified yet favored group and hiring members of the qualified yet disfavored group would still preserve the principle of merit. Another approach consistent with this principle is found in the United States, where the U.S. Supreme Court has allowed quota plans for hiring and promotion in "traditionally segregated job categories." Those are job categories where the evidence of historical discrimination is so well documented by past judicial findings and other forms of evidence that the court can assume that there are many qualified individuals in the minority labor pool; thus, a temporary quota plan aimed at increasing minority hires will not result in reverse discrimination.

Lovelace v. Ontario

Unfortunately, this approach, which would have been consistent with liberal justice, has been permanently foreclosed by a recent decision of the Supreme Court of Canada. In *Lovelace v. Ontario*, the Supreme Court held that the section 15(2) should not be treated as an exception to the general guarantee of non-discrimination provided by section 15(1). Instead, the Court read section 15(2) as an aspect of section 15(1). To see why this is problematic we have to return to wording of section 15(1). It states: "Every individual is equal before and under the law and has the right to equal protection of the law and equal benefit of the law without discrimination, and, in particular, without discrimination based on race, national or ethnic origin, color, religion, sex, age or mental or physical disability." The plain wording of this section clearly prohibits the state from discriminating for or against anyone on the basis of irrelevant criteria such as race or sex. And yet the Supreme Court has said that to achieve true equality, which it calls "substantive equality," it is necessary to read this section as though it allows discrimination in favor of government-designated disadvantaged groups. The court justified its contrived reading of section 15(1), in part, by appealing to the fact that the purpose of the equality provision is to promote "human dignity."[19] But how dignified do you feel when you're turned down for a job by a government department or publicly supported enterprise because you're not on the list of favored groups?

The facts of the *Lovelace* case demonstrate very clearly that court's equality analysis is pushing the country in a very troubling direction, which the "liberal-minded" advocates of employment equity never foresaw. In the mid-1990s, the Ontario government entered into negotiations with 133 First Nations aboriginal bands concerning the possibility of giving them the right to operate casinos on reservations. The negotiations ended in an agreement that allowed one group—the Mnjikaning First Nation—to build and operate a gambling house, which would be called Casino Rama. As part of the deal, the bands agreed that all proceeds from the casino would be shared among the 133 aboriginal groups that participated in the negotiations. The limiting factor on the distribution was that a group could qualify as a recipient only if it had been recognized as a "band" under the federal *Indian Act* and its members had been assigned a reservation. Problems arose when Ontario Indians who were descendants of the First Nations, but who were not registered under the Act or living on reservations, raised objections about being excluded from the distribution of proceeds. They argued that they possessed the relevant characteristic that entitled them to a share: they were members of historically disadvantaged First Nations groups. Robert Lovelace brought a class-action suit against the Ontario government, claiming that the government had discriminated against "non-status" First Nations Indians based on the irrelevant fact that they were not registered under the *Indian Act* and did not live on reservations. The government defended its action, in part, under section 15(2), claiming that it had the right to designate the disadvantaged group, in this case "status" First Nations Indians, that would receive preferential treatment. The case eventually proceeded to the Supreme Court of Canada.

The Ontario government's case for preferring "status" First Nations Indians in the distribution of proceeds was that they owned the reservation lands on which casinos were to be built. And that might have been true if all the bands had been given permission to build a casino. But, in fact only one First Nations band, the Mnjikaning, had been given that right. So, in effect, the other First Nations groups, as Lovelace rightly argued, were receiving the proceeds simply because they had registered themselves as bands under the *Indian Act* and were living on reservations.[20]

Lovelace's position put the ugliness of employment equity on display for all to see. Previously, Judge Abella had told the country that it shouldn't worry about the problem that group preferences could produce reverse discrimination because they would end the "hegemony" of advantaged groups (white males) over the "economic spoils." However, in this case, advantaged white people weren't being deprived of the spoils. Instead, members of one disadvantaged group, non-status First Nations Indians, were being robbed of the spoils by members of another disadvantaged group, status First Nations Indians. Or, to put it more accurately, members of one disadvantaged group were being robbed by members of their own group. That was the injustice as

Lovelace saw it. Thus, the Lovelace case witnessed the birth of a new government injustice: reverse discrimination by the victims of discrimination against the victims of discrimination.

The Supreme Court went through rhetorical contortions worthy of Cirque de Soleil to legitimize this unusual situation. One trick was to merge section 15(2) of the Charter, the employment equity provision, with section 15(1) the equality provision, thus ensuring that governments would have enormous leeway in deciding when and how to use group preferences. Another was to avoid facing the problem of reverse discrimination head-on by arguing that it would not get into the "unseemly" task of comparing the disadvantages of the two groups, arguing that this would be inconsistent with the court's commitment to "substantive equality." In the end, after bringing many other considerations to bear that had the effect of obscuring the problem of reverse discrimination, the court sided with the Ontario government and held that it could justify unequal treatment between members of First Nations Indians in the distribution of proceeds based on the fact that some members had the right status and others did not.[21]

With this decision, the court clearly signaled that it is not going to worry much about the problem of reverse discrimination. If the court is willing to go to these lengths to justify reverse discrimination between members of the same disadvantaged group, we could hardly believe that it will think twice about approving employment equity plans that produce reverse discrimination by favoring one disadvantaged group over another; and it certainly won't be concerned about plans that favor a disadvantaged group over an advantaged group.

The only saving grace of this decision is that the court held that a government that seeks to justify special programs favoring a disadvantaged group will have to provide some evidence that the group is, in fact, disadvantaged. That may open the door to arguments about whether women or certain high-achieving minority groups can be classified as disadvantaged. We will have to wait and see whether victims of reverse discrimination will seek to exploit this opening with a view to limiting the reach of preferential programs.

In the meantime, in the name of perfecting liberal justice by enacting what it calls "substantive equality," the Supreme Court has completely betrayed the basic goal of liberalism, which is to abolish group preferences based on irrelevant criteria such as race and gender. *Lovelace* buries the equal opportunity ideal in the public sector because governments will now feel free to distribute employment opportunities without any concern about being held accountable for reverse discrimination against individuals, whether they belong to advantaged or disadvantaged groups. We have to worry whether this attitude will carry over into the private sector. Once the highest court in the land has said that reverse discrimination is not an issue, ambitious unions may seek to bargain group preferences into collective agreements. And diversity councils, which are popping up increasingly in large corporations, may lobby for group preferences, wielding the threat that the under representation of minorities in certain job categories could lead to a complaint at a provincial or federal human rights tribunal.

Free Trade and Equal Opportunity

Free trade has given Canada a new imperative. To be truly competitive, our public- and private-sector companies must hire the most qualified candidates and do everything possible to maximize the potential contribution of every employee. This requires that we commit ourselves to the equal opportunity ideal, which holds that opportunities should be distributed on the basis of merit, not on the basis of irrelevant criteria such as race, religion or gender. The virtue of the equal opportunity ideal is that it combines justice and prosperity because when merit is recognized, every individual has the incentive to maximize personal wealth, which, in turn, increases the wealth of the whole.

Against this background, the employment equity movement must be seen as an immense mistake: it promises to destroy the equal opportunity society that we so desperately need if we hope to improve our standard of living vis à vis America, and other highly competitive nations. While many in the liberal vanguard believe that our commitment to equity is what makes our way of life so desirable, in fact, it's what holds the potential to undermine the widely shared prosperity that once made Canada, as some would say, the envy of the world.

While we should be focusing our attention on how to use our talents to compete effectively in the global economy, we're stuck with the false proxy of cultural representation. This is retrograde, even when measured by European standards. The European Court of Justice ruled recently that the city of Bremen could not hire a woman who was under qualified, in comparison to a male candidate, simply to increase the representation of women in municipal government. The court held that this practice, which aimed at achieving equality of result, offended the overriding principle of equal opportunity. Consistent with basic liberal principles, the court argued that the city of Bremen could give preferences to women in vocational training programs so that they could develop the skills needed to compete for opportunities with male candidates. In other words, the city could divert resources to women to improve their ability to compete for opportunities, but the city could not redistribute the opportunities themselves.[22] Since this ruling applies to the entire Common Market, Canada is now competing against 27 European nations with over 300 million people, who are committed by law to the equal opportunity ideal and the competitive advantage it confers.

The Misuse of American Jurisprudence

Regardless of what's happening in Europe, since 87% of our trade is with the United States, we need to focus our attention on the economic challenge presented by America's commitment to the equal opportunity principle. While the American practice of reserving educational and employment opportunities for women and minorities, referred to as "affirmative action," first began in the 1960s, the U.S. Supreme Court has played a significant role in curtailing its use to preserve the merit principle.

The court has consistently ruled that racial preferences violate the equal protection of the law granted to individuals under the Constitution. There are two exceptions, however, both of which preserve the merit principle. The first is that racial preferences can be used for a limited period to remedy specific acts of discrimination caused by a public or private employer. For example, in *Franks v. Bowman Transportation*, a trucking firm was found to have intentionally denied promotion opportunities to a specific group of black drivers by denying them seniority status. To assuage the effects of the discrimination, the Supreme Court issued an order that granted seniority and back pay to an entire class of black employees, who then automatically qualified for the promotions that had been denied. Although the order denied promotions to white employees who were next in line based on seniority, the court ruled that this could not be raised as an objection. In effect, the court held that its remedy would not result in reverse discrimination against the affected white employees since they would not have been eligible for promotions were it not for the discrimination against the black employees. Furthermore, the black employees who received the seniority award would have earned it were it not for the discrimination and therefore would have received their promotions based on merit.[23]

The second broader exception allows a private-sector employer to voluntarily use employment quotas for a limited period to remedy the effects of discrimination in "traditionally segregated job categories." These are job categories where minorities are drastically underrepresented and prior judicial findings and the weight of evidence support the view that minorities had been denied opportunities due to intentional and systematic discrimination practiced by unions or employers or both.[24] Here the merit principle is preserved because it's safe to assume that discrimination has created an untapped labor pool of qualified candidates.

The court has held consistently that group preferences cannot be used in the private or the public sector simply to ensure that minorities are more fully represented in the workplace, a practice referred to as "racial balancing," because it is an inherent violation of the equal protection guarantee to hire or promote anyone on the basis of race. The court has also ruled that group preferences cannot be used to remedy disadvantages suffered by minorities due to historical discrimination, which the court refers to as "societal discrimination." The reasoning on this point is that preferences that favor a particular racial group will produce reverse discrimination by excluding qualified members of other racial groups; since those who are excluded cannot be assumed to have caused any of the historical disadvantages suffered by members of the preferred group, such discrimination can never be justified.

It's very important to understand the American position because it reveals the limitations of the *Abella Report*. Judge Abella frequently cited American experts and American cases to justify her employment equity system. She cited a U.S. Supreme Court case, *Griggs v. Duke Power*, to support the notion that "adverse impact"—the underrepresentation of a disadvantaged group in a job category—was sufficient to prove the existence of systemic discrimination. But that was not the position taken by the Court in *Griggs*; it simply said that impact was one factor to be considered when assessing whether a finding of discrimination was warranted.[25]

As well, Judge Abella was clearly influenced by American authorities when she proposed group preferences as the solution to the problem of systemic discrimination. But, again, the U.S. Supreme Court had allowed group preferences only in the narrowest of circumstances. Judge Abella simply ignored the reasoning that had led the Supreme Court to reject simplistic standards for proving discrimination and simplistic group-based remedies for dealing with it. This proved to be decisive in putting Canada on the road to a legal regime that fails to honor the equal opportunity ideal. In particular, it allowed the advocates of employment equity to argue that group preferences could be justified in order to achieve racial balancing and to remedy societal discrimination—the two justifications that had been thoroughly rejected by the U.S. Supreme Court.

No Remedy for Societal Discrimination

Since societal or historical discrimination has become the most common justification for the use of group preferences in Canada, we should take a moment to review the reasons that the U.S. Supreme Court rejected this position.

Bakke v. Regents of the University of California

The court addressed this justification for the first time in 1978 in the case of *Bakke v. Regents of the University of California*. Allan Bakke applied for admission to the medical school at UC Davis, but was denied although he had received a benchmark score that placed him well within the range of qualified candidates. (A benchmark score is an accumulation of points based on grades, scores on the Medical College Admissions

Test, letters of recommendation and other criteria relevant to assessing a student's aptitude for medicine.) In pursuit of an affirmative action program, the medical school at UC Davis had reserved 16 spots in its first-year class for minority students, and had admitted minority candidates who had significantly lower benchmark scores than Bakke. Claiming that he had been excluded from admission due to the places reserved for minority students, Bakke argued that he had been discriminated against based on his race (he was Caucasian). He brought suit against the medical school citing Title VI of the *Civil Rights Act* of 1964, which guaranteed that educational institutions receiving federal financial assistance could not exclude anyone from participating in any program on the grounds of race or color. He also claimed that the school, which was chartered and funded by the state of California, had violated the Fourteenth Amendment, which holds: "No state ... shall deny to any person within its jurisdiction the equal protection of the laws."

All members of the court agreed that the medical school had been using racial classifications in its admissions process. The issue was whether the school could produce a convincing rationale for using what were otherwise prohibited racial criteria. The university would have to demonstrate a "compelling state interest" to justify the scheme. Among other reasons, the medical school justified the use of race on the basis that it would increase the representation of historically underrepresented minority groups in the school and counter the effects of societal discrimination.

In a strange 4–4–1 split decision, four members of the court rejected the school's justifications and found in favor of Bakke based on Title VI; four accepted the justifications and found against Bakke based on Title VI and the equal protection clause; and Justice Powell provided the deciding vote that produced judgment in favor of Bakke, relying primarily on the equal protection clause to reject the school's justifications.

Justice Powell's opinion was noteworthy because it was particularly tough on the issue of societal discrimination, and in this respect, embodied the view that has continued to hold sway with the court. Justice Powell objected to the notion the court could countenance programs that arbitrarily practiced reverse discrimination against members of the "white majority" on the basis that they had committed acts of historical discrimination against minorities. Since "the 'white' majority itself is composed of various groups, most of which can lay claim to a history of prior discrimination at the hands of the State and private individuals," that theory would open the door to preferential treatment for almost everyone, except perhaps "a new minority of white Anglo-Saxon Protestants." Furthermore, even if they wanted to, courts could never determine with any precision which groups to prefer because "[t]he kind of variable sociological and political analysis necessary to produce such rankings does not lie within judicial competence ... even if they otherwise were politically feasible and socially desirable." Thus, the decision to prefer some groups over others would become entirely arbitrary and fluctuate as some groups rose based on court-ordered preferences and others fell. In short, any court that embarked on working through the implications of societal discrimination would politicize the judicial process and produce entirely chaotic and unjust results. The injustice of the approach was clearly evident on the facts of the present case because the medical school's quota program imposed "disadvantages upon persons like the respondent [Bakke], who bear no responsibility for whatever harm the beneficiaries of the special admissions program are thought to have suffered."[26]

After rejecting the use of preferential criteria based on race, Powell held that race could be considered as one factor among many when deciding whether to admit an individual student who is part of a pool of qualified applicants. The consideration of race in this instance would be consistent with merit and could be justified in relation to the university's interest in creating a diverse student body that would promote a "robust exchange of ideas."

Thus, the limited use of race in the admissions process could be legitimized because it would contribute to the university's interest in securing the benefits of free speech as guaranteed by the First Amendment.[27]

The Uncertain Reach of Preferences

While the U.S. Supreme Court has placed restrictions on the use of preferential treatment, it's clear that the reach of affirmative action has not been clearly delineated. In two recent highly charged cases that involved the use of race in university admissions at the University of Michigan, the court applied Justice Powell's reasoning to arrive at results that are difficult to reconcile. In *Gratz v. Bollinger*, the Court ruled that the University of Michigan could not automatically add 20 points to the benchmark scores for undergraduate applicants based on their minority status. That, the court held, was inconsistent with the case-by-case strategy outlined by Justice Powell. The bonus points led to the admission of virtually all minimally qualified minority applicants, thereby creating a group preference that discriminated against non-minority applicants in the admissions process in violation of the equal protection of law guaranteed by Title VI of the *Civil Rights Act* and the Fourteenth Amendment.[28]

Yet, in the companion case, *Grutter v. Bollinger*, the court approved the University of Michigan Law School's practice of giving preference to minority candidates in order to promote a critical mass of minority students. The critical mass rationale expanded the diversity principle by admitting a range of considerations that were clearly not related to the First Amendment concern with freedom of speech. These included breaking down racial stereotypes, equipping students to succeed in a diverse global marketplace and sending a message to the nation that the path to leadership created by legal education is open to students from all backgrounds.[29]

Chief Justice Rehnquist, who wrote a dissenting opinion, argued that the critical mass justifications were shams designed to cover up a "naked effort to achieve racial balancing." Using statistical profiles entered into evidence, he demonstrated that the percentage of preferred minority candidates (African-Americans, Native Americans and Hispanics) in the applicant pool matched almost perfectly the percentage who were admitted on a yearly basis. And indeed, when we examine the Law School's explicit statement regarding its diversity policy, the very language suggests its minority program was explicitly designed to achieve racial balancing and remedy historical discrimination in violation of equal protection guarantees. In its policy statement, the law school claimed that its program was intended to achieve "racial and ethnic diversity with special reference to the inclusion of students from groups which have been historically discriminated against like African-Americans, Hispanics and Native Americans, who without this commitment might not be represented in our student body in meaningful numbers."[30]

While the use of race in university admissions has become somewhat elastic and may entail the use of previously forbidden group preferences, the legitimate use of group preferences in employment situations has expanded significantly. In *Johnson v. Transportation Agency,* decided in 1987, the court took the position that the underrepresentation of women in job categories traditionally held by men could justify the use of preferential programs to increase the number of female employees. Previously, the court had held that the underrepresentation of a group in a job category would not be sufficient to justify an affirmative action program, unless it was a matter of judicial notice that the job category had been "traditionally segregated." The court in *Johnson v. Transportation Agency* attributed the requirement of judicial notice to the fact that women were drastically underrepresented in the position of road dispatcher at the Transportation Agency as compared to their availability in the local labor pool. It thereby expanded the reach of the old doctrine. Justice Scalia made this point forcibly in his dissenting opinion, taking the position that the agency had not proved that the job category was traditionally segregated. The program, in his view, was simply an attempt to remedy societal discrimination, with all the attendant problems, notably the elimination of qualified male candidates through reverse discrimination.[31]

Another recent noteworthy expansion of preferential treatment occurred in 1990 when the Supreme Court held that the Federal Communications Commission could reserve broadcasting licenses for minority-owned businesses to promote the First Amendment interest in diversity in broadcasting. In her dissenting opinion, Justice O'Connor rightly stated that this decision had proceeded on assumptions that were completely alien to one of the most basic principles of liberal constitutionalism: "The Constitution provides that the Government may not allocate benefits and burdens among individuals based on the assumption that race or ethnicity determines how they act or think."[32]

Lessons for Canada

At an early stage in the affirmative action debate, the U.S. Supreme Court ruled that public- and private-sector bodies could not use group preferences to achieve racial balancing or rectify historical discrimination because both practices would produce reverse discrimination and destroy the equal opportunity ideal. That was a lesson Canada might have learned before it embarked on the project of making our country into a more equitable version of the United States. Sadly, our courts, our human rights tribunals, our federal government and even our legal scholars forgot about equal opportunity and turned a blind eye to the problem of reverse discrimination. Although the United States has moved slightly in the direction of Canadian equity by opening the door to the use of group preferences in university admissions, and expanding their use in public-sector employment and public broadcasting, the merit debate continues to rage within the courts and in the country at large. When the Supreme Court handed down its decisions in the University of Michigan cases in 2003, a week-long media circus ensued in which the supporters and critics of affirmative action argued their positions vehemently in print, on television and over the Internet. In Canada, there was barely a whisper when the Supreme Court delivered its decision in *Lovelace*, even though it signaled a radical step forward in the equity agenda by allowing the Ontario government to practice reverse discrimination against a disadvantaged group.

Canada should not have embraced preferential treatment without scrutinizing the American situation. If our political and legal elites had paid more attention to American jurisprudence, they might have applied section 15(2) of the Charter in ways that respect the equal opportunity ideal. Following the American cases, our elites could have decided that group preferences should be confined to cases where specific acts of discrimination are committed against clearly identified victims because their use in that context does not cause reverse discrimination. If decision-makers had taken that prudent position, section 15(2) would not have been eviscerated; it still would have authorized special programs that redistribute resources to disadvantaged groups to allow their members to acquire the skills they need to compete for opportunities. This would include measures such as loans to assist individuals in returning to school, day care for those who are seeking to improve language skills, or, as we saw in the European (City of Bremen) case, special access to training programs. Since these measures prepare members of disadvantaged groups to compete for opportunities, and fall short of redistributing the opportunities themselves, they are consistent with the merit principle and preserve the equal opportunity ideal.

Not long ago, we were well positioned to be the greatest place in the world in which to live. We had almost all the advantages that America has, and almost none of the disadvantages such as inner-city poverty, racial antipathies, high rates of violent crime and poor health outcomes for those who can't afford health insurance. Building on our strengths, we might have eclipsed the United States and laid claim to being the real land of equal opportunity. Instead, our political and legal elites decided to abandon the equal opportunity ideal and embrace progressive, politically correct theories of justice that make gender, culture and race more important considerations than individual merit. While America and Europe are proceeding on the assumption that the equal opportunity ideal will give them a decisive edge in the world economic competition, we are now moving inexorably toward a society where equal opportunity is the exception, not the rule. And so the brain drain continues, our prosperity suffers and even disadvantaged individuals like Robert Lovelace are complaining that they don't want to suffer the burden of reverse discrimination. If Sir John A. Macdonald could see us now, he would be grief stricken.

Myth Five

PAY EQUITY PROMOTES EQUAL PAY

The Confusion about Equal Pay

Do you believe that men and women should receive equal pay when they have the same qualifications and they're doing the same work? Of course you do. If a male teacher and a female teacher were both teaching the same number of hours in a high school, and they had the same seniority and similar educational qualifications, no one could plausibly argue that the female teacher should be paid less; anyone who approved of this would be condoning sexual discrimination.

Now consider the following situation. Let's say that cashiers at Zeller's retail outlets are paid less than forklift operators at the store's local warehouse. And let's assume that cashiers, most of whom are women, felt that they should be paid the same as the forklift operators, all of whom were men, because the cashiers believed that they were creating just as much value for the company as the operators. Would you agree that they should be paid the same wage? The cashiers would have a strong case, wouldn't they? Because they provide quick and friendly service, customers leave the store with a good feeling and want to come back and spend their money again. Good cashiers are essential to creating customer loyalty, and loyalty assures profitability;

cashiers are important indeed. And wouldn't we believe the cashiers when they told us that their claim is supported by the fact that they work in a female-dominated job category where their work has been undervalued by employers because it is assumed to be "women's work," which male managers have always assumed to be worth less than work that is done mostly by men? Wouldn't we have to agree that these women in these jobs are victims of sexual discrimination?

Of course, the manager doesn't see it that way. He says that it doesn't take long to train a cashier, and that the store is perpetually swamped with applications for cashier positions. So, he decided a long time ago to pay the cashiers $8 per hour because, in his experience, the store can hire good cashiers at any time for that wage. Forklift operators are another matter. The store manager has difficulty finding certified forklift operators in his area; sometimes he has to send a candidate to an expensive training course that lasts several days. Furthermore, the job has a high risk factor. Warehouse workers claim for workplace injuries on a regular basis. And should an operator mishandle a load, the cost to the store can be substantial. So, to get good forklift operators, who don't damage goods and don't cause injuries, the manager has determined that he must pay operators $15 an hour. Under these conditions, are the cashiers justified in asking for pay that is equal to the forklift operators?

The federal government and every provincial government in the country, save Alberta, would say yes. That isn't because governments in Canada guarantee equal pay for equal work. Clearly, that principle wouldn't apply here since the cashiers and forklift operators are doing different work. The cashiers would have a claim because governments have enacted a guarantee that employees should receive equal pay for work of equal value. This principle is referred to as "comparable worth" by some, because it allows the government to order an employer to pay equal wages for jobs that are dissimilar on the theory that the jobs have comparable value to the business. The government determines such value by bringing in experts to determine whether the jobs are similar when compared on the basis of skill, effort, responsibility and working conditions. And note, it can be applied to raise wages only in job categories where the majority of employees are female, because governments have made the assumption that employers have always undervalued "women's work."

This sounds nice in theory, but in practice it is beset with insuperable difficulties that make the entire process of determining comparable worth a total sham. Right from the start, there are two clear objections to this approach. It defies common sense to hold that jobs that are clearly different should receive equal pay. And then there's the problem that the criteria used by governments to determine whether these different jobs should somehow be deemed equal in value does not require officials to consider market forces. How can anyone determine the value of a job without reference to the laws of supply and demand and the role they play in setting prices for goods and services? It's a stunning shortcoming in the comparable worth doctrine. In effect, this allows the government to institute an archaic command economy, whereby the authorities determine wages in the marketplace for those job categories where women are in the majority.

The principle of equal pay for equal work, which first appeared in Canada in Ontario in 1951, and which was adopted by the federal government in the United States in 1963, is a liberal principle that promotes the equal opportunity ideal. To have a workplace that is truly free of discrimination, where individuals are paid what they're worth to a business without regard to race or sex, the government should prohibit an employer from paying women a lower wage when they're doing the same work that is performed by men in the same workplace. To allow otherwise would destroy the equal opportunity ideal because pay scales would not recognize individual merit.

However, virtually every government in the country, either by virtue of human rights guarantees, labor legislation or special pay equity statutes, is now committed to bypassing the equal pay for equal work principle in favor of the pay equity principle. Pay equity was first adopted in Quebec in 1976, where it now applies to both public and private sectors; the federal government adopted it in 1978 for all its public service employees and all federally regulated companies, then it spread to the various provinces, eventually reaching Ontario, which applied the principle to both the public and private sectors in 1987.

This radical shift from the liberal equal pay principle to the socialistic pay equity principle resulted from a lot of lobbying by feminist activists, mostly lawyers, who argued that women were still experiencing widespread discrimination in the workplace in spite of the fact that equal pay laws had been in effect throughout the country for well over 20 years. If the activists really wanted equal pay, and they believed that women were not receiving it, they should have asked governments to devote greater resources to enforcement of equal pay guarantees. Instead, they demanded that governments abandon equal pay in favor of pay equity based on the following theory.

They began by pointing out that the women were overrepresented in clerical, sales and service positions, which paid less than average wages, and in teaching and nursing, which paid better but where there was little opportunity for advancement. The clustering of women in these fields was said to be caused by employer discrimination, which prevented women from competing for the complete range of jobs for which they were qualified.

Feminists also claimed that the clustering phenomenon was due to a complex process of socialization. They said that a woman's work in the home in nurturing and supporting other family members had always been undervalued by men. As a result, when women entered the workforce, male employers assumed that they should be limited to working in supporting roles, where the pay was low due to the traditional under-valuation of women's work. This situation was perpetuated, it was argued, because women had been duped by men into believing that they should pursue positions only in these low-paying fields. From a purely econom-ic standpoint, the net result of clustering was an oversupply of women competing for jobs in these low-paying fields, which further depressed wages that were already kept artificially low by employer discrimination. Thus, the concept of the pink-collar ghetto was born.[1]

If women were stuck in low-paying jobs without any prospect of ad-vancement, the radical solution would have been to establish job quotas for women so that they could gain access to higher paying positions. Simply giving pay raises for women in low-paying jobs would have the unintended result of encouraging women to stay in positions where their economic prospects would still be rather limited. That, however, didn't stop feminists from arguing that the only way to solve this prob-lem was to use government power to compel employers to raise the wages of women in female-dominated occupations so that they equaled the wages of men in a male-dominated occupations, even if the men were performing different jobs. The human resource experts entered here to try to explain how fundamentally different jobs could be deemed to be equal in value. In other words, the scheme could work as long as some consultants were paid enough money to tell us that the world was flat and the moon was made of green cheese.

To justify this theory, pay equity supporters used one fact: the so-called wage gap between men and women. The advocates of pay equity always began by citing the statistic that men on average earn 60 percent more than women: for every dollar a man made, a woman made a mere 60 cents.[2] Clearly, the advocates argued, this was proof that women were being discriminated against in the workplace. But, the wage gap, when scrutinized, turns out to be one of the biggest lies ever told to the public in this country.

There Is No Wage Gap

To get a true picture of groups in the workplace, we have to begin by making sure that the groups are truly comparable, so that we aren't confusing apples with oranges. To understand how and where the pay gap originates, for every job sector in the country, we would have to compare male and female workers who are performing the same kind of work. In each sector, if we found women on average made less than men, then we would have to determine whether those differences resulted from differences in hours worked, levels of education, training or experience, or regional variations in pay within the sector. After taking all these differences into account, if men still earned more than women when performing equal work in a particular sector, then we would know that a true wage gap existed in that sector (and that the gap could be attributed to discrimination). That analysis could be duplicated for all sectors with a view to determining the true extent of the wage gap throughout the economy.

When feminists first started talking about the wage gap, however, they weren't too concerned about doing the research that was required to explain it. They made blanket comparisons that skewed their claim that a woman earned 60 cents for every dollar earned by a man. By comparing all working men and all working women to get that figure, they were confusing apples with oranges. Women have always held more part-time jobs than men, and men who work full-time tend to work longer hours than women who work full-time. That means that comparing all working men and all working women will produce a result that tends to make the gap between seem larger than it is.[3]

Fortunately, most economists made their comparisons more carefully than the pay equity advocates. As early as 1971, both Canadian economist Walter Block and American economist Thomas Sowell undertook to make the kind of nuanced analysis that compares working men and women who have similar characteristics. And they discovered something quite extraordinary. When they compared the wages of men and women who were working full-time but who had never been married, they found that their average wages were virtually identical! Furthermore, the finding on the Canadian side was confirmed 16 years later, in 1987, when Statistics Canada published a study that established that never-married single women over the age of 35 earned *more than* never-married single men.[4]

It turned out that the wage gap was entirely attributable to marriage. Block and Sowell discovered that the "wage gap" grew substantially when they compared married men and married women. In Canada, in 1979, single women earned 82 cents for every dollar earned by single men based on gross comparisons, but married women earned half that amount, a mere 41 cents.[5] Marriage had the effect of doubling the gap, not only because married women spend more time in the household tending to family responsibilities, but also because married men spend more time at work earning the extra income needed to raise a family. This conclusion is fully supported on the American side by Steven R. Rhoads, one of the world's leading experts on pay equity issues. He discovered that, in the mid-1970s, "... wives employed full-time averaged 25 hours of work in the home and 39 hours of work in the market each week, while husbands employed full-time averaged 13 hours of work in the home and 47 hours of work in the market." Furthermore, he found that the "... addition of each child enhanced the married man's earnings by another 3 percent while depressing that of the married woman by 7–10 percent."[6] The fact that women reduce their commitment to the work force or withdraw from it altogether to care for children has a profound impact on future earnings: "A worker who drops out of the labor force for five years earns one-third less on returning than an identical worker who has been employed continuously. Even five years after reentering the work force, the returning worker earns 15 percent less." Rhoads also believes that some women tend to prefer lower-paying jobs in the fields of teaching, health care, administration and child care, which are easy to exit and re-enter, and therefore attractive to women who want to take time off to care for their children.[7]

Any doubt about the findings of Block, Sowell, and Rhoads were confirmed by a comprehensive study of the wage gap published in 1989 by University of Toronto economist Morley Gunderson. His study established that the wage gap cited by activists could be explained away in relation to many factors that have nothing to do with alleged employer discrimination. These factors included differences in education, differences in the choice of jobs, differences in pay among different sectors of the economy where women tend to be employed, and differences in the duration and continuity of work experience, both of which affect seniority.[8] Once these factors were taken into account, he also found that marriage played a major role in explaining the wage gap. This study, which was based on a review of 117 books and articles on the subject of pay equity, should be read by every person who continues to argue for the pay equity principle. Clearly, when the "wage gap" cannot be attributed to employer discrimination, the case for pay equity legislation is completely undermined.

Of course, feminists would respond to these studies by arguing that women who choose family over a career are not choosing freely. They have, after all, been brainwashed by men into thinking that they must take on greater family responsibilities; and the price they pay for that is a wage penalty for which they should be compensated by a pay equity scheme. But we have to wonder whether it isn't the feminists who are suffering from the false consciousness they attribute to women who choose family over career. When you look at the women who sold this point of view to cowering, gullible male politicians, you'll find that they were people like lawyer Mary Cornish and professor Chaviva Hosek, who had chosen career over family. The pay equity advocates were careerists, based mostly in Toronto, who were totally out of touch with the lives of women in places like Windsor, Belleville, Red Deer and Harbourville, where choosing to take time out to raise a family was not seen as an apostasy from feminist orthodoxy. And then there's the problem that the feminists were doing exactly what they accused men of doing, that is, patronizing women by assuming they weren't capable of making their own decisions.

As early as 1971, before feminists started lobbying governments to adopt pay equity legislation to eliminate the "wage gap," women who chose a career over marriage were making as much money as men, if not more. Equal pay for equal work was already a reality for most women who were careerists. If feminists had done their homework, they would have discovered that the real cause of the wage gap was the differential impact that marriage has on the earnings of men and women. And that, in turn, would have led them down a different path, and we would never have had to endure the costly burden of pay equity legislation.

An Incoherent Scheme

Even if feminists could have proven that there is a significant wage gap that has been caused by employer discrimination, they could never have proven that pay equity schemes provide workable remedies. As we've seen, pay equity requires government officials to make comparisons between different jobs based on a composite picture of skill, effort, responsibility and working conditions. But that's the damning point—the comparisons have to be made because the jobs are different. The comparison process is artfully designed to obfuscate this fact. Unfortunately, many human resource specialists are willing to work creatively, particularly when it pays so well—it costs an Ontario employer more to establish a pay equity plan than to deliver the pay increases it mandates.[9]

Another major problem with the criteria is that the experts cannot agree on the weights that should be assigned to them. One expert might think that skill deserves more weight than working conditions; another that working conditions are more important than levels of responsibility, and so on. A pay equity plan, or a judgment delivered by a pay equity tribunal, will depend almost wholly on the biases of the experts who pronounce on the degree to which a male-dominated job category is similar to a female-dominated category. Based on scores of interviews conducted with pay equity advocates and experts in the United States, the United Kingdom and Australia, Steven Rhoads has concluded that,"[t]here is no agreement" among experts on factors to be included, on how they should be measured once decided, or even how factors (such as working conditions) should be measured once decided." As a result, the whole process has become politicized. Rhoads comments, "... comparable-worth advocates in private or at conferences among the initiated often stress the political, not the objective, nature of the job evaluation."[10]

The mischief that the evaluation process invites was brought home to me one afternoon in the late 1980s, when I was having a meeting with a lawyer in a large law firm in downtown Toronto. We started talking about the new pay equity legislation and she confided that she was extremely skeptical. The firm had just been visited by pay equity experts whose mission was to determine how much the legal secretaries in the firm should be paid under Ontario's Pay Equity Act. With a certain contempt in her voice, the lawyer told me that the "experts" had spent part of their time counting the number of steps that different members of the support staff took to get to the kitchen to fetch coffee for client meetings. I suppose that this counting was an aspect of determining how much "effort" each member of the support staff had to expend to get coffee. But, to be accurate, shouldn't the experts have taken into account that different people have different strides, which could make the effort of fetching coffee more or less demanding? And what weight would they assign to this effort, as compared to the effort involved in typing or printing a document, or sending out a courier package? This example speaks volumes about the pseudo-science of applying the various criteria.

And then there's the problem of defining the threshold for analysis. Pay equity provisions vary on the percentage of women that exist in a job category before it becomes suspect; some say its 70% female, while others say 60% or less. Can we determine with any accuracy when an occupational group has enough women in it to justify the assumption that the group has suffered wage discrimination?

The inherit arbitrariness of pay equity legislation has resulted in decisions that defy common sense. In Minnesota, for example, which adopted pay equity for the public sector in the early 1980s, the results have been outrageous. Steven Rhoads reports, "... utility and library directors have come out of the comparable worth process with higher pay than their city managers, and workers previously paid equally for equal work have been assigned unequal pay for doing equal work." Further, in St. Paul, nurses' wages in the public sector have been kept below the market rate by pay equity decisions, with the result that the state cannot offer the higher rates of pay needed to eliminate the shortage of nurses in the public health care system. And even though libraries had 40 to 60 applications for every open position, the pay police compelled the state to give librarians pay increases of anywhere from 20% to 60%.[11]

The incoherence of the pay equity doctrine was revealed in Ontario in the 1990s, when nurses demanded to have their pay raised on the basis that their profession was female-dominated (i.e., at least 60% of the employees were women). Their demand was rejected when pay equity evaluators could not find a male-dominated group in the hospital system to which to compare them. The only male-dominated group that received higher pay than nurses was doctors. And no one could plausibly argue that doctors and nurses could be compared in terms of skill, effort, responsibility or working conditions. So, the nurses argued that they should be allowed to have a comparison drawn between another male-dominated group in another sector of the economy. What? Another sector of the economy? This put the whole theory of systemic wage discrimination to shame.

As stated earlier, pay equity is built on the assumption that an employer in a particular workplace has discriminated against women in a female-dominated occupation by keeping the wages of that group artificially low, while paying members of a male-dominated occupation doing similar work a higher wage that reflects the occupation's true value to the organization. The *proof* of the employer's discrimination is that he is refusing to pay women the same wage that he's paying to men who are doing similar work, but the employer certainly cannot be discriminating in this way when his workplace *does not have a group of men doing similar work.* Thus, the nurses' claim of wage discrimination had no basis in fact under the legislation, and that made their demand to be measured against a male-dominated group in another sector of the economy a complete farce.

The nurses' inane position didn't prevent the Pay Equity Commission or the NDP government from taking action. After being lobbied by the union representing nurses and the Pay Equity Commission itself, the government amended the *Pay Equity Act* in 1993 to allow the commission to make "proxy comparisons" for the public sector. The commission was empowered to draw comparisons between female-dominated groups in the public sector and male-dominated occupations anywhere else in the provincial economy when a male "comparator group" could not be found in the public sector workplace where discrimination against women was alleged. This turned pay equity disputes into a free-for-all in which women in female-dominated groups in the public sector could allege discrimination and ask government officials to raise their wages in relation to any male-dominated group doing similar work anywhere in the province, with a preference, no doubt, for the highest paid male group.

After winning the provincial election in 1995, the Conservatives under Mike Harris brought in legislation to abolish the amendment that allowed for these proxy comparisons. The legislation was challenged in the Ontario courts by the union representing health care workers on behalf of a female Red Cross worker who would be a beneficiary of the proxy approach.

To make its case against the amendment, the government brought in its own human resource expert, who testified that the proxy comparison approach was a ruse because differences among groups in different organizations could be attributed to "non-gender related reasons" such as differences in location, working conditions, union strength and career opportunities, rather than discrimination.[12] That testimony, however, proved to be of no avail, and the court ruled against the government on the ground that its new legislation violated section 15(1) of the Charter, the equality provision that guarantees every citizen the equal benefit of the law. The court reasoned that the Pay Equity Act was intended to provide a remedy for all women in female-dominated job categories, which is to say, all women suffering from systemic wage discrimination. The court introduced the notion that the mere fact that a job category was female dominated was proof of discrimination. And thus it concluded that the government would be depriving some women of the equal benefit of the law if it excluded them from claiming pay raises under the

Act simply because they lacked a comparator group in the work-place.[13] With this decision, the perverse logic of pay equity was revealed, and at the same time, extended. But it would take another case at the federal level to reveal the ludicrous nature of the entire scheme.

Under the federal government's pay equity legislation, the Canadian Human Rights Tribunal made a decision in 1998 in which it awarded members of nine predominantly female job categories in the public service a $5 billion pay increase retroactive to 1985 based on a comparison with 53 predominantly male groups, also in the federal public service. The federal Liberal government, which had brought in the pay equity legislation in one of its previous incarnations, suddenly decided that pay equity wasn't such a good idea after all. So the Treasury Board offered a settlement worth roughly a quarter of the actual award.

Angry that the Liberal government wasn't living up to its own commitments, the Public Service Alliance of Canada (PSA) brought suit against the government in the federal court. Indicating that it was dead set on reducing the award, the government didn't rely on its own lawyers. Instead, it went to the private sector and hired superstar litigator, Sheila Block, who argued the government's case on the basis that the methodology used by the Human Rights Tribunal was flawed and that it established wage comparisons that were unjustifiably high. The entire case turned on lengthy, intricate, and often obtuse arguments about how an expert should make a comparison between female-dominated and male-dominated occupational groups.

The case was a testament to the fact that no one is able to agree on how to use the basic pay equity criteria—skill, effort, responsibility and working conditions—to make objective comparisons. Once parties begin the process of trying to determine how to define each factor and how much weight to give to each, they quickly get lost in a bog of statistics and graphs and a welter of conflicting and highly subjective political opinions. Just consider how the federal court described the lengthy, tedious hearings undertaken by the Human Rights Tribunal:

> The Tribunal formally started its hearings on September 9, 1991 and rendered its decision nearly seven years later on July 29, 1998. It held more than 250 days of hearings, and heard witnesses testifying for weeks and, in some instances, months on end. The reasons given by the Tribunal for the decision under review are 200 pages long; in addition, the Tribunal rendered two substantial decisions on preliminary issues...."[14]

In the end, the federal court rendered a decision in favor of the Public Service Alliance (PSA) and ordered the government to honor the award. But, unrelenting in its opposition to its own legislation, the Liberal government continued to negotiate with the PSA, which resulted in a settlement in the neighborhood of $3.5 billion. The full cost, however, would end up being much higher. Decades into the future, the cost of starting from an artificially higher starting point in the year 2000, when the federal court rendered its decision, would certainly amount to billions more. Currently, the country is indignant about the fact that the federal Liberals set up a phony national unity advertising campaign to reward supporters of the Liberal party in Quebec with $200 million of taxpayers' money. But the sponsorship scandal pales in comparison to the pay equity scandal. The pay equity legislation that the Liberals passed in 1978 has allowed federal civil servants to walk off with billions of dollars, with billions more yet to be paid, simply because the federal politicians wanted to appease the feminist lobby in the late 1970s with a piece of legislation that has no rational validity. Under pay equity guidelines, federal revenue—our tax money—has become a giant slush fund for female civil servants and the male employees who happen to be working in predominantly female occupations. When are we going to have an inquiry that will expose the immense corruption that this unwarranted transfer represents?

Whither the Market?

While the criteria used to determine pay equity adjustments are themselves internally incoherent, the real problem is that they exclude the market as a factor in determining wage rates. Obviously that's a huge problem given that most businesses, and even government departments, have no criteria other than the market to determine what they have to pay to get new employees or keep existing ones. To the feminists who lobbied for pay equity, however, that wasn't a problem because they believed the market was an oppressive, patriarchal instrument, which served to enhance male wealth and power by paying women less than they deserved. The feminists believed the economy was a giant white male conspiracy to deprive women of their due, and the only way to defeat it was to have government decree that women deserved a larger share of the pie.

While many of the advocates of this approach were highly educated people, clearly they'd never taken a first-year course on economics. Even a white male conspirator has to answer to the market. If he's in manufacturing, for instance, he will have to sell his goods at a price that people are willing to pay. And he will set his employees' wages at rates that will allow him to make a profit. But he can't get away with setting his wages too low because he may find that his best employees will go to work for someone else, perhaps even a competitor, who is paying better wages; or his employees might unionize and force him to pay higher wages; or he might be forced to hire underskilled workers who produce inferior products that people won't buy, and his profits will disappear. In this very basic scenario, the employer won't want to get away with paying women less for performing the same work as male employees. If he discriminates, the women will soon find out that they are being paid less than their fellow male employees; and, as a result, they won't work with the same zeal, their productivity will diminish and profits will suffer.

Now, the foregoing example assumes a world of perfect competition and we all know that world doesn't always exist. They teach that in first-year economics too. But the example expresses a basic truth: even white guys aren't powerful enough to control market forces. The market only discriminates between people who understand it and those who don't. And those who don't will soon go out of business if they set prices higher than the market will bear or they set their wage rates for male and female employees lower than the market will bear. The market is an impersonal mechanism that everyone must answer to eventually. To suggest otherwise is a fantasy. And yet the fantasy continues every time the federal or provincial government decides to make another pay equity award without taking market forces into account.

Counter-argument: The Market Is No Longer Free

Some would argue that I'm wrong to take free market economics as the basis for critiquing pay equity because the free market was given up in the early 20th century in North America in favor of the regulated market. Where market forces were once free, we have substituted minimum-wage laws, collective bargaining and myriad regulations that constrain market behavior to a greater or lesser degree in areas such as food processing and banking. And then we have to deal with the objection that businesses have been setting wages for decades using pay scales that are based on criteria such as skill, effort, responsibility and working conditions, the same used to determine wages under pay equity legislation.

First, let's deal with the objections concerning the vast number of regulations that the modern state has imposed on the private sector. The regulations that are in place, determining who can and cannot enter the banking or food-processing industries, or who can and cannot practice medicine, law or dentistry, just to take a few examples, certainly circumscribe the operation of the market; in that sense, the market is no longer truly free. But a truly free market would subvert public safety, which is a value that ranks more highly than the efficient production of wealth. If, for instance, there were no health guidelines in place for food processors, public safety would be compromised because the consumer would have to distinguish good processors from bad by incidents of food poisoning, and even death. If there were no licensing guidelines in place for doctors, again, public safety would be undermined as people lived or died depending on whether their doctors turned out to be highly trained professionals or charlatans. While regulatory requirements certainly keep some people out of the market, that's only to set the stage for the market to do its work in delivering goods and services in accordance with the laws of supply and demand. So, pay equity advocates can hardly justify abandoning market criteria in determining wage rates based on the fact that we now have regulated markets. The modern regulatory state serves to correct abuses in the functioning of the market, which has the effect of enhancing, not undermining, the dynamic effects of supply and demand.

As for minimum-wage laws, clearly they interfere with the laws of supply and demand since they sometimes force employers to pay their least valuable employees more than they're worth. However, that's one limit on one limited class of employees. For other employees, the laws of supply and demand continue to set their wages.

Collective bargaining is a greater challenge to free market economics since it's potentially available to any group of employees in the workforce. But, as a practical matter, it has little effect since less than 25% of the private sector workforce is unionized in Canada, and only about

10% is unionized in the United States. Even so, where unions do exist, their demands are necessarily constrained by the market since employees cannot bargain away an employer's profit margin, as determined by consumer demand, without forcing the employer into bankruptcy.

That leaves us with the objection based on the use of pay systems by large and medium-sized businesses. While it's certainly true that these systems are used to set wages in some organizations for the full range of job categories, it's not true that they ignore market forces. In fact, they take their cue from the market and they remain sensitive to it after initial wage rates are set. Typically, human resource experts will take one job category and assign it a "benchmark score" in relation to variables such as skill, effort, responsibility and working conditions. Then they will assign it a wage based on the average wage rate that would be paid for a job with that benchmark score within the industry in which the business operates. Other job categories in the workplace then have their wages pegged above or below that wage rate based on where their composite grades stand in relation to the benchmark score. Once these wage rates are set, they continue to be measured against market rates, and they are reviewed twice a year in some businesses to ensure conformity with market rates.[15]

Those who want to justify pay equity's failure to include market forces in its criteria—based on the belief that the market forces have been extinguished by the modern regulatory state or by bureaucratic pay scales—had better think again.

What Are the Real Costs?

Based on the award made in the Public Service Alliance (PSAC) case, we've already seen that pay equity has already cost the federal government billions of dollars with a final tally yet to be disclosed. But, beyond this award, which was made public because it arose from a federal court ruling, we don't really know the true cost of pay equity. That's very troubling. No one has ever attempted to tally up the costs of all the awards made in the public and private sectors across the country. Given that pay equity regimes have been in place in the federal public sector and in Quebec for almost three decades, and in most of the remaining provinces (except Alberta) for at least a couple of decades, we can imagine that the total cost of all awards would be overwhelming—billions more to be sure. It's hard to track the costs because governments have not been particularly forthcoming in disclosing how much money public and private employers have been forced to cough up in anticipation of or in direct response to government action. We should be told, however, because that money is coming from tax dollars that would otherwise be used for more pressing purposes. Just think of the federal government's multi-billion dollar payout in the PSAC case. What if those billions had been spent on our underfunded health care system? How many new hospital beds, operating theaters, chemotherapy treatments or MRI machines could have been funded with the initial $3.5 billion award? Someone at one of Canada's think tanks should undertake to calculate the past, present and future cost of pay equity schemes and publish the results because that's the only way the public will ever come to terms with the enormous burden that pay equity has placed on public spending. And let's not forget private-sector spending too. Every time a provincial government orders a private-sector employer to make a pay equity award, the employer is forced to divert revenue that might otherwise be invested in research and development or new machinery and equipment to unjustified wage hikes. The result is that businesses subject to pay equity awards are made less competitive and less profitable.

Certainly, pay equity regimes send a message to businesses that provincial governments are not truly interested in developing legal regimes that promote business development. We have to wonder whether Canada can afford to continue to send this message when we're competing for investment with the United States, and most U.S. jurisdictions long ago rejected the pay equity approach.

With the passage of the *Equal Pay Act* in 1963, the U.S. federal government rejected demands made by the Kennedy administration for the introduction of a pay equity regime and instead instituted the principle of equal pay for equal work for all businesses engaged in interstate commerce. It later affirmed the commitment to the equal pay principle in interstate commerce when it passed the *Civil Rights Act* of 1964, which, under Title VII, "... forbids wage and employment discrimination on the basis of race, color, religion, national origin, and sex."

The equal pay principle expressed in Title VII was put to the test in the early 1980s in the state of Washington, when the public service union, the American Federation of State, County and Municipal Employees (AFSCME), brought suit against the state, which had recently begun to phase in a pay equity scheme for its employees. The union argued that state had failed to bring in pay equity when it first became aware of wage discrimination against female employees based on a study completed in 1979, and that this failure was a breach of Title VII's prohibition of sex discrimination. The union sought retroactive pay increases and succeeded in its claim at the trial level. However, on appeal, the U.S. Court of Appeals reversed the trial judgment based on the ruling that Title VII instituted the principle of equal pay, not the principle of comparable worth. In reaching its decision, the court took full notice of the fact that pay equity fails to take the market into account in assessing rates of pay, and it considered that to be inconsistent with the purpose of Title VII. The court held that the statute was put in place to ensure that men and women doing the same work would be paid the same wage, while allowing the wage itself to be set by the market.

Because the pay equity scheme allowed the state to adjust wage rates without reference to market forces, it was deemed to be outside the ambit of Title VII. In effect, the court was saying that pay equity ruled out the consideration of the market forces because it deemed those forces to be inherently discriminatory, but nothing in Title VII indicated that the market could be characterized that way. The court stated: "Neither law nor logic deems the free market to be a suspect enterprise." And further, it held: "We find nothing in the language of Title VII or its legislative history to indicate Congress intended to abrogate fundamental economic principles such as the laws of supply and demand or to prevent employers from competing in the labor market."[16]

This case effectively terminated the pay equity principle in the United States. The state of Washington has continued to use pay equity principles to establish wage rates for female-dominated occupations, and Iowa and Minnesota have also adopted pay equity for the public sector. But, in the rest of the United States, pay equity enjoys little support.[17] This gives the United States a significant advantage over Canada when it comes to competing for investment in North American and world markets.

Where Is the Opposition?

Pay equity reveals everything that's wrong with political thinking in Canada today. Pay Equity:

- asserts discrimination where none can be found and falsely teaches Canadians to assume that they are living in an oppressive society
- creates misunderstanding about the role of markets in creating prosperity for everyone

• ignores the economic realities of competing for investment in the global marketplace

• creates special privileges for a group at the expense of the whole

• encourages the arbitrary rule of experts as a substitute for the rule of law administered fairly by our courts and our elected representatives.

Given all these problems with pay equity, you would think that at least some members of the Conservative Party, provincially and federally, would want to take a run at getting rid of the scheme. They're supposed to be in favor of free markets and limited government. But, so far, they've been reluctant to tamper with pay equity, and I have some idea as to why that is.

In the early 1990s, when the Conservative Party of Ontario was wallowing in third-party status at Queen's Park, I was asked to co-chair the party's Policy Advisory Council on Labor and Employment issues with the party's labor critic, Elizabeth Witmer. The council was comprised of business people, human resource professionals and labor lawyers, who were interested in developing recommendations for reforming the province's labor legislation. Although the council was a creature of the party and included many party supporters, it also included non-partisans who were interested in contributing to the process of reform with a view to improving Ontario's economic performance.

Since the party had already taken a strong position against employment equity legislation that had established job quotas for the public and private sectors, I assumed that it would also be willing to take a strong stand against pay equity. Many fellow council members made that assumption as well. However, I soon found there were strong dissenting voices. When I announced at one of the early meetings that I was hoping to develop a recommendation that pay equity should be scrapped in favor of equal pay, I had trouble recruiting some leading female Conservatives. Then I learned that Mrs. Witmer was also opposed to abolishing pay equity. She had her reasons. She was concerned that no one had quantified the costs of implementing the *Pay Equity Act*, and that the party couldn't take a run at it without having economic data to justify its opposition. Fair enough.

She also believed that the stakeholders were satisfied with the legislation as it stood. And it was true, no one in the business community was speaking out against the legislation in the early 1990s, which I found puzzling at the time. Later, I learned in the back halls of Queen's Park that business people who had criticized pay equity, when hearings were held in the mid-1980s prior to the passage of the Act, later found that their companies received special attention from the Pay Equity Commission. There were no dissenting voices by the early 1990s because the business community had come to understand that opposition, even when it was solicited by the government through public hearings, came at a significant price.

The silence in the business community in our most prosperous province was a measure of how much damage the pay equity movement had done. Feminists had persuaded the Ontario government to adopt a pay scheme that limited basic economic freedoms without any sound rationale and, in the process, they had also drastically curtailed freedom of speech.

Myth Six

PRIVATE PROPERTY IS NOT A FUNDAMENTAL RIGHT

Property Lines

Anyone who spends even a little time in the United States will quickly realize that most Americans worship private property and the free market; most Canadians, on other hand, aren't really true believers. Many of us tend to look down on the preoccupation with "success" that prevails south of the border. We often hear a fellow Canadian acknowledge that Americans are wealthier than we are but that their superior standard of living is a grand deception; the rich get richer but somehow the poor also get poorer. Gain for the few, or even the majority, is paid for with low tax rates that leave the state without the resources to deal with a chronic social deficit of illiteracy, high infant mortality rates, rotting inner cities, drug abuse, violent crime and inadequate health care for the unemployed and the poor. We fancy ourselves a kinder, gentler version of American capitalism that cures social ills by regulating private economic activity and redistributing wealth.

However, it's by no means clear that the rich get richer at the expense of the poor in the United States or that all of America's social problems, which are often overstated in the interest of making Canada look better than it is, can be attributed to smaller government. And, in any event, that debate has become passé. America has become so much more prosperous than Canada that it could finance a Canadian-style social agenda, but for the extraordinary cost of the war on terror.

The higher status that private property enjoys in the United States flows from explicit constitutional guarantees found in the Bill of Rights. Under the "takings clause" in the Fifth Amendment, the Bill of Rights states that "private property [may not] be taken for public use, without just compensation." This principle presupposes the belief that the individual has an undivided interest in his or her own property, whatever form it may take. Only that belief can explain the state's duty to pay a just price for what it expropriates. The Fifth and Fourteenth Amendments, which hold respectively that neither the federal government nor state governments may deprive any one of life, liberty or property without due process of law, also secure the individual's right of ownership. Both Amendments rest on the assumption that the individual has a prior exclusive claim on his or her assets; that is the only way to explain the fact that the state must have a strong legal justification before interfering with them.

Looking behind the explicit legal guarantees of the Bill of Rights, we find that the Framers of the American Constitution gave a special place in the pantheon of human rights to the right to acquire, hold and transmit property. Many Canadians will be familiar with the sublime phrase that Thomas Jefferson used in the Declaration of Independence: "We hold these truths to be self-evident, that all Men are created equal, that they are all endowed by their Creator with certain unalienable rights, that among these are life, liberty and the pursuit of happiness." While Jefferson and the signatories to the Declaration of Independence certainly believed that the new republic should give everyone the freedom to pursue happiness, what is not often recalled is that originally Jefferson had written that all Men "are endowed by their Creator with certain unalienable rights, that among these are life, liberty and *property*."

The Framers of the American Constitution were profoundly influenced by the English philosopher, John Locke, who had given property, which included ownership of one's person, freedom and possessions, a singular place in his political philosophy. Locke, who is recognized by many scholars as the chief philosophical architect of the modern liberal state, argued in his *Second Treatise on Government* that every political society should be governed by the Law of Nature: It "obliges every one, and Reason, which is that Law, treats all Mankind, who will but consult it, that being all equal and independent, no one ought to harm another in his Life, Health, Liberty or Possessions." Locke's teaching had a profound impact on the Framers, which was reflected in a series of public essays written by Alexander Hamilton, James Madison and John Jay shortly after the Constitution was drafted. Published in 1787 and 1788 in New York City newspapers, the *Federalist Papers*, as they were later called, were a series of articles that articulated the case for the adoption of the Constitution, which was then being considered for ratification by the states. In what would become one of the most well-known principles of American constitutional philosophy, Madison argued in *Federalist* #10 that "the first object of government" is "the protection of the different and unequal faculties of acquiring property."[1]

More than any other passage I've read in the *Federalist Papers*, this simple, eloquent formulation speaks to the animating spirit of the new republic. Note that Madison doesn't simply say that the first object of government is the protection of property; it's the protection of every individual's inherent right to express his or her unique abilities through the acquisition of property. This embodies the notion that there is no true freedom to pursue happiness unless the state gives free reign to personal invention and initiative in private economic activities.

This brief passage expresses perfectly the leading themes of liberal political philosophy, which established the new rational foundation for American political life. It reflected the beliefs that the individual was the building block of society, that the free market was an essential vehicle for expressing individual freedom and promoting general prosperity and, further, that the free market would advance the cause of justice by giving every individual an opportunity to live in accordance with his or her abilities. All this must be contrasted with the prevailing political situation in Europe where groups favored by the state for religious or political reasons stifled individual freedoms of all kinds, where rulers controlled the operations of the market for their own benefit, and justice consisted in giving government lackeys a piece of the action. The federalist vision, inspired by the "great Mr. Locke," as Madison called him, was truly revolutionary. And the status given to private property was at the heart of that revolution.

The federalist vision is of great interest to Canadians for a couple of reasons. The first is that leading political scientists, like Gad Horowitz, who believe that the Canadian personality has a socialist streak, begin with the assumption that Canadians, like Americans, are Lockean liberals in their basic political beliefs. The second matter of interest, related to the first, is that Sir John A. Macdonald's speech to Parliament recommending the adoption of the national policy expressed very nearly the sentiments of *Federalist* #10. You'll recall that the leading purposes of the national policy were to "bring out every kind of industry," "develop the minds of the people and their energies" and allow all Canadians "an opportunity" to "develop the skill and genius with which God has gifted them."

Although Canadians certainly are Lockean in spirit in some measure, we have not embraced the legal guarantees that would allow us to fully actualize Lockean ideals. The *British North America Act*, a rather dreary affair that aimed at dividing powers between the federal and provincial governments, didn't contain any reservations on behalf of individual rights. The Act said nothing about private property except that it could be regulated by provincial governments. Given its limited nature, the courts took almost 90 years to discover an individual right within the Act itself. In 1957, the Quebec Court of Appeal ruled that an individual right to freedom of speech was contained in the very scheme of the Act. Since the Act was put in place to define the division of powers within a democratic state, the court reasoned that it necessarily guaranteed the right of free speech because a democratic state could not function properly without a free and vigorous debate among its citizens. However, until the Charter of Rights and Freedoms was adopted in 1982, the courts said nothing more about individual rights in the Constitution.

Even political elites were silent on the issue of individual property rights. When Prime Minister Trudeau first held constitutional talks with the premiers in the early 1970s, he proposed a Charter of Rights, but his so-called Victoria Charter was a meager proposal that did not include a right to private property or a due process guarantee. And 10 years later, when the Constitution was finally brought home, and the Charter of Rights and Freedoms was entrenched, private property was left off the list of guaranteed individual rights again.

Prior to the adoption of the Charter, a few conservative-minded politicians demanded a guarantee for private property, but their voices were soon drowned out by a political chorus that sang the praises of big government. Both the Liberals and the NDP feared that a reservation on behalf of private property would interfere with their collectivist dreams for a Canada where government would eradicate all forms of social and economic injustice. As well, many politicians on the left and the right were concerned that property rights would limit their ability to use government to increase their power and influence.

On top of this, anti-Americanism reared its head in the form of intellectual posturing, which led certain political and intellectual elites

to argue that the American constitutional scheme gave too much power to the individual, particularly in economic matters. The reservation
on behalf of economic individualism and free markets, it was argued,
had created a state that could not regulate social and economic conditions to achieve a true common good; the result was a society with
glaring inequalities, a high incidence of poverty and inadequate health
care. The anti-American point of view had a respectable pedigree since
it could be traced to the Fathers of Confederation, who, as we've seen,
chose a parliamentary system over the American republican system,
because the latter was deemed to be too individualistic, free-wheeling
and unstable to be a suitable model. However, during the debate concerning the repatriation of the Constitution and the adoption of the
Charter, no one ever thought to link the anti-American position to the
rational, fully articulated viewpoint of the Fathers of Confederation;
for the most part, the position was presented formulaically and defensively. It also had the disadvantage of being utterly false. While it's true
that the American courts had used the takings clause and the federal
due process guarantee to hold up the New Deal legislation that was
designed to end the suffering associated with the Great Depression,
eventually the court saw the wisdom in allowing government a greater
role in regulating economic and social activities. As a result, since the
1940s, American governments have been free to regulate on a Canadian
scale. That, of course, didn't stop the Canadian critics from misrepre-
senting 40 years of American judicial history in pursuit of keeping
property rights out of the Charter.

Strangely, the intellectual resistance to the idea of entrenching property rights was never tackled in the academic arena, where there should
have been some powerful dissenting voices. Where were our great law
professors when one of the most important individual rights needed a
defense? Where were the papers, the books, the speeches, the courses?
I began my studies in law at the University of Toronto in 1980, when

the repatriation movement was in full swing, so I had the privilege of seeing how the debate was handled at one of the nation's leading law schools. Many smart people were watching over the patriation process, but I can't recall anyone taking on the issue of private property. In fact, across the country, legal scholars just weren't very concerned about it. In part, this was due to the prevailing intellectual atmosphere in law schools throughout North America, where new legal theories propounded by scholars such as John Rawls and Ronald Dworkin, held that fundamental human rights were simply legal fictions and historical curiosities that couldn't withstand the test of postmodern reasoning.

So, without any academic opposition, and almost no political opposition, the critics of private property got their way and the Charter was adopted without any reservation on behalf of individual property rights. Now, we might argue that this wasn't so bad in the end because, as I've already pointed out, since the 1940s, neither the takings clause nor the federal and state due process guarantees have done much to limit the reach of government in the United States. The American experience suggests that the few Canadians who favored entrenching property rights as a check on the expansion of government might have been very disappointed to find that their impact would have been quite limited. So why should we care about property rights today?

I believe that we should care because there is still a salient difference between Canada and the United States on an individual level, where rights are supposed to operate. In the United States, the takings clause and the due process guarantees allow the individual to raise a defense of his or her right to private property when the state truly overreaches. There is no such option in Canada. If the government decides to take your home tomorrow to build a new school or to allow a developer to put up a mall, don't expect a defense based on your inherent right to the fruits of your own labor. Or if a province decides to bring in punitive estate taxes to deal with government debt, don't expect a lawyer to come rushing to your door begging to defend the inherent right of your parents to transmit their property. Those rights simply aren't recognized by Canadian courts.

The other reason to be concerned about the lack of property rights takes us back to *Federalist* #10. As I've already argued, Madison didn't see the protection of private property as just another component of the American constitutional scheme. The "protection of the different and unequal faculties of acquiring property" was at the center of the new constitutional universe. It established several of the leading themes of American democracy—individualism, entrepreneurship and meritocracy. In other words, *Federalist* #10 laid the foundation for the elements that would produce the American commitment to the equal opportunity ideal. Those who fail to understand the almost sacred character of private property in the American system simply don't grasp that property rights are an essential expression of the American vision of liberal democratic justice. When you tamper with someone's property rights, you're not simply interfering with his or her particular rights—you're assaulting the Republic itself.

Thus, we can still make the argument that property rights should be protected under the Canadian constitution, not only to ensure adequate protection for the individual, but also to signal that Canada is ready to embrace the beliefs that would promote the equal opportunity ideal and improve our competitive position.

The Parochial Response

Some of my fellow citizens would object to this position on the ground that we shouldn't seek to Americanize Canada, which is what we'd be doing if we simply mimicked America's commitment to property rights. That would be wrong, they would argue, because our two countries have had different historical experiences, and we cannot assume that what works for Americans will automatically work for us. Perhaps we need to signal our commitment to equal opportunity in some other way that is more in tune with our political history, our habits and our fundamental laws.

There is one simple answer to this objection. Madison's arguments in *Federalist* #10 were not made from the standpoint that they were right for America at that point in its history. They were made in the sincere belief that they were given by reason, through the writings of the liberal philosophers such as Locke and Montesquieu, and that they were right for any society that was interested in promoting the twin goals of justice and prosperity. Those who would object to the priority given to private property in the American system have forgotten the teachings of the liberal philosophers who gave us the very idea of human rights. Whether we look at the writings of Locke, or other great liberal thinkers such as Montesquieu or Kant, we find that the first and most basic human right is the right to self-preservation. The second, without which the first could never be secured, is the right to acquire private property. Freedom of speech, religion and association are further down the list. Taking the view that every individual's primary and natural object is to secure his or her own physical security, and that other rights could never be exercised in any event without it, liberal thinkers gave pre-eminence to the right to self-preservation and the right to acquire property. This must be contrasted with the Canadian view that property rights don't deserve constitutional recognition. The Canadian position is simply not rational when seen from the perspective of liberal democratic justice.

Here I must refer to the views of the late Honorable Pierre Trudeau. I admired many of Trudeau's ideas and his many outstanding personal qualities, and I agree with John Turner, who reckoned that Trudeau was the leading citizen of his time. However, his status as a liberal thinker has been greatly overrated. In 1967, the late prime minister gave a speech to the Canadian Bar Association, in which, as Justice Minister in the Pearson government, he advanced the idea that Canada should constitutionalize the guarantee of basic human rights. Trudeau referred to fundamental rights such as freedom of speech, freedom of association, freedom from sexual and racial discrimination and the right to a fair trial. He even made reference to Thomas Jefferson, citing his famous statement: "Nothing then is unchangeable but the inherent and unalienable rights of man." But Trudeau mentioned nothing about reserving any individual rights for private property. Either Trudeau had disagreements with his preceptors or he had read them selectively. Any hope that Trudeau would include property rights in his emerging constitutional philosophy was squelched when he spoke critically about the due process guarantee in the American Bill of Rights. Taking the standard Canadian view of its impact, he stated:

> What of a constitutional guarantee of "due process of law?" In the United States, this phrase has, in the past, created many problems because of its vagueness. At times, the Courts have construed it so broadly as to invalidate some social legislation which we would now accept as essential.[2]

In this statement, we can see that Trudeau was both a liberal democrat, who believed that limited government was needed to secure individual freedoms, and a social democrat, who believed in the unlimited use of government to achieve social justice. He was clearly signaling to the country that he was willing to ignore the essential liberal right to private property in order to promote his social democratic vision. This uneasy alliance of liberal and illiberal views would become a recurring theme in his political thinking. It would eventually manifest itself in his schizophrenic willingness to limit the reach of government by introducing the Charter of Rights and Freedoms, while allowing public spending to run wild, leaving us with a crushing public debt that has strangled our ability to deliver essential social services such as health care and education. His conflicted philosophy was also revealed in his willingness to constitutionalize employment quotas under section 15(2) of the Charter, which, as we've seen, had the effect of promoting the socialist ideal of equality of result at the expense of the liberal ideal of equal opportunity.

While Trudeau, and other political and legal elites, may have thought that Canada would be better off by refusing to embrace the liberal democratic principle of protecting property rights, they clearly failed to consider the ultimate impact that would have on the nation. By leaving private property off the list of protected rights in the Charter, they missed an important opportunity to affirm the beliefs in individualism, entrepreneurship and meritocracy, which have been so instrumental in giving the United States its lead in the race for talent and wealth. If we still hope to instill those beliefs as a step in the direction of improving our competitive position, we need to reconsider how and why liberal thinkers first developed the idea that government should protect fundamental rights, such as the right to private property. To correct the inadequacies of our legal regime, we must promote a new civic education that teaches that citizenship in this country requires an awareness of the rights we should honor, and why we should honor them. The starting point is found in the writings of the "great Mr. Locke," who argued that all human beings are by nature endowed with a specific set of fundamental rights, which must always be respected by government because they exist prior to its creation.

The Original Philosophy of Natural Right

When we hear the phrase, "the state of nature," we are naturally led to thoughts of a canoe trip in the Canadian wilderness. And this is not a bad way to begin thinking about what Locke means when he says that we must return to the state of nature to discover justice in its pristine form. But Locke isn't recommending that we become political sociologists and study the practices of aboriginal peoples living in isolation to determine how to organize ourselves in civil society. Locke's journey is a journey of the mind that can be taken at any time by anyone, regardless of whether he or she lives in a large city or on the Serengeti. And that journey consists in comparing and examining all the conflicting claims made about justice within society and eliminating those that can be attributed to bias, self-interest or prejudice. The final destination is a completely rational account of justice that is derived from first principles that are objective and indisputable. Locke refers to that account as the state of nature because it expresses the truth about human nature and what it means for the determination of our respective rights and duties.[3]

To get us to the state of nature, Locke gives himself the task of taking on all the false claims about justice that had been foisted on societies since the time of the ancient Greeks. In particular, he directs his attack against those who argued that people could become fully human only by living up to certain standards of excellence, which consisted in devotion to a particular religion or the cultivation of moral or intellectual virtues. According to Locke, there is no rational support for the notion of an absolute end for human activity: "... the philosophers of old, did in vain inquire, whether *summum bonum* consisted in riches, or bodily delights, or virtue, or contemplation; and they might have as reasonably disputed, whether the best relish were to be found in apples, plums, or nuts, and divided themselves into sects upon it." By rejecting these so-called teleological doctrines, Locke dispenses with the traditional notion that justice consists in taking care of others before taking care of oneself.[4] This leads to the vindication of selfish interest, and the belief that human ends are relative. The good is redefined as the selfish pursuit of pleasure and the measure of pleasure is reduced to individual desire.

In spite of the fact that human ends turn out to be relative, Locke argues that people can still recognize the existence of common interests in self-preservation and personal freedom. These common interests are the necessary outcome of Locke's attack on traditional thinking: no one can doubt the value of life when there is nothing worth dying for, and no one can doubt the value of the freedom to pursue happiness when there is no authoritative account of the good life.

So, Locke begins his teaching with a principle that speaks to our universal interest in living safely and living well. He argues that those common interests would lead each one of us to recognize that everyone has a natural right to "comfortable self-preservation." However, we cannot enjoy this right unless we have the means to enjoy it. We must have some way of acquiring the things that ensure our well-being or the right to it is useless. Thus, Locke argues that the right to comfortable self-preservation logically gives us a right to appropriate and transform the products of nature, and labor is what gives us title.

At first, this position seems problematic because Locke takes the side of modern environmentalists and argues that nature is owned in common. Thus, to take anything from nature, we need everyone's consent or each of us must share whatever he or she takes with everyone else. Locke argues that we must reject both options because they would prevent anyone from using nature to preserve him- or herself. By the time you asked every person for permission to eat the apple you just picked, it would have rotted; if you bypassed consent and sought instead to share the apple with everyone else, your share would be so small that you would starve. The only way out of this dilemma is to give each person an absolute individual right to acquire land and transform its products. But note that we are entitled only to as much land as we need to preserve ourselves and to pursue happiness. The rest belongs to all other people for their survival and happiness.

If each of us were entitled to only as much land as would be needed to live in simple comfort, everyone would end up with roughly the same amount of property. The small farmers who lived on the frontiers of the early West would be Locke's model citizens. However, only for brief moments have societies ever followed the limits established by natural right. Every civilized society is and has been characterized by great inequalities in wealth, with a minority controlling most of the productive assets, including the land.

Given that inequality is a practical reality, Locke is forced to ask whether it can ever be justified. Surprisingly, his answer is yes. Extreme inequality can be justified if it enhances the right to personal security and the right to pursue happiness, the two rights that are contained within the right to comfortable self-preservation. But how is that possible? Isn't it clear that when a few people control the wealth of a society, they leave less for their fellow citizens, depriving them of security and personal freedom? On the contrary, Locke argues that concentrations of wealth produce greater wealth and freedom for the entire society. We can recognize the truth of this argument, according to Locke, by reflecting on the fundamental problem that we face as human beings: the world is a niggardly place. Nature is hostile to our aspirations. To use it for our benefit, we must attack and subdue it. Nature gives us plenty, but only when we invest it with our labor. Labor is so important to the fulfillment of our needs that nature is dwarfed in comparison. Labor increases the value of nature a hundred times, and in many cases a thousand times. So, the political problem for Locke becomes, how can we encourage people to mix their labor with nature to "increase the common stock of mankind"?[5]

The solution is already in our midst. Society must introduce a currency. With money, people can acquire more land than is required for their immediate needs because they can exchange the surplus product, which is perishable, for a form of wealth that is permanent. Money creates the possibility of accumulating personal wealth, which is *the* incentive people need to accelerate the conquest of nature, or, to put it in more modern terms, to promote economic growth.

Obviously, this development leads to growth for some, that is, for the "industrious and rational" few who cornered the market on land and other capital assets. Yet everyone else is also better off, at least potentially, due to the division of labor that results. Those without land find jobs working on the land itself or transforming its products.[6] The members of this latter group, even though they are completely separated from the means of production, become guarantors of prosperity. Because others are monopolizing the society's productive resources, this group is forced to be energetic, creative and innovative in finding ways of adding value to what the owners and their employees produce. The ability to add value to primary products plays an essential role in promoting economic growth. The most recent development to confirm the truth of Locke's teaching is the advent of computer technology. Today, the greatest value added to products is not provided by owners of land and other forms of capital, or their employees, but rather by an independent class of software specialists.

So, the monopoly held by some on the land, and later, other capital assets, is justified because it creates the condition for economic development that makes everyone better off. When inequalities exist, everyone has a better chance of securing his or her life, liberty and happiness. This is the original trickle-down theory of economic growth.

We might agree that most people are better off in societies that have adopted Locke's free market approach, a fact that has been proven by the dynamic growth recently experienced in China and other Asian countries. Yet we must also recognize that some people can end up unemployed and even homeless in such societies. We need only spend a day walking the streets of New York City or Toronto, dodging the homeless and penniless, to understand that harsh reality. Some of the champions of capitalism believe that this proves the justice of the Lockean system; those who worked hard and trained well were rewarded and those who didn't were punished, as they should be. On the other hand, the critics of capitalism believe that the persistence of poverty proves the injustice of the system; many of those who were qualified and industrious were ignored, laid off or underpaid, and then left to fend for themselves because the system doesn't do enough to help the disadvantaged.

Both the champions and the critics fail to realize that Lockean liberalism is not nearly so harsh. Indeed, Locke maintains that what anyone earns or acquires by his or her own labor is the product of his or her talent, creativity and industry; as such, no one else can claim a share in it. This means that immense inequalities of wealth that result from individual effort are insulated from state control. But let's be clear about what we mean by state control. A liberal democratic state cannot confiscate or dictate the use of any citizen's property. It may, however, "regulate" the use of property under certain conditions.

To understand how public control re-enters the picture, we must return to Locke's starting point. Remember that the right to comfortable self-preservation is the primary right in Locke's system. The right to the fruits of our labor is a secondary right that secures the first. So, if the exercise of the right to acquire and use property does not guarantee to everyone the bounty needed to secure comfortable self-preservation, the state has a right, and in fact a duty, to tax the rents and income accruing from capital and labor to provide for the disadvantaged. And the state remains the judge of how much redistribution is needed to achieve the comfortable self-preservation of every citizen.[7]

The Liberal Betrayal

Locke's original teaching about the role of private property in the liberal conception of justice reveals the limitations of the Canadian perspective on property rights. When our political elites decided against putting property rights in the Charter, many thought they were perfecting our commitment to liberal justice by giving the state the greatest possibly leeway to regulate social and economic activities. In other words, they thought they were giving the state the freedom to expand the welfare state to secure the public interest. However, when we look at Locke's account of the origins of basic human rights, we discover that a state cannot really call itself liberal unless it guarantees property rights to its citizens. Furthermore, we can see that our political elites wrongly believed that entrenching property rights in the Charter would severely limit the state's regulatory role. Locke gives the state the right to regulate the market to redistribute wealth, prevent undue concentrations of economic power and promote a merit-based society.

From this standpoint, we can also see that Canadian politicians misinterpreted the meaning of the American judiciary's struggle to define the limits on state action imposed by the property rights contained in the Bill of Rights. The American Supreme Court eventually ruled in a series of cases decided in the 1940s that the guarantee of property rights did not prevent the state from taking the actions needed to deal with the pressing social and economic problems caused by the Great Depression. And, now with Locke's principles in clear view, we can see that when the court handed down these rulings, it was perfecting those principles by allowing the state to exercise the regulatory functions that Locke reserved for it. If Canadian political elites had done their homework, they would have seen that the American jurisprudence on private property embodied a progression that led to the fulfillment of the original principles of liberal justice, and that it deserved respect, not contempt.

Just as Canadian political elites ignored the implications of these important American judicial decisions, they also ignored the trend that they set in motion. Once the U.S. Supreme Court gave the green light to government actions designed to deal with the effects of the Great Depression, the new concern among small "l" liberals was that the state would gain too much latitude in determining when it could restrict individual property rights. Their concern was justified as courts gradually chipped away at what remained of the individual's right to secure his or her property from governmental interference.

The individual's natural right to control his own property was eroded yet further in a United States Supreme Court case, *Kelo et al. v. City of New London et al.*, which was handed down on June 23, 2005. This case dealt with the issue of whether the municipal government for the City of New London (Connecticut) could use the takings clause to condemn and expropriate family homes to promote general economic development.

In an attempt to resurrect its depressed local economy in the late 1980s, the municipal government of the City of New London had been taking steps to create an urban renewal plan. The opportunity to develop a specific plan was presented in February of 1998, when Pfizer pharmaceuticals announced that it was going to build a $300 million facility in the area. Three months after Pfizer's announcement, the city presented a plan that called for the demolition of family homes on two parcels of land adjacent to the Pfizer site—one to be used by private developers to build an office tower; the other to be used for undefined future development in "support" of a nearby park site. The city justified its renewal plan by relying on the takings clause in the Fifth Amendment, which states that "private property shall [not be] taken for public use, without just compensation." The city believed it had met the standard of "public use" because the proposed development served several "public purposes"—it would create jobs, generate revenue, encourage revitalization of the city core, improve the aesthetics of the area and provide new recreational opportunities. Families whose homes had been condemned had brought suit to challenge the city's justification of the plan; they had lost their case in the state appeal court, but successfully moved to bring the matter before the Supreme Court.

The case raised a tricky question concerning the meaning of "public use" under the takings clause. Normally public use entailed expropriation by the government to build a public road, a public hospital or a military base. If the expropriation involved a transfer to private individuals or companies, the resulting development would still have to be for public use; for example, a public utility, a railroad or a stadium. However, in this case, since the city was allowing transfers of private property to private developers to build an office tower that would be "used" by "private" individuals rather than the "public," the takings appeared to be illegitimate. The aspect of private use was enhanced because Pfizer's decision to locate in the area had given rise to the plan and Pfizer would clearly benefit from the development.

A five-member majority held that the takings were legitimate even though the office tower and other possible future developments would be used by private individuals, because the plan was justified in relation to clear "public purposes" such as creating jobs and increasing tax revenue. The wording of the takings clause, which called for actual use of expropriated land by the public to justify expropriation, was rejected as unworkable because no court would ever be able to decide with certainty how much public use would be required to satisfy the standard. Thus, as long a legislative body could prove that it had a public purpose in mind, and its development plan was reasonably connected to achieving that purpose, it could expropriate as many family homes as it pleased.

The four dissenting members of the Court argued, rightly in my view, that this ruling would allow governments to expropriate anyone's home for the benefit of any private developer and its clients because virtually any form of development could be justified in relation to some beneficial public purpose; every new condominium project or new office building creates new jobs in construction and holds out the possibility of a larger tax base due to higher density or the arrival of more affluent taxpayers. Thus, this ruling totally eliminated the protection for private property provided by the takings clause and, as the minority noted, it thereby undermined the federalist belief that "the security of Property" is one of the "great ob[jects] of Gov[ernment]."[8]

If, prior to the adoption of the Charter of Rights and Freedoms, Canadian political elites had given serious thought to the ever-diminishing role of individual property rights under the U.S. Constitution, they might have considered that entrenchment was needed in Canada to sustain the original liberal commitment to property rights. Those who wanted us to improve on the American model might have argued that we should not only entrench property rights, but that we should do so in a way that truly ensures that the individual is fully protected from arbitrary state action.

A commitment to property rights that corrected any lingering imperfections in the American approach would have allowed Canada to lay claim to being the Western world's foremost liberal democratic nation. We would have secured individual rights to the greatest possible degree, and at the same time, signaled to the rest of the world that we were fully committed to the beliefs in individualism, entrepreneurship and meritocracy that define the equal opportunity ideal.

When the Charter was introduced in 1982, there was virtually no awareness of what was at stake in the refusal to provide a guarantee for property rights. Now that time has taken its toll, the failure to address the issue of property rights is reflected in a weakness of conviction that has hampered our ability to compete with the United States under the free trade regime. When Canadian politicians failed to entrench property rights, they missed the chance to promote the beliefs in individualism, entrepreneurship and meritocracy, which would have made us more competitive in the 21st century. The price of looking down on America, and ignoring our liberal heritage, has turned out to be higher than anyone could have imagined.

Myth Seven

CANADIANS HAVE A
SOCIAL DEMOCRATIC BIAS

Two Nations – Two Visions of the Role of Government

I have argued that the size of government must be reduced and its activities aligned with the equal opportunity ideal before our nation can realize its creative and productive potential—and close the prosperity gap with the United States. While that's what Canadians need, it isn't necessarily what Canadians want. It's a fact that Canadians have always had a marked tendency to rely on government to provide solutions to social and economic problems, and that we've accepted the state's intervention in areas where Americans have shunned it. We have supported a publicly owned trans-national railway, a public broadcasting system, a state airline, public utilities (notably electricity generation), a national health care system, national marketing boards for farm products, and an "equalization" program that redistributes wealth from the most prosperous provinces to the least prosperous. Other examples of public intervention, such as the National Film Board or the Canada Council, could be cited, but they don't begin to approach the foregoing examples in scope or cost. In the U.S., the state is not involved in most of these areas, and where it is, its participation is minimal in comparison, with the exception of public health care, where the U.S. spends only slightly less than Canada (6.7% of its GDP vs. 6.8% in Canada).[1]

The question then arises: If Canada and the U.S. are both liberal democratic countries, why are they so different in their attitude toward the role of government? There's a stock answer to this question that you can read in any introductory textbook on Canadian government or in recent books on Canadian–American relations, such as Michael Adam's *Fire and Ice*. The stock answer is that while America was explicitly founded on the principle of *limited* government, Canada was founded on the principle of *responsible* government, which placed no constitutional limit on government action.[2] And the answer is true enough. The Framers designed the American system to frustrate ambitious politicians, who would naturally desire to extend their sphere of influence. To solve that problem, one as old as civilization itself, the Framers created a new political science that consisted of three measures that would guarantee that power would be limited and exercised in the public interest.

The first was to divide power between the federal and state governments to make it less likely that any one legislative body could oppress the people. The second measure was to set up an institutional framework at the federal level whereby the different branches of government (the executive, legislative and judicial) would check and balance each other in their selfish pursuit of power and produce government that would confine itself to protecting the rights of the people. This idea was expressed concisely and elegantly by James Madison in *Federalist #51*, where he advocated a "policy of supplying by opposite and rival interests the defect of better motives."[3] The third measure, adopted in 1791, was to entrench a Bill of Rights to provide additional safeguards against government infringement of individual freedoms.

The system of checks and balances, as established in the constitution of 1787, is reflected in the many steps still required for a bill to be passed into law at the federal level. If a bill is lucky enough to make it through committee hearings and actually reaches the floor of the House of Representatives, it must be approved there by a majority; then it moves on to the Senate, where it must also be approved by a majority. To become law, it must be signed by the president, unless he decides to veto the measure, in which case, it goes back to the Senate, where it must receive a two-thirds majority in a second vote before coming into effect. Even if that happens, the new law can still be challenged before the courts and annulled if it is deemed to be outside the federal government's jurisdiction or in conflict with constitutionally guaranteed rights, such as freedom of speech or freedom of association.

While the Framers thought that liberty was best achieved by establishing a limited government that respected the natural rights of individuals, the Fathers of Confederation reached entirely opposite conclusions about the arrangements needed to secure precious gift of freedom. Although they endorsed the device of dividing powers between the two levels of government, and the establishment of an independent judiciary, they believed the leeway given by the Framers to the States and to individuals had contributed to the outbreak of the Civil War. They were also concerned that entropy in the American system had been encouraged by the practice of allowing the direct election of chief officers, notably the president, governors and judges.[4] To ensure that government had the power it needed to secure peace, order and good government, they instituted a federal parliamentary system that weighted power in favor of the federal government. As well, they insulated government representatives from the whims of the people by setting up a process whereby government leaders—prime ministers and premiers—and their cabinet ministers were selected outside the electoral process. Party members would choose government leaders, and leaders would choose cabinet ministers, but before they could take office, they would have to be approved by the Queen's representatives—the Lieutenant-Governors in the provinces and the Governor-General in Ottawa. As a final step, the Fathers of Confederation made all federal legislation dependent upon approval by the Governor-General and an unelected Senate, and provincial legislation dependent upon the approval of the Lieutenant-Governor.

While much was hoped for with these checks in place, in practice, both the consent of the Senate and the G-G became a routine matter; the same result followed in the provinces where the L-G became a passive participant in the legislative process. As a result, Parliament and the provincial legislatures became sovereign for all practical purposes within the matters assigned to them under the *British North American Act*. Without any serious counterweights in the parliamentary system, soon after Confederation politicians were free to pursue their selfish agendas, in the way the Framers of the American Constitution would have predicted. The result has been ever-burgeoning government at all levels of government in Canada, a trend that has been arrested only recently by two events. The first was the entrenchment of the Charter of Rights and Freedoms in 1984, which placed limits on the government's regulation of individual freedoms. The second was the discipline imposed by international lending markets when they set higher interest rates on government bonds issued by Canadian federal and provincial governments in the early 1990s to compensate for the higher risk of default associated with rising levels of government debt. In response, federal and provincial governments were forced to reduce program spending and allocate a larger share of public revenue to debt reduction; together these measures placed serious financial constraints on the growth of government.

So, we can explain the rise of big government simply by the fact that the Canadian system, as compared to the American, has given politicians much greater latitude to expand their powers. And although the Charter has done much to limit governmental infringement of individual rights, the power of the provincial and federal governments to tax and regulate remains unlimited; thus, the Charter has only partially checked the expansionist potential inherent in the parliamentary system.

We could rest with this explanation, as many others have, and simply attribute Canadian statism to the parliamentary system. This "institutional" explanation would allow us to conclude that Americans would probably have more government were it not for the system of checks and balances. As neat and simple as this explanation may be, and though it expresses an important truth, it must be regarded as incomplete. The fact that Canada does not have a system of checks and balances does not mean that Canadians have had to put up with politicians who are intent on expanding the state. Obviously, in a parliamentary system, citizens can vote for parties that favor limiting the role of government. Nonetheless, while some provincial parties have risen to power promising to reduce the size of government, notably Klein's Conservatives in Alberta and the Harris Tories in Ontario, we've never seen a federal party that has run successfully against big government, although Harper's Conservatives took a good run at it in 2004. (I don't consider Mulroney's governments to be major Conservative successes since they moved within the orbit of Liberal ideas and made very little progress in reducing the size and scope of government.)

Even more striking than Canadians' failure to elect parties that favor limited government is the fact that they have a tendency to elect governments that favor the expansion of government. The socialist New Democratic Party has been elected with majorities in Ontario, Manitoba, Saskatchewan and British Columbia; and although it has never held power in Ottawa, it did hold the balance of power at the national level in a minority Liberal government in 1972, and it currently holds the balance in the Liberal minority government elected in June of 2004.

Then we have to deal with the Canadian love affair with the Liberal Party, which has wracked up more victories provincially and federally than any other party in Canadian history. In Ottawa, they've been in power for 75 of the past 105 years, a fact that has led everyone from *Globe and Mail* columnist Jeffery Simpson to New York novelist Tracy Quan to refer to the Liberals as Canada's "natural governing party."[5]

With the exception of the national railway, which was part of Prime Minister Sir John A. Macdonald's National Policy, and hydro projects, which were initiated by colonial governments and supported after Confederation by all governments, Liberal governments have led the way in increasing the size of the state. They gave us national health care, national bilingualism, a full-blown national unemployment insurance system, the Canada Pension Plan, foreign investment review, the National Energy Policy, regional development schemes, equalization programs, affirmative action programs and expanded entitlements across the board. At the very least, we must conclude that a socialist party with a few major successes, a Conservative party with only a few minor successes, and a left-of-center Liberal party that has dominated the pack indicates that the Canadian tradition of big government can't be attributed simply to nature of parliamentary government; it must also be attributed to the public's innate preference for big government.

The Canadian Preference for Big Government

So, why do Canadians have a preference for big government? Historians and political scientists have offered three possible explanations. The first is based on a theory about the development of Canadian political culture. Although every citizen in Canada is a distinct individual with his or her own political beliefs, each nonetheless shares certain beliefs that define a general trend in the nation's thinking about the aims and limits of government action.

When those common beliefs persist, they become the basic elements of a nation's political culture.

Those political scientists who want to explain the Canadian preference for big government in terms of political culture have isolated the beliefs that have led Canadians to prefer government. They believe that this preference is attributable to socialist beliefs that were brought into Canadian society by a group of extreme British patriots known as the United Empire Loyalists, who were based in the United States and fled to English Canada at the time of the American Revolution.

Those who favor this theory believe that the Loyalists had a strange mixture of political beliefs—some came from the modern world of liberal individualism and others from the pre-liberal world of feudalism. The feudal beliefs of the Loyalists imparted an "organic" element to our political culture, which later expressed itself in the preference for big government. To see what political scientists mean when they talk about this organic element, we have to consider the basic beliefs that defined the feudal outlook. The world of feudalism, which still existed in some measure in Britain and the European continent, was based on the belief that the divine order revealed itself in the secular world, and that it resulted in the division of society into naturally ruling and naturally ruled classes: priests and ministers ruled over church members, landowners who were members of the nobility ruled over commoners who worked the land, and the Crown ruled over all its subjects. In this system, the rulers were obliged to promote the welfare of the ruled and the ruled were obliged to submit to the rulers—this is the organic element in the feudal view.[6]

The Loyalists supposedly still believed in the legitimacy of the old feudal order to some degree when they entered Canada; as a result, they added an organic element to our political culture, which expressed itself in the belief that the ruling political and social elites had a duty to use their power for the benefit the people and the people had a corresponding duty to submit to the rule of the elites. This organic element was a minor addition to Canada's dominant liberal political culture, which gave up on the idea of naturally ruling and ruled classes, and substituted the idea that the people should rule themselves through elected representatives. Nonetheless, the organic element introduced by the Loyalists was powerful enough to give rise to attitudes that encouraged political elites to use government power actively and the people to accept and even welcome that development. The result was a sustained socialist movement in party politics and a general preference for big government in English Canada, which would increasingly express itself in the belief that government should promote equality of result rather than equality of opportunity. (The belief in equality of result is reflected in redistributive taxation based on high marginal rates, equalization programs that transfer wealth from more prosperous to less prosperous provinces, employment equity policies and pay equity schemes.)

Although the Loyalists did not settle in Quebec, the preference for big government among the French can also be explained in relation to organic political beliefs, which were present because France established a feudal system when it settled the area in the 1600s, and major aspects of the system survived well into the mid-20th century.

This explanation of Canadian statism is expressed unconsciously in the present by Canadian nationalists who take great pride in the fact that we have a greater willingness than Americans to use the state to ameliorate and regulate. For them, Canadian identity—and Canadian moral superiority—rests on this very fact. Our tolerance for big government means that we're more compassionate and more concerned about the common good than Americans. If those who hold this view had to explain our greater concern with the welfare of the whole, they would have to resort to some explanation about the comparative evolution of Canadian and American political beliefs. And that would force them into the camp of those who believe that our willingness to use the state to promote the common good is rooted in feudalistic beliefs that were present when English and French Canada developed their distinctive political personalities.

The second explanation for our statist tradition is that Canadians were more influenced by the tradition of British colonial rule, which emphasized deference to appointed colonial leaders based on a distrust of popular government. This in turn translated into a greater willingness to tolerate the expansion of government. It's easy enough to see how this argument is made. While Americans rejected British colonial rule in the Revolution of 1776, Canadians continued to respect the Crown, very slowly and respectfully evolved toward independence, receiving it officially in 1931, when the Statute of Westminster was passed by the British Parliament. This explanation also has another dimension that is a little less obvious. The presence of the deferential streak in the Canadian personality can also be attributed to United Empire Loyalists, whose intense devotion to the Crown may have reinforced the existing willingness of Canadians to defer to the authority of the state.

The third explanation for the Canadian preference for big government is based on the idea that our statism has been a response to the challenge involved in attempting to unite an underpopulated, relatively poor and geographically vast country along the east-west axis, while resisting the southern pull of the United States. This formidable project has required a series of massive public works projects, the first and foremost being the National Railway. Seen in this way, the tradition of big government is less an expression of any particular preference for big government, or even a sympathetic concern with the common good, than it is a pragmatic and necessary response to unique historical circumstances.[7]

So we're left with three possible explanations for the rise of big government in Canada—a feudalistic organic streak was introduced into Canada's political culture by settlers in French Canada and United Empire Loyalists in English Canada; Canada never fully rejected the colonial tradition that stressed deference to authority; and Canadians have been forced to rely on the state to facilitate the process of nation-building.

These competing explanations deserve serious consideration because they bear on the advisability of the project of reform I have proposed. To reiterate, I have argued that Canadians must embrace the equal opportunity ideal *and* reduce the size of government if they want to liberate the creative and productive potential of the nation and improve our standard of living. Both the wisdom and the practicality of this recommendation depend on these explanations. To understand why that is so, we have to begin by recognizing that the explanations are interpretations of the national character that have been used as guides to political action.

Explanation #1: Feudal-Organic Influence

For instance, those who believe the Canadian preference for big government is rooted in a organic element in our political culture, which arises from feudal beliefs that were supposedly present at our founding, would reject my project of limiting government based on an appeal to small "l" liberal democratic principles. They would argue that it would be wrong to expect Canadians to fully conform to liberal principles, which are based on asserting individual rights and claims against the authority of the state, and promoting equality of opportunity. Why? Because the nation's personality has also been formed by organic beliefs, which are based on asserting the authority of the state over and against individual rights and claims, and promoting equality of result. Since those who favor this theory assert that Canadians are not thorough-going liberals, and never have been, they also believe that it would be wrong to expect Canadians to endorse a project that would require them to perfect the liberal ideal of equal opportunity. It would also be wrong to ask Canadians to consider reducing the size of government because they are naturally inclined, by the same organic beliefs, to accept big government. This argument rests upon an implicit analogy between the individual and the nation. Trying to compel Canadians to change their attitudes toward government would be like trying to force an adult with a well-formed character to suddenly become a different person. It would lead to madness or a great deal of very expensive therapy. In either case, it wouldn't be desirable. Thus, we should accept ourselves as we are and be proud of our willingness to use the state for constructive purposes.

This is a powerful objection. If we accept the view that there is a permanent organic element in the Canadian personality which expresses itself in the belief that government has a duty to use its powers actively to promote the common good, understood as equality of result, then we might just have to resign ourselves to living with a society that fails to achieve its potential because it prefers to live with a conflicting pastiche of liberal and illiberal tendencies.

Explanation #2: The Colonial Tradition

The second explanation—that the preference for big government results from the colonial tradition, which encouraged deference to appointed colonial rulers based on a distrust of popular rule—is less harmful to the cause of reform. This explanation does not require us to explain our statism in relation to illiberal tendencies in the political culture. Therefore, it gives us greater leeway to argue for the adoption of the equal opportunity ideal. It also gives us greater leeway to argue for reducing the size of government. Since Canadians have been self-consciously liberating themselves for the last 50 years from the cultural and political influences that developed during our long association with Great Britain, they might very well be inclined to completely throw off the latent colonial attitude that inclines them to accept big government.

Explanation #3: Historical Conditions

Based on historical necessity, this theory is even more favorable to the cause of reform. While it may have been necessary in the 19th and 20th centuries to use the state to hold the country together and avoid absorption by the United States, in the 21st century, a different solution might be required because different historical forces are at work. While the circumstances of one era might recommend government intervention to achieve basic political and economic goals, the circumstances of another era might require less government to achieve the same ends. Clearly, in the epoch ushered in by free trade, Canadians are compelled to consider reforming their views on the role of government in order to maintain our competitive standing. If we want to avoid a situation where our only hope for a higher standard of living is to join the United States, we must reduce the size of government to make our country more hospitable to investment, and completely embrace the equal opportunity idea.

The Prevailing View

The most influential explanation for the Canadian preference for big government is the first—that Canadian political culture has an organic streak inherited from the Loyalist and French settlers. This view was first expounded in 1966 by Gad Horowitz, a professor of political science at the University of Toronto, in an article entitled "Conservatism,

Liberalism and Socialism in Canada: An Interpretation." Although published in a relatively obscure academic journal, due to its boldness and sweep, this 18-page article soon became the definitive interpretation of Canadian statism in political science departments across the country. For the last 40 years, it has been de rigueur reading for tens of thousands of students of political science. As a result, two or three generations of politically active people—some exercising enormous influence from positions in academia, journalism, law and government—have been shaping the public agenda based on a hostility to the equal opportunity ideal and a belief that big government is the Canadian way. A lot of the bad thinking at the elite level in Canadian politics can trace its roots to the Horowitz thesis, or some version of it.

Fortunately, we need not take the Horowitz thesis as the definitive explanation of Canadian statism. The thesis rests on a very shaky assumption, which is that the Loyalists held political beliefs that contained traces of the old feudal outlook. The historical evidence suggests, however, that they did not.

The Beliefs of the Loyalists

The facts and figures on Loyalist emigration from the American Colonies certainly bear out Horowitz's assertion that the Loyalists may have set the tone of early Canadian political life. After the American Revolution of 1776, somewhere between 40,000 to 50,000 Loyalists emigrated to Canada, which at that time was sparsely populated. Roughly 30,000 settled in and around Nova Scotia and the remaining 6,000 to 10,000 settled in areas along the shores of Lake Ontario and the St. Lawrence River, which later became parts of Upper Canada. These Western areas were populated mostly by the Loyalists until the late 1700s, when large numbers of American settlers entered Upper Canada.[8]

What kind of impact did the Loyalists have on the emerging political culture? To answer this question, we would have to look to historical writings to determine the political beliefs that held sway with the Loyalists in the Colonies where they were most heavily concentrated. If we could determine what the Loyalists believed before they entered Canada, we could determine whether their beliefs reflected the feudal-organic viewpoint that supposedly shaped Canada's early political culture. Unfortunately, historians provide very little hard evidence regarding the beliefs of rank-and-file Loyalists, most of whom came from the Middle American Colonies—Massachusetts, Pennsylvania, New York, New Jersey and South Carolina.[9] However, the historical record does give us access to statements made by Loyalist leaders at the time of the Revolution. We can refer to these statements on the basis that they might reflect the views of rank-and-file Loyalists. This approach is problematic because we can never assume that the views of political leaders accurately reflect the views of their followers. Regardless, by default, it's the only approach we can use to determine the views that may have been held by rank-and-file Loyalists in the Middle Colonies.

This is where the Horowitz thesis really hits a brick wall. To prove that the Loyalist leadership in the Middle Colonies in the 1770s was still influenced by feudal doctrine, it would necessary to prove that they believed, in some measure, that the divine order revealed itself in the secular world and that it took the form of naturally ruling and naturally ruled elements, whereby priests and ministers ruled over church members, feudal lords over vassals, and the Crown over all its subjects, and that rulers felt duty-bound to exercise their power, in some measure, for the benefit of the ruled. But the fact is that the historical record does not prove that leaders in the Middle Colonies held such views.

The evidence presented by historians suggests that Loyalist leaders in the Middle Colonies were advocates of strong government, insofar as they argued for the preservation of British rule in some form as an alternative to the Revolutionary position, which, of course, called for the end to colonial rule. Loyalist leaders tended to favor a new form of colonial government in which the American colonists would enjoy some degree of participation through the appointment or election of an American parliament. Did the Loyalist leaders favor this arrangement because they were still affected by the feudal-organic view of the world, which stressed the need to treat the colonial elites as beneficent natural rulers? Or did they favor the continuation of British colonial rule based on the stodgy British tradition of deferring to the authority of the Crown? The work of colonial historians suggests that the latter belief was the motivating factor for many of the Loyalist leaders.

This conclusion is supported by the work of historian Robert Calhoun, who argues that the feudal-organic vision had become "antique" by the time of the Revolution. Calhoun maintains that the appointed colonial politicians and officeholders, who were the real spokesmen for the Loyalist viewpoint, argued for their continued rule based on the British colonial tradition, which was founded on a distrust of popularly elected government and a corresponding belief in the need to defer to the authority of appointed rulers. The leaders' justification of strong government was therefore totally secular—it did not depend on religious notions regarding man's place in an organic whole. Loyalist leaders did not express views that raised the specter of angels blessing the three estates or feudal lords on horseback throwing sticks of bread to the poor.[10]

Given that the leadership in the Middle Colonies argued for British rule in secular terms, and most of the rank-and-file Loyalists came from the Middle Colonies, we can infer that the Loyalists who emigrated to Canada *were not exponents of the feudal-organic view.* These Loyalists could probably best be described as moderate secular conservatives. They had accepted the liberal goals of peace, prosperity and freedom, but they believed that those goals could be achieved without increasing popular participation in government. The historian Wallace Brown argues that "one looks in vain for Loyalists who were opposed to liberty or the rights of Englishmen."[11]

Any remaining doubts about the lack of organic beliefs among early Loyalists can be put to rest by considering the impact of later emigration. The Americans who emigrated to Canada during the late 1700s and early 1800s were so numerous that, by 1812, only 20,000 of Upper Canada's 100,000 inhabitants were Loyalists or their descendants and the remaining 80,000 were American-born. Even if feudal organic beliefs had been lingering in the minds of the original Loyalists, those beliefs would have been diluted by the liberal beliefs of an additional 80,000 American settlers. (Horowitz does not mention the later American settlers, perhaps out of a desire to avoid this conclusion.)[12]

Loyalist Acceptance of Undemocratic Government

To counter the evidence that the organic well had dried up, Horowitz would point to the Loyalists' acceptance of authoritarian colonial rule as proof that they were still clinging to the feudal outlook. In Nova Scotia, the Loyalists willingly subordinated themselves to a government run by an oligarchy of Halifax families. The system there followed the old colonial model whereby a governor-general and a ruling council, which were appointed by the Crown, exercised almost total control over the colony's affairs; the small legislature was granted very limited powers. In New Brunswick, the same system prevailed. Like the Loyalists in the East, those in the West also willingly accepted the appointed government, which was run by an established social and commercial oligarchy (the "Family Compact"). Horowitz attributes this aspect of Loyalist behavior to an organic belief that the rulers should be trusted to act in the interest of the ruled. However, as I've argued above, quite clearly the

Loyalists were motivated by British colonial tradition, which stressed deference to authority, rather than any lingering beliefs that can be traced to the feudal tradition. The supreme influence of the British tradition was reflected in the Loyalists' "conservative" reluctance to disturb the existing order even when appointed ruling cliques favored their selfish interests at the expense of the public interest. For instance, when "radicals" in Upper Canada rebelled against the arbitrary and selfinterested rule of colonial elites in 1837, they were put down quickly because they weren't supported by the public.[13]

While the cautious conservative beliefs of the Loyalists explain their tolerance of undemocratic government, they fail to explain the settlers' willingness to use the state dynamically to support massive public projects. Was this the product of a lingering feudal-organic commitment to the welfare of the whole community? Not necessarily. The early Upper Canadian "mega-projects"—for instance, the construction of the St. Lawrence and Welland Canals—can be explained in practical terms. These projects were motivated by a general desire for public improvements, which reflected the fact that the settlers were struggling in their efforts to subdue the harsh Canadian wilderness. And since the colonial rulers were the only settlers who possessed the expertise and the financial resources to undertake the conquest of the harsh environment, by necessity the state became involved in developing the colony's infrastructure.

The second motivation for state intervention was rooted in fear related to the construction of the Erie Canal to the south. The canal, which linked Lake Erie to the Hudson River in New York state, created a shipping route to New York City that was much quicker and less expensive than transport by land. Canadians feared that the canal, which quickly became a great commercial success, would divert trade away from Upper Canada and undermine its economic aspirations. In the absence of a strong private sector, the government was forced to intervene to protect Upper Canada's commercial interests. So, the early growth of public ownership in Upper Canada was driven by sheer economic necessity and was no doubt facilitated by the Loyalists' habit of submitting to governmental authority. It did not result from feudal-organic beliefs that inclined the settlers to treat the colonial elites as beneficent natural rulers who were interested in promoting the good of the community. Our earliest interventions were not fueled by a pre-existing sense of community; they were the product of the need and the willingness to use government *to establish a community*.[14]

To summarize, all the historical evidence points away from the possibility that there was a pronounced feudal-organic element in the beliefs of the Loyalists. The original settlers were essentially secular conservatives whose trust in authority can be explained on the basis of beliefs engendered by the British colonial tradition.

What about Socialism?

So, how can we account for a socialist movement in Canada, which was first championed by the Canadian Commonwealth of Farmers (CCF) in Western Canada in the 1930s and later led by the New Democratic Party (NDP)? Our analysis suggests that socialism did not develop in relation to the beliefs of the original Loyalist settlers. The settlers lacked the feudal organic beliefs that would give rise to a political movement based on a belief that rulers could be trusted to use government power expansively to promote the interests of the community. Thus, the socialist movement must have been produced by another immigrant group. Given that the CCF first emerged as a political force in Western Canada in the 1930s, the party's base can probably be traced to the British immigrants who arrived in Canada in the late 1800s and early 1900s, some of whom had been exposed to socialist doctrines that were then circulating in Britain and on the Continent.[15]

Since Canada's socialist movement, which has always been the enemy of the equal opportunity ideal, cannot be traced to the ideas on which Canada's political culture was founded, we need not accept socialism as an essential aspect of the Canadian personality. Neither, therefore, need we see it as an obstacle to liberal democratic reforms that would reduce the size of government and promote the equal opportunity ideal.

Implications for the Equal Opportunity Ideal

As we've seen, the Canadian preference for big government can be explained in three possible ways, and each is more or less favorable to the project of reducing the size of government and promoting the equal opportunity ideal. The first explanation—the presence of a feudal-organic streak in Canada's political culture—was seen to be unfavorable to the cause of reform because it would force us to conclude that Canadians are naturally inclined to accept big government, and to prefer the socialist view that government should promote equality of result than equality of opportunity. Since this explanation has been found lacking based on our analysis of the Horowitz thesis, we are free to consider embracing smaller government and the equal opportunity ideal without being concerned that these measures would be impractical or unjust.

The other two explanations for our interventionism now seem closer to the truth, and they are indeed very favorable to the cause of reform. The idea that the Canadian preference for big government is rooted in the British colonial tradition of deference to authority is friendly to small "l" liberal reform because it does not require us to assume Canadians have illiberal beliefs that would and should defeat the equal opportunity ideal. Nor does it require us to assume that Canadians should accept big government. As I've argued, since the British connection has been weakening in the minds of Canadians for over 50 years, we are justified in rethinking whether we should hold on to outdated beliefs about government that are rooted not just in a British tradition, but in a British "colonial" tradition.

The final explanation—that our preference for big government is the product of historical necessity—is also favorable to the cause of reform. Although, in the past, it may have been necessary to use the state to establish the links that would promote prosperity and national cohesion, today we are facing entirely different circumstances that require a different solution. To improve our standard of living in a free trade environment, we must consider reducing rather than increasing the size of government. That's the only way we can create an environment that can attract the investment and stimulate the economic creativity and productivity that will allow us to close the prosperity gap. At the same, we must also use government in a positive way to promote the equal opportunity ideal because it is the best guarantee of collective prosperity and the only guarantee of individual justice.

Myth Eight

DOING IS MORE
IMPORTANT THAN THINKING

Crossing the Tracks

A couple of years ago I was invited to lunch by an editor to discuss the possibility of writing a new book on inheritance issues for Canadian lawyers. We decided to meet at her office, which was located on the outskirts of the city in one of those isolated office towers that stands as a testament to Toronto's insufferably high property taxes. Our luncheon took place in a nearby hotel that had decor that was reminiscent of the disco era. Lunch began with an appetizer that consisted of a quick resume of each other's professional accomplishments. It turned out we were both former practicing lawyers, who had ended up in media and publishing after working on Bay Street. The editor went on to discuss the twists and turns of her career, which allowed us immediately to go to the main course, which was a frank discussion about how careers are made and broken in Toronto.

She had been a successful attorney with a downtown firm during the 1990s, but she had chosen to give up her practice to go to Montreal, where her husband had been offered a lucrative job in business. The editor had trouble finding work in Montreal because she was trained as a common law lawyer and Quebec is based on the civil law system; to qualify for practice, she would have to go back to school and take another set of bar exams. Since there was no guarantee of employment if she requalified, she decided to take a job in the stock market, where she became a successful trader.

A few years later, her husband was transferred to Toronto. The editor looked forward to returning because she wanted to resume the practice of law. But, to her chagrin, she found that her many years of success in a well-respected Toronto firm were no longer relevant. No firm in her area of practice would take her on.

On reflection, she realized that Toronto law firms followed employment practices that governed the business world throughout Toronto. In her view, Toronto ran on a series of career tracks that rarely crossed. If you got off your track, even due to reasons beyond your control, you would not be allowed to hop back on. Neither would you be allowed simply to hop on to another track. If you were allowed to cross over, you'd mess up the system. You would displace employees who were proceeding along their tracks and would annoy employers who weren't willing to eschew formal criteria and consider special cases. So, if you got off your track, you could be committing career suicide; and, at the very least, you'd be forced to start over again in another field at a much lower rung on the career ladder.

Since we had both attended university in New York City, we shared similar insights into how the American system worked. We agreed that it's much easier in the U.S. to cut across career tracks and that employers often see value in someone who has a diverse professional background. American lawyers in particular have had great success taking their expertise into other fields, and some have done it without closing the doors on practice. One sees this in Washington all the time. A lawyer might leave practice to take a position in government and is later welcomed back into the profession because his or her contacts and knowledge of public affairs are regarded as assets that can contribute to the firm's expertise and business profile. Granted, this sometimes happens in Canada, but not to the same degree.

The American acceptance of diversity in job experience reflects the greater value accorded to generalists in the United States. In Canada, most employers value the employee who sticks to his or her particular expertise. In the United States, employers place a greater value on the person who has the ability to handle a variety of tasks because it's assumed he or she can add value in many different ways and can provide leadership based on an understanding of how to organize specialized tasks in pursuit of common objectives.

This discussion with the editor had a profound impact on the way I saw the city and the way I saw myself. It helped me to understand why I so often found myself at loggerheads with the way business is done here. My own *modus operandi* was to cut across the tracks in search of new ideas and opportunities. I had been working on that basis for years without giving it a second thought. I realized that this approach, which had become so deeply ingrained in my outlook that I was barely conscious of it, was rooted in the training that I had received in the late 1970s at the University of Toronto while studying under the direction of Allan Bloom, who would go on to become an international celebrity due to the success of his 1987 work, *The Closing of the American Mind.*

I first encountered Bloom when a graduate student suggested that I check out Bloom's first-year course, POL 101, *Introduction to Political Philosophy.* At that time, I was already in the third year of a political science program, but this proved to be an advantage because the course was considerably harder than the average first-year course. In the first five minutes of the first lecture, Bloom announced that we should regard POL 101 as a course in "remedial reading." Bloom was going to teach us how to read great books word by word, line by line, so that we would begin to appreciate the depth and subtlety of philosophic thought. In this way, hopefully, we would begin to see that those texts challenged our most strongly held opinions about the most important matters.

This experiment would involve reading the books in relation to fundamental questions such as: what is justice? what is piety? what is nobility? what is the good life? Bloom limited the reading list to a small number of texts, which made it possible to read carefully and truly reflect on these questions. While other teachers had assigned so many texts that I had been forced to read them like they were paperback novels, Bloom limited the reading list to Machiavelli's *Prince*, Plato's *Republic*, de Tocqueville's *Democracy in America* and Hobbes' *Leviathan*, with a little bit of Swift and Flaubert thrown in for good measure.

Bloom's pedagogic approach challenged all the approaches that I had been exposed to in previous courses in the humanities—a small number of esoteric books were substituted for endless reading lists; rumination on a few essential ideas imparted by those books was preferred to a superficial survey of the entire Western tradition; great books were not treated as historical curiosities but as living texts that might challenge our own cherished views and potentially change our lives for the better.

Judged by the standards of the academy in the 1970s, one of Bloom's most heretical ideas was that great books did not belong to any one department of the university. Bloom had made this point very early in his career when he published a series of essays entitled *Shakespeare's Politics*. There he presented works such as *Julius Caesar* and *Coriolanus* as works of political thought that could address the concerns of students of political science, though they were regarded by the academy as works that should be studied in English departments and treated primarily as works of art. In his foreword, he states:

... Shakespeare is not the preserve of any single department in the modern university. He wrote before the university was divided as it is today, and the knowledge he presupposes cuts across these partly accidental lines. He presents man generally, and it is not to be assumed that a department literature possesses any privileged position for grasping his representations comprehensively. Consider a work like Rousseau's *Nouvelle Heloise*—does it belong primarily to a philosophy department, a literature department, or a language department? Surely to all and to none; perhaps most of all to the educated amateur.[1]

I was enthralled by the idea that academic boundaries were artificial and that one shouldn't be afraid to chase an idea across the boundaries in search of the truth. I immediately put the idea to work in my studies. I brought political philosophy into my courses in English, history, and political science and brought ideas in those courses to bear on my studies in political philosophy. I took courses on Shakespeare to further explore the lines of argument that Bloom had pursued in *Shakespeare's Politics*. I didn't adopt this approach simply out of respect for Bloom or because I wanted to be on the cutting edge of some academic trend. I did it because I experienced it as real thinking. I understood so much more when I tried to see how one idea could be developed and expressed within different fields of study.

I had gone to university with one aim in mind: To learn how to make judgments about the world. Before I ran into Bloom, I had been having a rather disappointing time and didn't feel that my education was amounting to much. I certainly didn't feel that it was helping me to make perceptive judgments about life. But, armed with Bloom's course in remedial reading and the view that we could cross academic boundaries in search of the truth, I suddenly found that I had the method and the substance needed to get the education that I wanted so badly. I was experiencing for the first time the *liberation* that a liberal education was supposed to provide. Liberation, though, might be too mild a word to describe the experience. I felt as if Bloom had tripped a switch in my mind and dormant neurons had finally started to fire; soon circuits were overloading and I became an electrical storm of insights and opinions.

When I went into law school, I carried over this idea and experimented with inter-disciplinary approaches to the study of law. This freed me from the stultifying common law approach, which bowed down before precedent and treated certain cases as authoritative without giving thought to whether they were grounded in first principles that were truly rational and objective. While my inter-disciplinary approach meant that my studies in law were frequently experimental, it allowed me to pursue the truth of the matter across the boundaries of areas such as contract, tort, property and constitutional law. Eventually I took this approach to Columbia Law School where I wrote a thesis on the legal philosophy of the German thinker, Immanuel Kant. Kant himself had self-consciously integrated all the different approaches to knowledge within his major works. Some legal scholars, however, had regarded Kant's work of legal philosophy, the *Philosophy of Right*, as a separate vessel of thought that was moored to its own independent principles. I tried to show that one couldn't understand the *Philosophy of Right* unless one understood that its foundations were connected to Kant's thinking about history, politics, moral philosophy, political philosophy and metaphysics.

Before graduating from Columbia, where I studied in three different departments as part of my inter-disciplinary approach, I had already experienced the power of this approach in practice, having used it to great advantage as a political advisor in the 1984 federal election campaign. But, when I returned to Toronto for full-time employment in law and business in the late 1980s, I received a rude shock. I discovered that no one wanted someone who could think across the boundaries. There was a lot of talk around this time about the importance of thinking outside the box. And it wasn't long before "forward-thinking" types were saying that inter-disciplinary scholarship would become the model for higher education in the 21st century. All this seemed to bode well. I had trained myself not simply to think outside the box, but to make the connections between the boxes. But I didn't see much demand in Toronto, or the country, for thinkers who could manage information and knowledge in a comprehensive way.

Looking back on this period, I realize that this was when I began to understand that Canadians prefer specialists who work within their boxes and stay on their career tracks. And this, I came to believe, is what gives Canada it's prosaic tone. Specialists are essentially doers. That's because their goal is simply to complete a specific task. They don't have to worry about how their work fits into the greater scheme of a business, a profession or society at large. The preference for specialists is what has made Canada into a nation of doers who live by the mistaken view that doing is more important than thinking.

I say mistaken view because it's now so obvious that we are living in an age of innovation where the future belongs to societies that encourage people to think critically and creatively. Here we should recall that we've already linked Canada's declining standard of living to its low rate of innovation, which is reflected in its low rate of patent registration and its low investment in R&D. These problems speak very clearly to the Canadian preference for the practical-minded specialist, who prefers to keep on doing things as they've always been done because that's the way they've always been done or because that's the way the bosses want them done. The specialist mentality, which defeats the generalist who dares to think outside the traditional boundaries, is one of the greatest impediments to encouraging the kind of innovation that we need to improve Canada's economic performance.

The Tension between Thinking and Doing

When thinking about how to correct the Canadian tendency to value doing over thinking, I find it helpful to reflect on de Tocqueville's analysis of the democratic mind in *Democracy in America*. Tocqueville provides a framework that allows us to see the Canadian problem in the context of the natural tendency of democratic regimes to produce a bias in favor of doing at the expense of thinking. Tocqueville argues that this tendency undermines the effectiveness of practical activities because those activities ultimately depend for their efficacy and progress on the results of theoretical research. If, for example, we want engineers to build bigger, stronger bridges, Tocqueville would argue that we have to support researchers who investigate theories of mechanics that give rise to new, more effective principles of application. If we want more effective medical treatments, we have to fund research activities, even when they don't promise an immediate return. Certainly, Tocqueville would approve of the human genome project, even though it won't produce immediate practical remedies for human disease because, in time, it will.

It would be a mistake, however, to simply connect Tocqueville's concern with theory and research with projects like the human genome. His ultimate concern was with keeping alive the spirit of theoretical inquiry as end-in-itself, untainted by any prospect of a practical or material result. He wanted to carve out a place for those truly rare human beings who pursue scientific inquiry simply for its own sake because those individuals represent a form of human flourishing that has independent value, and that we all, in some measure, feel compelled to recognize through our longing for wisdom. Tocqueville argued that those who pursue purely theoretical research also bring great benefits to civil society because their insights sometimes have great practical value for the applied arts and sciences.[2] Einstein's work presents many examples in this regard. In 1916, for instance, Einstein produced a statistical theory that predicted that when light was passed through a particular substance, it would produce more light. This theory, which would later become part of quantum mechanics, eventually led to the creation of the laser; and, of course, the laser has produced an ever-expanding array of industrial and commercial applications.[3]

Even though liberal democratic societies, by virtue of being free societies, make way for theoretical inquiry, they also tend to discourage it. To explain this problem, Tocqueville draws a contrast with the attitude toward theory in aristocratic and democratic regimes. Because the ruling classes in aristocracies didn't have to worry about paying the bills, they had the leisure to develop a taste for theoretical pursuits. This taste was reinforced by the fact that aristocrats thought highly of themselves and developed exalted notions regarding their own pursuits. They preferred activities that were grand, delightful, beautiful or subtle over those that were practical or useful. That outlook greatly encouraged thinking as an end in itself; Tocqueville states:

> In aristocratic ages vast ideas are generally entertained of the dignity, power, and the greatness of man. Such opinions influence those who cultivate the sciences, as they do all others. They facilitate the natural impulse of the mind toward the highest regions of thought, and they naturally prepare it to conceive a sublime, almost divine love of the truth.[4]

By contrast, in democratic regimes, the social order itself tends to suppress theoretical activity. Since there is no leisure class, everyone starts off in roughly the same social and economic position, and, in the effort to rise, is engaged in a perpetual struggle for wealth and power. As a result, the democratic mind is always agitated, which makes it resistant to theoretical studies: "In the midst of this universal tumult, this incessant conflict of jarring interests, this endless chase for wealth, where is one to find the calm for the profound researches of the intellect."

The struggle to get ahead also encourages a taste for superficial thinking that is equally harmful to theoretical inquiry. To *survive* in the rat race, people have to make judgments hastily without all the facts and without fully testing the truth of ideas and principles: "In democratic centuries when almost everyone is engaged in active life, the darting speed of a quick, superficial mind is at a premium, while slow, deep thought is excessively undervalued."

One further consequence of the rat race is that people tend to value knowledge only in so far as it promises to deliver an immediate financial return, which means that thinking that is tied to practical results is more highly valued than thinking that is purely theoretical. The general taste for practical knowledge, in turn, tends to influence scholars and intellectuals, who soon learn that they can gain wealth and fame by focusing their minds on inventions that promise to quickly better the human condition. As a result, the energies of the most promising minds are channeled into applied science and away from theory.

Tocqueville's analysis leaves democratic peoples with a paradoxical problem. They want the benefits of applied science, which means that they must support theoretical science. But it's unlikely that they will, given that democratic conditions tend to produce habits of mind that discourage a taste for and appreciation of pure thinking. How does one solve this problem? Tocqueville's solution is to enlighten democratic leaders regarding the need to persuade the people to support theoretical research. Wise rulers will create rewards for those who devote themselves purely to theory, because that will promote the betterment of all in the long-run and reconcile the tension between democratic and aristocratic inclinations in the human spirit.[5]

If Tocqueville were alive today, he would probably be surprised to find that the United States has become the world's leader in theoretical research and alarmed to see that Canada is not reaching its full theoretical potential. Clearly, the United States has effectively counterbalanced the democratic tendency to prefer practice to theory while Canada has not. We've already seen that Canada spends proportionately much less than the United States on research and development and that Canada spends less on university education on a per capita basis. These two facts alone say a great deal about the different value that each society places on thinking.

There are other signs. In the U.S., think tanks are more lavishly funded and play a more influential role in shaping debate in both government and the media. Thinkers are also more highly valued in government itself. Over the last 45 years, presidents have made a practice of seeking out the best and brightest to serve and advise. This has made intellectuals like Kissinger, Brzezinksi and Rice into household names. Can anyone name a professor who has been given such a prominent position in the prime minister's office during this same period? The employer's preference for the practical-minded specialist is yet further proof of the overall problem. Even one of our great novelists, the late Robertson Davies, felt the need to comment on the anti-intellectual streak in the Canadian personality; in a television interview aired in the 1980s, he stated that Canadians have a "grumpy" and "peasant-like quality."

The Findings of the Ontario Task Force

If one had any doubt about whether Canadians have less respect for theoretical activities than Americans do, the Ontario Task Force provides revealing evidence to put it to rest. The task force conducted a public opinion survey that revealed that Ontarians and Americans differ dramatically on the importance of university education. The task force asked the general public and business community what advice they would give to a young person concerning educational goals. Over 30% of Ontarians recommended a community college or technical diploma as compared to 10% of Americans. Further, nearly five times as many Americans would recommend a bachelor's degree, and three times as many would recommend a professional or graduate degree.[6]

The task force found that the American preference for university education was also reflected in vast differences in university enrollment. While a study demonstrated that 29% of grade nine students in Ontario were enrolled in university five years later (2001), the median figure for leading American states was 33%. And in several states, enrollment figures were much higher: Massachusetts was 47%, New Jersey 47% and Pennsylvania 41%. In 2003, the Canada Millennium Scholarship Foundation released a study that revealed that 50% of students who were eminently qualified to pursue a post-secondary degree decided not to do so; and *77% of those students cited non-financial reasons for their decision.* These findings suggest that the lower esteem in which Canadians hold university education may be fostering attitudes that prevent younger people from maximizing their academic potential.[7]

The Ontario bias in favor of recommending a college or technical diploma reinforces my point about the Canadian preference for specialists and the drag that places on our economy. Clearly, one of the reasons that we have a society that discourages innovative thinking is that one-third of the population believes that community college training, which prepares people to perform highly specialized tasks, is superior to university training, which, in the best case, foregoes specialized training in favor of studies designed to impart the generalist's perspective. This bias toward specialist training is likely to intensify because, according to the Conference Board, Canada is already facing a serious "skills shortage," which will only get worse in coming years when baby boomers begin to retire in large numbers. The tradespeople who will be most in demand include heavy-equipment operators, industrial mechanics, industrial electricians, construction workers, auto workers, steel workers and welders. In response to this problem, the federal government has begun an advertising campaign to encourage young people to take up a trade.[8]

Although the skills shortage is real, and good money is to be made by those who opt for community college training or apprenticeships, we should not assume that such training will secure the economic future of the country. We may win the skills battle only to find that we've lost the economic war because we've reinforced the specialist mentality that devalues the innovative thinking and theoretical research that create new forms of wealth.

Based on the foregoing comparisons, we can see very clearly that Canadians and Americans differ considerably in their attitudes toward higher education, and this, I would argue, has played a major role in creating a competitive advantage for the United States. Americans expect to compete with their minds, as much as with their hands and their hearts. A society that places so much emphasis on university education, particularly post-graduate education, will necessarily be more innovative and prosperous because it places a higher value on cutting-edge research and intellectual creativity.

The Liberal Arts in America

One of the striking differences between Canada and the United States in the realm of higher education is that America has over 900 liberal arts colleges, while Canada has perhaps three—St. Thomas College, King's College and Mount Allison University. To understand what this difference represents, we have to consider what a liberal arts college really is. In the U.S., generally speaking, a liberal arts college provides a four-year program of study that gives students an opportunity to sample a variety of subjects in the sciences and the humanities. The goal of liberal education is not to enforce specialization on students in the hope of turning them into "marketable" commodities. The overriding purpose is to teach students how to think critically so that they can excel at whatever they choose to do in life. It's generally assumed that critical thinking is encouraged by giving students broad exposure to a core curriculum in the arts and sciences in their first years of study, after which a more focused program is encouraged. As I learned when working under Allan Bloom, this approach works best when the curriculum includes the study of great books.

The liberal arts curriculum can be found at universities in the United States, and notable examples can be found at schools such as Columbia and Chicago, where the great books approach has been followed for over half a century. However, the liberal arts college has carved out its own unique place in the American system and it represents an important force in American society. The liberal arts college embodies the American belief in the value of critical thinking. And, in practical terms, that belief is reflected in the willingness of American employers to hire generalists trained in a liberal arts setting. The lack of any corresponding tradition in Canada helps to explain the lower status given to university education in general and liberal education in particular, and the lower esteem in which the generalist is held in the world of employment. Although our most practical-minded citizens may have trouble believing it, America has a true competitive economic advantage over Canada due its liberal arts tradition, which reflects the fundamental value that Americans place on the power of thinking.

Toward a New Magnetic North

The problem of making room in Canadian society for innovative young thinkers is being addressed by a new organization called Canada25. On its website, Canada25 describes itself as a "non-profit, non-partisan organization that brings the voices and ideas of Canadians, aged 20 to 35, to the nation's public policy discussion and takes action on issues of local and national significance." In a paper entitled, *Toward a New Magnetic North*, presented to the TD Economic Forum on Canada's Standard of Living, Canada25 argues that the key to encouraging the innovation that will substantially improve Canada's standard of living is to keep Canada's talented young people at home; but to keep them at home or give them the incentive to return to Canada from the United States and other countries, we have to innovate to create an environment that is more welcoming. To create a more dynamic atmosphere, Canada25 has proposed the following solutions:

- Give younger Canadians access to world leaders in various fields by establishing more visiting fellowships and lectureships;
- Create new think tanks that are non-partisan and that provide opportunities for internships and entry-level positions for young people;
- Provide a more inclusive employment environment for skilled immigrants;
- Create opportunities for interdisciplinary experience by encouraging the public and private sectors to share ideas and personnel (for example, companies could provide incentives for employees to serve for short periods in government; universities could more actively appoint non-academics to contact positions in teaching or research).[9]

In a more detailed version of this paper, which is available on Canada25's website, additional solutions are proposed. These include:

- Making a concerted effort to attract top researchers to the country during the next decade when over half of Canada's university teachers will be retiring;
- Providing tax incentives to encourage private donations to universities;
- Consolidating the funding under the Canada Research Chair program so that research grants for professors can be increased from $500,000 to $1 to $2 million, which would ensure that Canada can attract the best researchers.[10]

I've taken great solace in the work of Canada25 because it's shown me that some of the problems I've addressed in this book are already being discussed and debated by younger Canadians who may occupy important leadership roles in the near future. When reading *Toward a New Magnetic North*, I came across a statement made by a Canada25 member based in Boston that was particularly illuminating. It's fitting to end the chapter with this statement because it so clearly expresses how Canadians and Americans differ on the value of thinking, and, in particular, how Canadians tend to undervalue our most highly educated young people by preferring doers to thinkers and specialists to generalists:

In Canada, employers are caught up with trying to make sure they get the right skill. For example, if you have a degree in anthropology you could never work as an investment banker in Toronto. In the United States they care more about your mind. Can you think critically and creatively? Can you learn quickly? Employers in Canada need to learn to hire minds, not skills.[11]

Myth Nine

A COMPASSIONATE SOCIETY IS A JUST SOCIETY

Trudeau's Egalitarianism

The Just Society. That's what Pierre Trudeau promised to deliver during the 1968 federal election campaign that resulted in another Liberal majority in the House of Commons. As Trudeau saw it, Canada was a country that had already achieved a remarkable degree of freedom. The only way to improve our situation, he believed, was to promote equality to ensure that everyone enjoyed that freedom in the appropriate measure. In an essay he wrote in 1990 entitled "The Values of a Just Society," Trudeau stated that his overriding goal had been to establish an equal opportunity society:

> At a time like this, what led me to enter politics was not a desire to fight for freedom; in a way, that was already yesterday's battle. In my thinking, the value with highest priority in the pursuit of a Just Society had become equality. Not the procrustean kind of equality where everyone is raised or lowered to a kind of middle ground. I mean equality of opportunity.[1]

By establishing a uniform minimum standard of living across the country, and instituting legal reforms designed to eliminate discrimination, Trudeau hoped to create a framework of just conditions that would give every citizen the opportunity to rise within Canadian society. In the "Values" essay, Trudeau singled out the following measures in the 1968 platform as proof of the Liberals' commitment to the equal opportunity ideal: the imposition of a capital gains tax, full implementation of Medicare, reform of the penal code, institution of a bilingual civil service, the provision of subsidies to promote economic development in the less prosperous regions of the country, and revision of our foreign policy (presumably to help equalize opportunities around the world).

So, from the start, Trudeau and the Liberals were committed to an egalitarian politics that aimed at redistributing income and leveling social and economic conditions across the country. During the 16 years that Liberals were in power, the egalitarian politics of the Just Society unfolded in three distinct stages. In the first stage (1968 to 1974), the Liberals slowly expanded the fiscal boundaries of the modern welfare state; transfers to the unemployed were increased under the Unemployment Insurance plan, as were transfers to seniors under Old Age Security, the Canada Pension Plan and the Guaranteed Income Supplement, transfers to the poor under the Canada Assistance Plan, and transfers to everyone else under Medicare and Family Allowances. In the second stage (1975–1984), the government expanded the welfare state itself by creating new government programs and agencies, such as the Foreign Investment Review Agency and Petro-Canada, while allowing spending to increase vastly across the board on all existing programs. In the final stage (1978–1984), which overlapped the second, the government concentrated on changing the rules of the game in its relentless pursuit of equality. During this period, it allowed group rights to replace individual rights as the basis for determining wage scales and employment opportunities in the federal government, and all federally regulated bodies, which included all of the country's banks. This meant that pay equity schemes and quota systems for women and minorities were established for over 20% of the full-time Canadian workforce.

As Liberal egalitarianism went into high gear in the late 1970s, Canadians were asked to endorse the new high-spending, interventionist Canadian state based on a compassionate concern for minority groups. The Just Society became the Compassionate Society. This transformation was dictated by the overriding imperative of helping the disadvantaged, which proved to be the enduring theme of the Just Society. It was also dictated by the changing base of Liberal support. When taxes and regulations began to multiply, the business community felt that the helping hand of the Just Society had become a heavy hand, and a similar feeling emerged among most Western Canadians when the federal government ignored their concerns about the practicality of bilingualism, the mounting debt and the government's partial expropriation of the oil patch. By the 1980s, the Liberals were forced to seek support from youth, women, minorities and the poor. If there was any doubt about this development, we need only consult the writings of Tom Axworthy, Trudeau's Principal Secretary, who made the following statement in *National Forum* in November of 1984:

By the mid-1980s, the affluent, and especially members of the business community, had deserted the Liberal Party in droves. They had been replaced, however, by an almost classic social democratic core of the young, women, ethnic supporters, and the disadvantaged.[2]

Under the influence of the politics of compassion, Trudeau's Liberals had changed fundamentally the way in which Canada was governed.

In 1968, they had begun with a liberal democratic agenda that guaranteed equal opportunity, but by the late 1970s, they had moved to a social democratic agenda that was designed to equalize outcomes in the name of helping disadvantaged minorities. They had moved us from a society where everyone would be given the freedom to define his or her standing in life to a society where selected groups would have their standing defined by government action. In the process, the Liberal party brought us many of the ills that have eroded our standard of living. By spending recklessly, they burdened us with overwhelming public debt, high taxes, high inflation, high interest rates and low rates of investment in infrastructure and post-secondary education. And, by changing the basic rules of the game, they took us from a merit-based society, which gave everyone the incentive to produce wealth, to a politically correct society where individual justice and national prosperity were eclipsed in favor of an obsessive concern with the status of minority groups.

I've already explained in the chapters on employment equity and pay equity how the transition to a society devoted to group rights and equality of result has cost us dearly. In the next section, I will track the arc of public spending to demonstrate how the politics of compassion resulted in a spending binge that produced cruel results for everyone.

Welcome to the Party

In the years immediately preceding the election of the Trudeau Liberals in 1968, public finances at the federal level were in remarkably good shape. The debt was at an all-time low in the post-war period and interest charges on the debt consumed a mere 11 cents of every tax dollar paid by Canadians. At first, Trudeau's new Liberal government seemed to be respecting the fiscal prudence of its predecessor by bringing in a balanced budget during the 1969-70 fiscal year. (In other words, the government spent only as much as it received in tax revenue.) Thereafter, for the next 14 years, interrupted only by Joe Clark's six-month interregnum in 1979, the Liberals ran deficits every year. This meant the government had to borrow money domestically and internationally by floating government savings bonds and treasury bills to finance the shortfall between spending and tax revenue. However, every time this was done, the government was adding to the national debt, and thereby the yearly sums owed to investors in the form of interest payments. Thus, the Liberals put Canada on the path to fiscal disaster.

As the Liberals increased the provision of public services, they would spend more, but to spend more they had to borrow more. And every time they borrowed more, they had to pay more in interest. So, as the debt grew and interest charges grew with it, eventually the government had less money to devote to services. (By 1984, interest charges consumed almost a third of every tax dollar.)[3] Eventually, the debt would become so large that the Liberals had to borrow money just to pay the interest on it. This kind of thing happens in the developing world all the time. That's why impoverished countries need foreign aid and low-interest loans from the World Bank.

When Trudeau started running budget deficits in the early 1970s to finance the Just Society, no one foresaw, perhaps not even Trudeau himself, that this spending, which was aimed at making Canada into the most advanced of all Western nations, would eventually turn it into a debtor nation that resembled a developing country in its dependence on foreign capital. The basic figures tell the whole story. By 1985, the federal government was spending twice as many real dollars on each citizen ($4,750 per capita) on a yearly basis as compared to 1968.[4] This vast increase was reflected in the 1984 budget, in which the Liberals spent 55% more than the government actually received in tax revenue for the year. The government's total debt also reflected the mania for spending; in 1968, the total government debt was $58 billion but, by 1984, it came in at around $350 billion, an increase of almost 600%![5] And then there's the problem of interest charges on the debt. In 1967–68, the interest on the debt totaled $1.3 billion; by 1984–85, it grew to the monstrous sum of $22.5 billion, which, as I noted above, consumed almost a third of every tax dollar.[6]

Although the Liberals ran deficits from 1970 to 1975, and the total public debt increased substantially, this was a period of high growth, which meant that the size of the debt relative to the Gross Domestic Product (GDP) of the country actually decreased. In other words, while the debt grew, the country produced goods and services so much faster that the debt was shrinking when compared to our accumulated wealth. In 1975, the debt-to-GDP ratio fell below 20%, a record low in the post-war period.

However, as *National Post* columnist, Andrew Coyne, has argued, spending reached truly dangerous levels during the period from 1976 to 1985, which he calls the "lost decade." That's the decade in which the government was willing to pay any price to deliver us into the promised land of the Compassionate Society. As the yearly deficits increased and the debt began to mushroom, the government was totally unprepared for the 1981 recession. With interest rates rising due to inflation prior to the recession, and revenue going into decline when the recession hit, the government faced a fiscal crisis; it didn't have enough cash on hand to meet the increased cost of servicing the debt. The Liberals were between a rock and a hard place. To reduce inflationary pressures and reduce the need to borrow, they could cut spending to reasonable levels. But if they did that, they might prolong the recession by reducing the stimulus created by public spending. Of course, when you're driven by the project of creating a truly compassionate society, there's only one choice: keep on spending!

Coyne has provided one of the definitive accounts of how and where the Liberals overspent during the "lost decade." He isolates four different areas of government activity, which together account for the massive increases in government spending. The first source of increased spending was the expansion of the number of people administering government programs. During Trudeau's rule, the federal government created 114 new boards, agencies and commissions, and seven new government departments; it added 44,000 new employees to the public payroll, and 19 additional members to the Cabinet. To top things off, it allowed public-sector pay scales, which had been set in relation to private-sector scales, to exceed the private-sector benchmarks by 20%— and this happened as early as the mid-1970s.

The second cause of deficit spending was the decision to substantially increase transfers to the provinces for health care, post-secondary education and social assistance. This increase was accelerated by the fact that the Liberals had entered into a shared cost agreement with the provinces whereby the federal government was committed to providing 50% of provincial funding in the aforementioned areas. So, as the provinces continued to increase their spending, in part because they had the incentive of federal contributions, the federal government's transfers became ever larger. Between 1967 and 1975, transfers were increasing at the rate of 10.8% per year.

To put a lid on these never-ending increases, the federal government eventually moved to a block grant system, which tied increases to the rate of economic growth. But, as part of the deal, the federal government gave up tax points to the provinces. That cost the government $38 billion in for gone revenue between 1978 and 1985. The provinces also profited from large increases in equalization payments, which were designed to improve the standard of living in the less prosperous provinces. In total, the various transfers proved to be a heavy burden. Coyne states: "By 1984–85, the value of all federal grants, transfers, equalization payments and tax points ceded to the provinces totaled $26 billion, equal to one-quarter of all federal spending in that year."

In its third aspect, deficit spending can be attributed to increases in transfers to individuals under various social programs. During the entire 17-year period stretching from 1968 to 1985, these transfers rose at 7% per year after inflation. The most egregious example was the 1971 "reform" of the Unemployment Insurance (UI) system. The government increased benefits from 40% of earnings to 66%, allowed benefits to kick in for anyone who had worked for eight weeks and increased the duration of benefits to 51 weeks. Under this dispensation, UI essentially became a welfare scheme, and yearly payments rose from $700 million in 1970 to more than $10 billion by 1985. In addition, in the 1970s, yearly increases in pensions and family allowances were allowed to exceed the rate of inflation, and in the early 1980s, the Guaranteed Income Supplement for seniors was hiked several times. Seniors also benefited from a drop in the qualifying age for Old Age Security from 70 to 65. Together, these increases put significant pressures on federal coffers.

The fourth and final source of deficit spending was comprised of transfers to agencies, interest groups, Crown corporations and businesses (in the form of subsidies). According to Coyne, the government allowed these transfers to run wild. During Trudeau's first two governments, subsidies and capital assistance to businesses increased at the rate of 17% per year, with much of the money going to underperforming regions under programs administered by the Department of Regional Economic Development. Subsidies for Crown corporations grew throughout the 1970s and 1980s; by 1985, these corporations were receiving $6 billion per year. (Canada Post alone was receiving $1 billion per year at its peak, and the total multi-year bill for Petro-Canada reached $14 billion.) And then there were all the transfers to interest groups under programs administered by the Secretary of State.[7]

While these transfers hardly constituted the major source of revenue drain, they nonetheless contributed disproportionately to the expansion of government in my view. The government provided funding for these groups—primarily women's groups and multicultural groups—knowing full well that they would lobby the government for special privileges. This increased the external pressure for the federal government to continue expanding its spending commitments to disadvantaged groups and regions. Furthermore, these groups were largely responsible for persuading the government to change the rules of the game by introducing pay equity and employment equity schemes in the public sector.[8]

Needless to say, all this reckless spending led to higher taxes because borrowing alone couldn't satisfy the state's voracious appetite. In 1970, federal, provincial and municipal taxes consumed about 36% of the Gross Domestic Product (the total value of all goods and services produced in the nation in the year); but by 1982, they consumed around 50% of GDP. By the mid-1980s, individuals were paying, on average, over 50% of their gross incomes in taxes.[9]

In summation, Coyne points out that many people believe erroneously that spending on social programs is what really ramped up the debt. In fact, transfers for health, education, old age security, federal housing and labor-market programs increased but didn't "unduly" strain federal revenue. However, when these transfers were combined with greater transfers to interest groups, agencies, Crown corporations, businesses and to government itself, the total effect was staggering. If increases in these latter two categories had been held constant in 1968 dollars, total program spending in 1984–85 would have been reduced by $20 billion.[10]

Even though social programs didn't get the lion's share of federal spending increases during the Trudeau years, Liberals often treated them as their crowning glory. When the opposition, a few sober-minded academics and business leaders, began to call for cuts to these bloated programs during the last Trudeau government, Liberals often responded sanctimoniously, charging that their critics were asking them to breach a sacred trust with the Canadian people. But, it was the Liberals themselves who had broken faith with the country. By running up the debt, the Liberals virtually guaranteed that future governments, both Conservative and Liberal, would have to cut social programs to get the country out of the red.

To see why that was so, we need only consider how the federal Progressive Conservatives struggled with the debt when they were elected in 1984. Although they had run on a platform that stressed fiscal responsibility, they soon found that interest payments on the debt made it virtually impossible to stop the bleeding. Even though they eventually brought in several successive operating surpluses (i.e., they spent less than they received in tax revenue), the interest payments on the debt were so high, eating up well over one-third of every tax dollar, that they continued to run budget deficits; as a result, they had to continue to borrow funds to prevent default, and this, in turn, caused the debt to grow further.

During their first year in government, the debt rose to $378 billion; four years later, it had risen to well over $500 billion. We can clearly see the gravity of this situation when we consider that Tax Freedom Day in 1988 was July 7—all the money made by Canadians from January 1, 1988 to July 6, 1988 went to the taxman.[11] We can certainly blame the Conservatives for failing to make the radical spending cuts that were necessary to prevent the debt from expanding, particularly given that they had run on the promise of fiscal restraint and had won the largest number of seats in Canadian history. However, the fact that they eventually ran operating surpluses but could not bring the debt under control demonstrated how much damage had been done by the previous government.

The debt problem continued to plague the federal government when the Liberals returned to power in 1993. Ironically, they were

the ones who would have to face the unpleasant task of making dras-
tic cuts to social programs to deal with the fiscal problems created
during the Trudeau years. As the federal debt approached $600 bil-
lion, and the *Wall Street Journal* was speculating that Canada might be
facing devaluation of its currency and a severe downrating of its bond
rating, Finance Minister Paul Martin was forced to act. In the 1995
budget, he slashed $25 billion in program spending over a three-year
period, which allowed the federal government, two years later, to finally run a true budget surplus for the first time in 27 years. Those
who complain about the quality of public health care and the decline
of our post-secondary institutions should not be pointing their fin-
gers at Mr. Martin's program cuts. Instead they should direct their
animus toward Mr. Trudeau, whose reckless spending turned the
debt into a juggernaut, and Mr. Mulroney, who didn't have a plan or
the fortitude to bring the debt under control.

The transition from the Just Society to the Compassionate Society
came at a great price, one that was so great that it undermined the
very goals that Liberals had hoped to achieve. The Compassionate
Society can hardly qualify as the Great Society or the Just Society
when its generosity resulted in reckless spending that compromised
the agenda of helping the disadvantaged, as well as the broader
agenda of maintaining middle-class entitlements.[12] This failure
doesn't mean that compassion is a bad thing. On a private level, it's
the virtue that we most value in our friends and family members.
On a political level, however, its effects are inherently destructive.
The political commitment to compassion necessarily produces four
conditions that make it impossible to achieve a compassionate society: reckless spending, dishonest leadership, unprincipled policies
and low productivity.

Dishonest Leadership—How the Ambitious Use Compassion

One of the first and most pronounced effects of the politics of compassion was that they attracted disingenuous political types who were instrumental in running up the debt and compromising the disadvantaged groups they championed. This happened because the appeal to compassion became a moral claim that trumped other more sensible claims to rule. In this respect, the politics of compassion were distinctly illiberal.

The founders of liberalism, notably Hobbes and Locke, understood that the problem of political life is that the most ambitious political actors justify their self-serving actions in relation to a higher moral standard. This approach is not necessarily a conscious strategy because the super-ambitious are often true believers, who have perfect confidence in their own privileged insights. In some cases, however, their moral claims are well-conceived deceptions designed to legitimize their selfish pursuit of power. Liberals wanted to limit the influence of these ambitious ideologues because they had been the cause of the great religious wars of the 16th and 17th centuries, which had utterly destroyed public peace in England and the rest of Europe.

The liberal solution was to banish from the public domain transcendent moral claims, based on religion and culture, that "hellish spirits," had used to wreak havoc and legitimize their predatory rule over the people.[13] That solution, which was given its fullest expression in the late 17th century by the English philosopher, John Locke, consisted of two strategies. The first was to assign religion and culture to the private realm where they would become matters of personal choice. The second was to make an appeal to economic self-interest that would reconcile the ambitious few and everyone else to the authority of the state. That was accomplished by establishing free markets where everyone would have the chance to satisfy his or her selfish desire for gain, and the super-ambitious would satisfy their longings for honor and power by getting rich.

Compassion entered the picture later, when Jean-Jacques Rousseau launched a broadside attack on the liberal solution in the middle of the 18th century. He argued that by encouraging people to make morality a private matter and otherwise appealing to economic self-interest as the basis for establishing a common good was bound to fail. In his view, the appeal to self-interest would eventually lead people to act in their own interests in all matters, which would lead to a great deal of cheating, lying and malicious conduct that would eventually produce disorder and widespread unhappiness. Based on his study of ancient cities like Rome and Sparta, Rousseau believed that a stable regime had to be founded on public-spiritedness, which required public education in moral matters, a solution that liberals had forsaken by assigning moral matters to the private realm. However, given that the small, closed ancient city could not be revived in the diverse, enlightened conditions of modernity, he believed that the liberal project had to be rescued from the shoals of selfishness by making compassion the foremost social virtue. Rousseau believed that a true common good, a caring society, if you will, could be constructed only if the pursuit of self-interest were moderated by an appeal to the heart. Social virtue was identified with active sympathy for the suffering of others.[14]

Although Rousseau's reliance on compassion was a correction of the liberal solution, it was directed in some measure at solving the liberal problem—how to rein in the ambitious ideologues and prevent them from becoming political tyrants. The solution was not to put the super-ambitious into a race for wealth, which, he believed, would just lead to new forms of oppression based on economic power. Instead, he hoped that the ambitious would seek to distinguish themselves by their concern for the less fortunate.

Unfortunately, Rousseau didn't foresee that this solution had the potential to invite the ambitious to become a new priestly class that would seek political power based on claims of a superior, quasi-religious concern with the sufferings of others. These were the individuals who exerted tremendous influence in the late 20th century in both the Liberal party in Canada and the Democratic party in the United States. In his superb article, "Moist Eyes—from Rousseau to Clinton," North America's leading expert on the subject of compassion, Clifford Orwin, argues persuasively that Bill Clinton is the post-modern apogee of Rousseauian heroism, with all its faults.[15]

In my experience, the ambitious ideologues in the Liberal party, fell into two basic camps. The first camp was the morally ambitious. These people advanced through the ranks of the party and society by fighting for the rights of the disadvantaged. They often did a lot of good, but they were driven more by the desire to be recognized as morally superior than by any real concern with the downtrodden. These individuals found a natural home in a Liberal party that preached compassion for the disadvantaged, while selling them out by ramping up the debt.

The second category was the purely ambitious, who were often running things in the second Liberal campaign in which I was involved. They loved to meet with campaign volunteers and talked a lot about helping the disadvantaged. But, as soon as the rank and file weren't around, they were just as eager to demote or betray a fellow campaign worker to preserve their influence or get ahead. These people were the natural friends of big government because they wanted to increase their personal power by serving in a government that was increasing its power. And yet they justified their personal ambitions in moral terms, chattering incessantly about the need to help the victims of society, about whom, by the way, they knew very little, since most of them had grown up in privileged households. In another age, these same people would have been corrupt priests, using the authority of religious doctrine and the concern with the poor and downtrodden to rationalize their capture and abuse of political power.

I don't mean to suggest that all Liberals fall into one of these camps. The Liberal candidates and House members I've had the privilege of advising did not belong to either camp. The ambitious ideologues in the party were in the minority, but they exercised enormous influence. The most striking example of this kind of person in Canadian public life today is Tim Murphy, Chief of Staff to Prime Minister Martin. I worked with Tim in the 1988 federal campaign and witnessed how he made nice with the ethnic voters while being less than kind when exercising power in the back rooms.

It took someone with that mentality to spearhead the grassroots campaign to oust Mr. Chretien in favor of Mr. Martin. However, Mr. Martin has now discovered that the kind of person who knows how to wage that kind of campaign against his confederates is not the kind of person who will know what to do when he reaches high office. Since becoming leader, Mr. Martin has failed to take the country in any clear direction and, as a result, as this book goes to press, he is mired in the sponsorship scandal. My own view is that Mr. Martin's fuzzy leadership can be traced directly to his apparatchiks—Murphy and his team in the Prime Minister's Office—who don't have what it takes to develop a real vision for the country. Mr. Martin got to become prime minister by relying on the nasty, ambitious elites of the Liberal party, and he's now paying the price.

In the 1970s and 1980s, the movers and shakers in the Liberal party "used" compassion to justify their political ambitions and their willingness to relentlessly expand the reach of government. And, once compassion had become the goal of political action, it attracted the ambitious ideologues, who admonished everyone to become more responsive to the disadvantaged while they eliminated anyone who wouldn't fully cooperate with their personal agendas. While some hoped that the politics of compassion would bring out the best in our political leaders, instead it brought out the worst. The result was that we suffered through years of reckless spending and power-hungry, irresponsible leadership. The religion of compassion hasn't done the damage that other public religions did in the 16th and 17th centuries, but, in the end, like them, it has damaged the conditions that promote good government.

How Compassion Can Subvert Justice

While the politics of the Compassionate Society encouraged irresponsible leadership, it also encouraged irresponsible thinking about social justice and the role of government. And this thinking is what encouraged both leaders and citizens to endorse the harmful expansion of government.

In the history of modern political thought, we are presented with two different ways of encouraging people to practice social virtue. The first, popularized by Rousseau, is to make an appeal to the heart by holding out compassion, understood as a visceral sensitivity to the suffering of others, as a standard of human nobility. The second, advocated by the German philosopher, Immanuel Kant, is to bypass the heart and make an appeal to reason, which informs us that justice consists in helping those who are in need; this position is also linked to a conception of nobility since Kant believes that we live virtuously only when we live in conformity with the dictates of reason.

Each solution is in itself incomplete. In Kant's case, it's hard to understand how helping others can be disconnected from any feeling of social empathy. In Rousseau's case, without the aid of reason, it seems difficult to make principled distinctions between people who deserve help and those who do not. In fact, good decisions don't simply come from the heart or the mind, but from both, because the mind can and should limit what the heart demands.

Do you feel sorry for the gambler who wasted his life savings at the roulette table? If you knew that he had an addiction to gambling, you might. But if you knew that he was simply a foolish person who wanted to gain notoriety as a high roller, you might think he deserved what he got. This simple example expresses a basic truth about the limits of compassion: we don't feel sorry for those who deserve their fate. Pity is ultimately controlled by reason. Though our hearts may be moved by suffering, the depth of our feelings and our willingness to alleviate suffering are determined by our conception of justice.

If this is true on a private level, it is certainly true on the public level because the supreme goal of politics is to achieve justice. The politics of compassion, however, goes directly for the heart, and asks us to use government to help the disadvantaged without considering fully whether those who are classified as disadvantaged are truly disadvantaged (in the sense of being unwilling victims), whether policies that favor the disadvantaged are effective and whether those policies unfairly penalize others. It's this unrefined appeal to the heart that drove Liberal government during the late 1970s and 1980s, and, as we've already seen, it produced self-defeating results by giving us big government that we cannot afford and that does not reach its professed goals.

And what if you were a dissenter during that period when the Liberals were running up the tab in the name of compassion? What could be more stinging than the accusation that you were lacking in compassion? The emotionally charged, moralistic language of the time turned out to be an early form of political correctness that shut down any meaningful debate about the justice of the Compassionate Society.

Compassion and Productivity

Yet another problem with the politics of compassion is that it helped to create the conditions that have reduced our productivity, giving us high taxes that prevent individuals and corporations from making investments machinery and R & D, and draconian budgets that prevent governments from making essential investments in infrastructure, post-secondary education and health care. And then there's the most damaging legacy of the Compassionate Society—the false belief that the fate of society is tied to the fate of the disadvantaged.

In Chapter 1, I argued that a truly prosperous society must be based on the principle of equal opportunity because it gives each individual the opportunity to maximize his or her productive potential, which, in turn, maximizes the prosperity of the whole society. And I've also argued that this solution doesn't work unless the state plays some role in helping members of disadvantaged groups to gain the support and training they need to maximize their potential. However, making that the primary goal of politics misses the entire point of the liberal project. Liberal politics are supposed to liberate everyone's potential, that's true, but the focus is on liberating the potential of the most talented and hard-working among us because they contribute disproportionately to the creation of the opportunities and the wealth that make it possible for everyone to improve their lot in life.

The founder of Microsoft, Bill Gates, and the founders of Apple, Steve Jobs and Steve Wozniak, for example, created millions of new jobs with their inventions, and generated billions of dollars in new wealth. The goal of a liberal society is to make sure that exceptional people like these get a chance to make their mark, whether they start off rich or poor, because they can play such a large role in affecting outcomes for the entire society. Contrary to the teachings of the Compassionate Society, a truly liberal society will tie its fate to the advantaged—the natural aristocracy of talent—which Locke referred to as "the Industrious and the Rational." Liberals argued that the disadvantaged should prefer such a society because they, along with everyone else, would be made better off by the wealth created by its most enterprising members. And, as I've argued, a truly liberal society will regulate economic and social conditions so that members of disadvantaged groups can aspire to become enterprising and successful too.

Seen from a liberal perspective, then, the Compassionate Society must be judged an abysmal failure. By focusing government activity excessively on helping the disadvantaged, it changed the very logic of liberalism. It tied our fate to our willingness to do anything to improve the situation of the disadvantaged instead of tying the fate of the disadvantaged to our willingness to do anything to ensure that people who seek to become advantaged through hard work, innovation and risk-taking are honored and rewarded. This reversal has produced many of the developments that have so grievously affected our competitive position: profligate spending, the creation of affirmative action programs that undermine the merit system and the exodus of some of our most talented citizens to the United States.

Why Compassion Is Widespread but Weak

To understand how compassion has failed to fulfill its promise on a political level, it's necessary to recognize that, in a democratic society, compassion never accomplishes as much as we might hope. Here I borrow my analysis from Tocqueville's *Democracy in America*. Tocqueville tried to understand social virtue, as it was practiced in the United States, by considering how it was practiced in the aristocratic regimes of Europe. In aristocratic regimes, where people were divided into social castes by the feudal system, Tocqueville found that nobles and commoners were exceptionally sympathetic toward their own kind, but not to each other. As a result, nobles made heroic sacrifices for their friends and took great delight in claiming or believing that they were acting from the highest of motives: "It gratified them to make out that it is a glorious thing to forget oneself and that one should do good without self-interest, as God himself does." At the same time, they could be exceptionally cruel toward commoners, not because the aristocrats were barbarous or uncivilized, but because they lived in such a rarified milieu that they could not begin to conceive what it was like to be a commoner, and therefore lacked the ability to empathize with the plight of those who served them. (The same could be said reciprocally about commoners toward their masters, given the wretchedness of the commoners' condition.) So, within the feudal castes of aristocratic societies, social sympathies were strong but between the castes almost nonexistent. Tocqueville saw, however, that the new democratic order of America, where people lived in social and economic conditions that were roughly equal, had broadened their sentiments. Since Americans were not separated by classes, they could easily identify with each other and sympathize with each other's sufferings.[16]

While compassion had become a democratic virtue, it did not call forth the same kinds of sacrifices as it had when aristocrats prided themselves on grand gestures. That was partly due to the fact that people living in equal conditions made Americans self-regarding because they had to rely on their own hard work and initiative to survive. Just as important in diminishing the power of compassion was the pervasive influence of "the doctrine of self-interest properly understood." Under the influence of that doctrine, Americans rejected the view that virtue was to be practiced for its own sake, or that it consisted in denying one's selfish desires. Instead, its goodness stood or fell according to its utility. Americans were willing to help each other on the condition that they were simultaneously helping themselves: "It gives them pleasure to point out how an enlightened self-love continually leads them to help one another and disposes them freely to give part of their time and wealth for the good of the state."

By founding virtue on self-interest rather than honor or some grand conception of the higher self, virtue lost the power it had to lead people to make great sacrifices. Nonetheless, it made everyone sociable and cooperative in some measure. Tocqueville states that the doctrine of self-interest properly understood "... does not attempt to reach great aims, but it does, without too much trouble, achieve all it sets out to do."[17]

It is in relation to the doctrine of self-interest properly understood that we can see why compassion is widespread but weak in democratic times. It's widespread due to the leveling of social and economic conditions, but it's weak because it is constrained by the selfish race for gain and the belief that morality should serve selfish ends.

For our purposes, these conclusions create the backdrop for understanding the limits of the politics of compassion. From the start, we can see that those politics would necessarily become abstract and ideological because they asked people to give compassion an exalted place in their lives when, in fact, compassion, tempered by self-interest, would necessarily remain a prosaic and limited affair. In other words, the politics of compassion was phony from the start, and it brought phony claims, phony promises and phony players into the political arena. And the result has been what we might expect—self-defeating policies and punishing public debt.

Canadians Are More Compassionate Than Americans?

Back in the late 1980s, I tuned into a television program that featured Robertson Davies, who had had just come out with a new book. He was being interviewed by Adrienne Clarkson and, as you might expect, the conversation eventually turned to the issue of Canadian identity. Ms. Clarkson asked Mr. Davies whether he thought that Canadians were more compassionate than Americans, while effecting a presumptuous tone that assumed the answer had to be yes. Mr. Davies' answer was a peremptory no. I can't remember what Ms. Clarkson said next, but I remember vividly the surprise and discomfort that was reflected in her voice. Rather than pursue Mr. Davies' troubling answer, she moved on to the next question.

I saw Ms. Clarkson's attitude as an indicator of the mentality prevailing among so many of our political and media elites. They believed that Canadian identity and self-esteem rested on our superior compassion, and that we needed to confirm our superiority by allowing the state to expand relentlessly in the name of helping the disadvantaged.

Like Robertson Davies, I certainly doubted that Canadians were more compassionate than Americans. As elite opinion weighed uncomfortably on my brow, I decided to embark on a lengthy study of Canadian political culture to determine whether there was any truth to what the elites were saying. And that led me to the conclusion that I've discussed in Chapter 7: As Canadians we tend to prefer big government because we're still holding on to colonial attitudes that stress deference to authority, and we've grown accustomed, by necessity, to using the state in the process of nation-building.

I do not subscribe to the view that we are more compassionate than Americans; on average, I feel we are somewhat less compassionate. My opinion is grounded to some degree in facts and personal experience.

First, I have to point out as others have that Canadians are not as charitable as Americans. In 1970, American corporations and individuals together gave charitable contributions equal to 1.92% of their GDP, while Canadian corporations and individuals only gave .86%; in 1980, the disparity was 1.7% versus .67%; and in 1985, it was 1.87% versus .72%. If we look just at Canadian individuals, the figures show an exceptionally deep decline, going from .97 of GDP in 1970 to .43 in 1985.[18]

Not surprisingly, as the government grew larger, spent more and taxed more, people simply had less to give. But, that problem aside, there was a charity gap separating the two countries before the spending onslaught began. And that gap is still with us in the 21st century. In the year 2000, the average American charitable donation was US$3,494, while the average Canadian donation was CAN$915. Even before taking differences based on exchange rates or purchasing power into account, either of which would substantially increase the gap, we can see that Americans have been spending around four times as much as Canadians on charitable causes. And our poor performance is not mitigated if we make a comparison based on our most charitable provinces. British Columbia and Alberta, our most giving provinces, posted an average donation of CAN$1,129 in 2000, which is just a shade above the national average.[19]

Some people believe that the charity gap is simply a reflection of the fact that, historically, Americans have relied less on government and more on themselves, and the ethic of private action has manifested itself in a larger commitment to charitable causes. We, in fact, are just as charitable, they say, but we prefer to manifest our concern using the state as our proxy. I tend to have doubts about that argument from a commonsense standpoint. When I pay my taxes, I don't think about all the needy people I'm helping with my tax dollars. Paying taxes is a rather impersonal affair. Taxpayers have some idea where all the money is going, but we can never be quite sure, especially when budget commitments vary from year to year and government to government.

However, when people donate to the Cancer Society, often they do it because they have friends or family members who are battling the disease or have succumbed to it. When they give, donors are focused on the suffering of others, and, in that moment, they are moved by compassion. I have trouble believing that when we, as taxpayers, give indirectly through government, we are giving with our hearts in the same way that private donors are. In the end, the figures don't tell me that Canadians don't give from the heart, but that more Americans do so more often. For anyone making comparative assessments of compassion, this difference is hard to miss.

It may be that Americans give more because they believe more in private action. But, I think there is something even more powerful at work, and that is patriotism. The fact is, patriotism is less powerful in Canada than it is in the U.S. Love of one's country and the willingness to make sacrifices for it are greatly enhanced when citizens live in similar social and economic conditions. When similarly situated, citizens can more easily imagine themselves in each other's shoes, which, in turn makes them more willing to make sacrifices that reduce suffering and promote the public good. In democracies such as Canada or the United States, where social and economic conditions are roughly equal (almost everyone is a member of the middle class), patriotism tends to thrive. However, in the last thirty years, Canada has been divided by language, regional loyalties and culture much more dramatically than the United States. As a result, patriotic sentiments have been less intense, and this is reflected, in part, in lower rates of charitable giving

American Compassion Revisited

Let's look at it from another perspective now. If we concede that Americans are more charitable than Canadians, that may not mean that they are necessarily more compassionate. The American preference for limited government has meant that millions of unemployed Americans cannot afford adequate health care, and that, compared to Canada, the country has higher rates of poverty, as well as greater inequalities of wealth. Recent OECD statistics tell the whole story. American governments spend 14.8 of the GNP on social programs, while we spend 17.8%; American unemployment insurance covers 6% of someone's previous earnings in the United States, while Canadian insurance covers 20%; 17.1% of Americans live in poverty as compared to 10.3% of Canadians; 21.7% of American children are living in poverty as compared to 13.6% in Canada. To measure income inequality, the OECD resorts to the gini coefficient, which measures inequality based on a scale of 0 to 1, with 0 indicating perfect equality and 1 perfect inequality. On this basis, the United States has greater inequality, scoring 35.7 as compared to Canada, which comes in at 30.[20] If Americans are willing to tolerate these outcomes, surely we cannot give them so much credit for their charitable giving. In fact, we might take the argument one step further and point to the greater gap between the rich and the poor as evidence that greed trumps compassion in the American system. This view depends on the assumption that the rich get rich at the expense of the poor, or, at the least, that the rich stay rich because they don't give enough to the poor.

Here we have to confront head on the fact that many of the advantages that have allowed America to become more productive and more prosperous can be attributed to lower tax rates. American businesses have had more revenue on hand to invest in new machinery, ICT and R&D, because the United States has lower corporate tax rates than we do. And many American families have had more disposable income to spend on education because the United States has lower personal tax rates than we do. Also, American governments have spent more on post-secondary education and urban infrastructure—two of the major determinants of America's economic success—because they spend less on the sick and poor than we do.[21]

All that is true. However, it is not just that Americans tax less but they also invest public and privately in the factors that promote higher productivity. And higher productivity has given the United States a standard of living that is now 20% higher than Canada's. By focusing its investments on the factors that promote growth, the United States has the wealth on hand to deal more equitably with the disadvantaged. And, as I've argued above, if it weren't for the stupendous cost of the war on terror, the United States could easily afford a Canadian-style social agenda. We, on the other hand, cannot afford a Canadian-style social agenda. We've spent too much on the welfare state and not enough on the factors that promote future growth. Who should be deemed more compassionate in the end: the country that spends for future growth so that it can finance a higher standard of living for everyone or the country that spends to satisfy all social needs in the present and thereby stymies the growth that makes it possible to make everyone better off?

The strange paradox of the compassion debate is that Americans have to spend more on the disadvantaged to become truly compassionate, and we have to spend less. But spending less won't be enough if we hope to substantially improve our economic performance. The United States didn't become more prosperous simply because it taxes less. It has many advantages that are either situational (a greater number of business clusters) or attitudinal. And the attitudinal advantages, which can be expressed as differences in our two political cultures, are numerous:

- greater commitment to individual rights (and a corresponding rejection of group rights)
- greater belief in the power of the individual
- greater belief in meritocracy
- higher tolerance for risk-taking
- greater respect for private property
- greater respect for markets
- greater willingness to compete in global markets
- greater respect for higher education (and post-graduate education, in particular)
- greater commitment to business education
- greater belief in the benefits of theoretical research
- greater openness to "new talent" among immigrant groups

Canadians will have to find some way of assimilating these advantages if we hope to raise our standard of living and produce the revenue stream that will sustain our public commitments. Ultimately, the project of building a just society is as much an appeal to the mind as it is to the heart. Or, as George F. Will once wrote, "statecraft is soulcraft."

Myth Ten

THE SUCCESS OF THE INDIVIDUAL DEPENDS ON THE SUCCESS OF THE GROUP

Selling an Idea

Four years ago, on a hot summer afternoon, I was sitting in my office browsing the International Management Group's (IMG) website for some information about a skating event. (IMG is the world's foremost sports marketing company.) I discovered that IMG runs a large sports academy in Florida, which provides state-of-the-art training facilities for amateur and professional athletes. I was amazed by the scope of their programs, particularly those for tennis and golf, where they were training thousands of young people who aspire to attend college on athletic scholarships or enter professional sports directly. The whole concept of the IMG Academies piqued my interest because I had been a varsity basketball player in high school, and during summer vacations, had attended Willis Reed's basketball camp in New York. The kind of training and coaching I received there was very similar to the kind provided at the IMG Academies.

All student athletes have to deal with the problem of finding the time to do well in school, have a social life and still excel in sports. It's tough to do, and I was wondering how IMG dealt with the larger issue of making sure that their athletes achieved a successful balance. As I scrolled, I learned that the academy had been farming out students to local high schools for their academic training but that it was about to open its own school on site. I had an epiphany: this new school would provide an excellent opportunity to develop a comprehensive philosophy to guide student athletes in achieving life success. There was a book in this. It could be a valuable resource for students at the academy, and with IMG's support, it could be distributed to student athletes around the World.

I decided to take the idea to the IMG office in Toronto. With a written introduction from a friend who provided consulting advice to IMG Canada, I sent a letter to an agent asking for a fifteen-minute meeting. I received a letter of reply from the head of human resources who informed me that IMG didn't talk to anyone unless the company was trying to fill a position. Okay, I thought, I'll take a second run at this; so I sent a letter to a top executive. No response. That's when I decided to write directly to the president and founder of IMG, Mr. Mark McCormack.

I called the New York office, got a receptionist, and told her that I wanted to contact Mr. McCormack. She said, "I'll put you through to Mr. McCormack's line." A direct call was not what I'd had in mind, but, before I could object, I was on hold. I had a moment of panic as I tried to quickly formulate what I was going to say if Mr. McCormack picked up. Fortunately, I got his executive assistant. I told her a bit about my idea, and she advised me to send a letter to Mr. McCormack at the home office in Cleveland, and she would bring it to his attention. I sent a letter by courier, and a few weeks later, I received a personal letter from Mr. McCormack. He said that he thought my idea had merit and that he would bring it to the attention of senior management. Eventually, Mr. McCormack sent me the phone number for IMG publishing in New York, and invited me to speak to the division's executive editor about my proposal. I got right through to the editor, but I couldn't get him to see the value in the idea. So I decided to let the matter die on the drawing board. But the lesson of this episode was one that I've learned over and over again. In the United States, even if you're an unknown individual from another country, if you've got an idea that might have value, someone at the top is always willing to give you five minutes to make your pitch. Five minutes is all you'll get, but that's all you'll need if your idea is good enough. In Canada, even if you're well connected, it's often difficult to get a meeting with one of the managerial elites.

If I had been dealing with two different companies, one Canadian and one American, then the different reactions to my pitch might simply have reflected differences that were particular to the companies themselves. However, given that I had been dealing with the Toronto and New York offices of the same American company confirmed my perception that the differences in treatment reflected differences in the cultures of the two societies.

Experiences such as these helped me to grasp more fully the extent to which Americans and Canadians differ on the status of individuals. Eventually, I articulated the difference this way: Americans believe the success of the group depends on the success of the individual; Canadians believe the success of the individual depends on the success of the group.

Americans simply have a greater belief in the power of the individual to make a difference. As a result, individual achievement is rewarded more handsomely, recognized more conspicuously, and pursued more eagerly: every American wants to be named the most valuable player.

The true American economic advantage is the belief that developing individual talent is what is best for the individual and society as a whole. In a sense, America is a great talent contest. This is a fact that screams at me every time I read an American newspaper or watch American television or visit a major American city: the obsession with competitive sports, the non-stop proliferation of award shows, the overwhelming success of *American Idol*, the never-ending top-10, top-100, top-500 lists. Even the JonBenet Ramsey murder investigation, which became such a long-running media soap opera, speaks to the overwhelming concern with rank and talent. As a lawyer, I might have been interested in the case based on the legal issues it raised; otherwise it might have held my interest because it presented so clearly the contradiction in American thinking, which holds the accused innocent until proven guilty and yet tolerates the media convicting and crucifying accused parties on prime-time television. For me, the fascinating and truly American fact about the case was that John and Patricia Ramsey, a wealthy couple with all of life's advantages, would put their little girl in a local beauty contest. (Remember the video that was played endlessly, showing JonBenet performing on stage in make-up and costume?) Mr. and Mrs. Ramsey felt the need to put their seven-year-old daughter into the race for distinction with everyone else, even if family wealth had already guaranteed her a place in the winner's circle.

Canadians simply don't place the same emphasis on the cultivation of individual talents. The measure of the difference between the two countries is that the great local tradition in America is the talent show; in Canada, it's the multicultural festival. Could there be any more glaring contrast between the American concern with the status of the individual and our concern with the status of groups?

The Group Mentality in Practice

This striking difference in attitude toward the individual in the United States and Canada has become evident to me in a myriad of ways over the past two decades, particularly during the late 1980s when I lived and studied on both sides of the border. When I attended the University of Chicago in 1985, I was surprised to find that large private banks and government agencies came to campus to recruit students from the political science department. When I studied political science at the University of Toronto, I had never once heard of any organization coming to the department in search of talent. Even when I was at the University of Toronto Law School, firms didn't come to the school to recruit. Students in search of full-time employment had to go down-town and compete in a week-long interview process for a chance to be taken on by a firm. When I was studying at the graduate level at Columbia Law School in New York City, I saw how the recruitment system worked at the highest level. My classmates didn't have to go to Wall Street or the center of any other major city in search of opportu-nity. Law firms, consulting companies, banks and the like were so keen to get the chance to hire a Columbia graduate that they came to the school to recruit on site for an entire week. The same held true for undergraduates attending Columbia College. Employers from govern-ment and the private sector attended the school frequently in the hope of getting talented twentysomethings to sign up.

The recruitment drives at American colleges clearly represent how we differ from the United States on the status of the individual. American companies, and even government departments, were constantly trolling for that one person who could really help the organization. In Canada, students were constantly trolling for the chance to join that one organization that would be so kind as to help them.

The difference between the two systems has changed in some measure since the late 1980s, when I was completing my education. At the University of Toronto Law School, for example, firms now come directly to the school to provide information sessions and make pitches. But, they started doing that only under pressure brought to bear by American law firms, which had been stealing the top graduates.

Other striking examples in the educational field also come to mind. In 1994, in its annual ranking of Canadian universities,

Maclean's ran a short piece on the American college system and interviewed Ryan Craig, a Canadian, who, along with his younger brother, was attending Yale University. Mr. Craig pointed out that his brother had been rejected by several Canadian schools due to his "grades," but had nonetheless been accepted at Yale "after seeing how well-rounded he was in high school." That comment was made in the context of pointing out that Canadian schools can be more elitist than top private American schools due to the overwhelming emphasis that Canadian institutions place on grades. It was also a clear testament to the fact that American schools spend more time and resources on assessing whether a student is well suited to a particular program. In reaching their decisions, most American schools consider a wide range of factors, including grades, scores on college entrance exams (SATs), letters of recommendation, extra-curricular activities, personal statements and interviews. Not only do American schools spend more time assessing individuals, they also have a broader conception of what it means to assess individual talent.

The limits of the Canadian university system were revealed a little over two years ago when an Ontario teenager, Eva Vertes, was accepted at Princeton, but rejected by McMaster, University of Western Ontario and the University of Toronto, even though she had won the Intel International Science Fair for a project investigating the death of brain cells in Alzheimer's patients and had never had less than a 91% average throughout high school. As a result of winning the Intel award, Ms. Vertes had accepted an invitation to continue her research at a university lab in Italy, where she worked full time while completing her final year of high school by correspondence. Because she was studying by correspondence, she failed to meet the admission guidelines set for all students by Ontario's centralized university application center; she wasn't able to submit mid-term grades and did not complete all her courses on the center's rigid time line. As a result, an exceptionally promising student was never considered for admission to an Ontario university. There was no room in the warehouse approach used by the application center for someone whose background was unusual. The more individualistic American approach was reflected in the response that Ms. Vertes's mother got when she inquired about admission at Harvard:

> She called Harvard, where admissions officials told her not to worry. Her daughter would be evaluated according to her overall achievements, rather than specific course requirements. Harvard even said Eva could complete high school during the summer.
>
> "I think the American application process is much better for choosing students who are not only academically successful, but who have had life experiences and have done other things," Ms. Vertes said.[1]

Forces favoring the group at the expense of the individual are also at work in some parts of the corporate world in Canada. One can see them very clearly just by comparing the career pages on the websites of America's largest bank, Citigroup, and Canada's largest bank, the Royal Bank of Canada (RBC). The Citigroup pitch begins with politeness: "Thanks for visiting Careers at Citigroup!" And then it gets right to the point: "We are looking for talented people to join us." RBC's career page begins with some trite talk about the bank's passionate commitment to serving clients. Isn't that what every ambitious young person wants? A chance to serve clients? It takes 10 lines for the bank to answer the important question: what's in it for me? And the answer is that new recruits will be working with a group that will help them to advance: The website states: "Now this sounds like a team of people that'll help me get to where I want to go!"

The difference in emphasis isn't a minor point. At Citigroup, the message is that the organization needs talented individuals; the message at RBC is that talented individuals need the organization. Better not rock the boat.[2]

I ran across quite a telling point on the same theme in a newsletter published by a Canadian speakers bureau. It advised clients that Americans and Canadians have different tastes in motivational speakers and that it is wise to consider these differences when planning an event. The newsletter states: "Canadians may closely relate to an individual who was part of a successful team, or who achieved their goals through successful planning, organization and implementation. Americans may relate better to a person with outstanding individual achievements or who succeeded against the odds." Here is clear market-based evidence that attests to the Canadian aversion to individualism.

The group mentality in the Canadian corporate world is reflected in the great emphasis that is sometimes placed on "paying your dues." That is perhaps nowhere better reflected than in the legal profession where the articling system is used to train "students-at-law." In Canada, articling was originally a form of apprenticeship that formed the core of a lawyer's training in the 19th and early 20th centuries; aspiring lawyers learned most of their trade by spending several years working as underlings in a law office. Eventually, though, law became a heavy-duty academic discipline and the apprenticeship was reduced to a one-year stint with a firm after graduation, followed by several months of examinations leading to the call to the bar.

The official rationale for holding on to the articling system was that young lawyers needed the steady hand of experienced practitioners to learn how to apply their knowledge of law. And that's true enough. However, the apprenticeship year quickly became a veiled exercise of enforcing hard labor on young lawyers in exchange for a meager wage—with no guarantee of future employment. After the year of articling, firms decide to hire back some students as associates, and the rest are left to fend for themselves. For anyone who doesn't make the cut, which is often based on arbitrary reasons, the system can be unforgiving because no one really learns enough in one year of doing menial work to actually run a law practice. So, if you're not hired back, a promising career in law might be terminated at an early stage, and four years of training can go down the drain. Firms don't care much about the carnage because they've gotten their added value from hard-working "students." I can't think of any other profession that imposes such draconian conditions on its younger colleagues. The articling year is the ultimate Canadian, dues-paying, conformist experience. As one of my colleagues at a Toronto law firm once said about her success as a rising associate, "I realized during articling that I couldn't afford to piss off one person." That's a tall order in a firm of over 200 lawyers. Succeeding in such an environment isn't about talent, taking initiative or thinking creatively and critically. It's simply about ingratiating yourself to everyone and his cousin until you're ready to drop.

The American legal system gave up on apprenticeships a long time ago and that ended the enforced bargain and all the kowtowing that goes with it. In the United States, the summer after they graduate from law school, law students take the bar exams and get their call and actually become full-fledged lawyers before they ever join a firm. So they join as working professionals and don't have their jobs terminated based on an arbitrary time line. Generally, young lawyers can stay on for several years, during which their work is reviewed and their suitability for partnership track is considered. In the meantime, they actually get to practice law and, if they are forced to leave or want to leave, they have a strong base of experience that allows them to start their own practice or seek work in another field. There's a weeding-out process in American firms, but the bargain struck with young lawyers is based on a certain degree of respect for their talent, and generous starting salaries reflect that attitude. (Articling salaries have gone up considerably in Canada in recent years in major centers, but only because Canadian firms now have to compete with American firms for new hires.) In Canada, the concept of talent is eroded by the articling system and the value placed on conformism as the criterion of success.

Politics and the Individual

When comparing American and Canadian politics, one also sees fundamental differences in the approach toward individuals. In the United States, it's very clear that the political system welcomes contributions from promising younger people. That's reflected at the highest level in presidential fellowships, which give accomplished young Americans a chance to work in the White House for a year; it's also reflected in the general willingness to promote younger people within the party system.

A Canadian beneficiary of the American system is Daniel Casse, who rose to the highest levels in American political life not long after graduating with a degree in political science from the University of Toronto. Upon graduation, Daniel got a job in New York City as an editor for *The Public Interest*, a highly influential public policy journal. From there, he went to Harvard, where he did a Master's degree at the Kennedy School of Government. He then participated in the 1988 presidential election campaign, after which he took a position as speechwriter and special assistant to Bill Bennett, head of the national drug policy office. Within a year, Daniel was recruited to the White House Office of Cabinet Affairs, and went on to serve as special assistant to President George H. W. Bush. During this time, Daniel remained a Canadian citizen, he eventually received American citizenship, but not until the last day of the Bush administration's mandate in 1993. Can you imagine an American college graduate coming to Canada, working as an editor at a newspaper or magazine, and rising from that position to become a high-ranking advisor to the Prime Minister? It would never happen, not only because so many of our political and media elites would regard it as an act of treason to promote an American to the highest level, but also because the people running the system are not looking for talented individuals who can make a difference.

Even when a Canadian political party goes on a campaign to recruit highly qualified people, there is no guarantee that they'll be heard in the halls of power. In the early 1990s, Frank Klees, a long-time Conservative party member who would go on to win a seat in the legislature in 1995 and later become minister of transport, and Floyd Nixon, a party stalwart, spearheaded a policy initiative that created policy advisory councils to provide independent advice on policy matters to Conservative members. Initially, there were 17 policy councils that advised on everything from governance to criminal justice. What made this initiative unique was that no one had to be a member of the party to join. One simply had to have demonstrated expertise or interest in a particular policy area and a willingness to bring forward new ideas that might be helpful in setting the agenda for the party in the next election.

At the urging of a good friend and former student, Tony Clement, who later became minister of health in the second Mike Harris government, I took on the job of acting as co-chair of the council that advised on labor and employment issues in 1993. I had a chance to see how this experiment worked from the inside. And the results were impressive. The party was extremely successful in recruiting well-informed party members and independent experts. Some of the councils exerted considerable influence on the party's 1995 electoral platform, the Common Sense Revolution. But, when Mike Harris won the election, I know of only two council members who were asked to serve at Queen's Park. I'm sure there were more, but I didn't hear about them, and I was on the executive. I was extremely disappointed that Harris and his cabinet had not seen fit to use the policy advisory councils as a talent pool for government positions. Power within the government eventually came to reside in the premier's office, and even cabinet members were grumbling that they were shut out of the policy process by the premier's coterie of personal advisors. As often happens in the Canadian system, a few advisors at the top controlled the show and didn't show any sincere, sustained interest in drawing on the ideas and talents of the rank and file. No wonder there is such widespread dissatisfaction with the political process in this country.

Unfortunately, the parliamentary system itself tends to prevent members with new ideas from coming forward and making a difference. The parliamentary system depends above all else on party solidarity in the House of Commons and the provincial legislatures. A party can form a government only by winning a majority of seats, and it can hold that majority only by commanding a majority of votes when attempting to pass a bill. Any time a ruling party cannot muster a majority of votes, it will "lose the confidence" of the people and be forced to call an election. This feature of our system means that differences between members of the ruling party must be resolved behind the scenes, where matters will almost always be resolved in favor of the prime minister or the premier. The leader determines the work assignments of each member and so disagreeable people with criticisms or new ideas are going to find themselves on the backbench instead of at the cabinet table. If members of the majority had the option of voting against their party, they would gain the freedom to express their views and bring new ideas to hear on public debate. That approach would make the leader think twice before refusing to address the views of thoughtful members. However, under the rules of the current system, loyalty to the leader and the party effectively blocks individuals from making effective contributions that would improve the quality of government.

This group-think that parliamentary government encourages reached new heights during the Chrétien years due to Mr. Chrétien's obsession with loyalty. His zealous concern with personal loyalty became evident after he won the federal election in 1993, and he made a point of denying cabinet positions and committee chairmanships to members who had not supported him during his 1984 leadership bid. (Nine years is a long time to hold a grudge.) Throughout his years in power, Chrétien ran the prime minister's office like a mafia don, with Eddie Goldenberg, his Chief of Staff, playing the role of enforcer. The result was three successive governments that placed an overwhelming emphasis on fidelity to the leader and the party at the expense of vision and innovation.

One shouldn't be at all surprised that the sponsorship scandal occurred under Chrétien's watch. A leader who makes party loyalty the overriding goal of government sends the innovators to the sidelines; the resulting vacuum is filled by operators who are more than willing to buy party loyalty, as long as they get a piece of the action and they know the people at the top are willing to look the other way. At a time when we needed new ideas and perspectives to deal with our declining standard of living, Mr. Chrétien used his folksy bonhomie to convince us that everything was just dandy—and it certainly was for those who had their hands in the cookie jar.

Although one might give credit to Chrétien's Liberals for attacking the public debt, overall, Mr. Chrétien's leadership has had an enormously harmful impact on the country. It reinforced the Canadian tendency to believe that the group should prevail over the individual and prevented the country from moving toward a new imperative that linked the maximization of individual potential to the goal of raising our standard of living. In the end, Mr. Chrétien's concern with group solidarity prevented the Liberal government from addressing fundamental questions about the relationship between individuals, groups and government, which must be answered if we hope to close the prosperity gap with the United States. If Canada is not successful in improving its competitive position during the next five to 10 years, I have no doubt that historians will see the Chretién years as the period when this country lost its chance to stay in the global economic race.

The Underlying Causes of the Group Mentality

The belief that the success of the individual depends on the success of the group is a problem that harkens back to the origins of our political culture. The Loyalists who entered Canada after the American Revolution were steeped in the British Colonial tradition; they believed that citizens should defer to the authority of the state and that social and economic changes should be effected incrementally These beliefs blended nicely with the existing colonial outlook in the emerging colonies in Upper and Lower Canada. The deference to authority translated as willingness to subordinate individual rights and claims to the authority of the the colonial government. The belief in gradualism translated into a lack of tolerance for enterprising individuals who wanted to change the existing order. Consider how quickly Upper Canadian reformers were put down when they rebelled against oppressive colonial elites in 1837. This bias in favor of groups has been reinforced over time by politicians and academics who persist in thinking of Canada as a coalition of groups rather than a collection of individuals sharing common rights of citizenship. This view, expressed by historians such as Kenneth McNaught, has been aided and abetted by the policy of multiculturalism, which, of course, teaches that we should think of ourselves primarily as members of ethnic groups. And it's been strengthened by the policies of employment equity and pay equity, which reserve special employment privileges for government-designated groups. It's been supported as well by our anti-Americanism, which leads some Canadians to reject individualism on the ground that it's an American tradition.

We're left with a country that presents as schizophrenic, combining a commitment to individualism, reflected primarily in the individual rights guaranteed in the Charter of Rights and Freedoms, and a commitment to groups that is reflected in a host of misguided beliefs, practices and policies. This strange pastiche of beliefs was clearly manifested by Pierre Trudeau, who simultaneously favored a limited government that protected individual rights and an unlimited government that doled out favors to groups and regions. Rather than being the great reconciliation of French and English, and left and right that so many thought he embodied, in retrospect, Trudeau, in spite of his many virtues, seems instead to express the contradictions and ambiguities that were present in Canada from the time of its founding and that undermine the very individualism that Trudeau himself lived out on a personal level with such panache.

I am sorry to say that the Canadian willingness to link the fate of the individual to the fate of the group has given rise to a resentment of success in some parts of the country. This phenomenon seems to be based on an unarticulated belief that success is a zero-sum game. In other words, some Canadians tend to believe that one person's success is another's failure, and that individual financial success is often achieved at the expense of the community. (While it's certainly true that some individuals have attained wealth at the expense of the others, we cannot treat the exception as a general rule; if we did, we'd be in conflict with the most basic premise of economic theory, which holds that individuals can create new forms of wealth that make everyone better off.) The low-level buzz of *ressentiment* that's in the air in some parts of Canada has been commented on by Derek Burney, a former ambassador to Washington, who also served as CEO of Canadian Aerospace Enterprises. In a paper written for the TD Economic Forum on Canada's Standard of Living, Mr. Burney stated: "We don't celebrate the success of others; in fact, one could argue that we resent 'winners' who stand out from the crowd or 'raise the bar.'"[3]

The mistaken belief that success is a zero-sum game tends to be aggravated by other aspects of Canadian society. The fact that Canada is a relatively small market means that many of the best opportunities are located in one or two major cities, which sometimes makes it seem that the country is much smaller than it is. One person's promotion can appear to be another's demotion. Our declining standard of living, which is shrinking the base of opportunities in relative terms, supports that idea in a very real way. As long as our standard of living continues to fall, we'll be stuck with the fact that many hard-working and meritorious Canadians will not be able to achieve their dreams. And that will perpetuate the notion that individual achievement is somehow suspect. And that, in turn, will fuel the belief that liberating individual talents will undermine the welfare of the group.

Our *ressentiment* leaves us with a chicken-and-egg problem. In order to achieve greater prosperity, we must change our attitude toward the individual and be willing to liberate individual talents within organizations. But to feel secure about liberating individual talents, we first might have to achieve greater prosperity so that everyone feels optimistic about the new approach.

The Failure To Embrace Lockean Liberalism

I've traced the belief that the success of the individual depends on the success of the group to the way in which Canadian political culture developed under the influence of colonial values of deference and gradualism. There is, however, another way to see the problem. It can be expressed as a failure to fully embrace the liberal democratic beliefs that played an essential role in the development of political life in North America. I've noted earlier that even academic socialists, such as

Gad Horowitz, agree that Canadians, like Americans, are Lockean liberals at heart, which means that they accept the basic principles of the liberal political philosophy as they were articulated by the influential English philosopher John Locke, whose ideas exerted an enormous influence on the development of North American politics throughout the 18th century.

The starting point for all of Locke's thinking is that the individual is the building block of society. As we've already seen in chapters 6 and 9, Locke's system is grounded on the following beliefs: each person is the best judge of his or her own interests; each person has the right to pursue his or her own conception of happiness; the pursuit of individual self-interest, particularly economic self-interest, can produce a stable, prosperous and just society. This last belief is essential in determining the viability and the vitality of liberal individualism.

The longest chapter in Locke's *Second Treatise on Government* deals with property. And there Locke argues for a version of what has come to be known as the "invisible hand" (i.e., the belief that the pursuit of self-interest can produce a common good). Locke argues that a properly organized society, which guarantees fundamental rights to its citizens, should allow the ambitious few to profit handsomely from their selfish economic activities because they can produce new forms of wealth that make everyone better off. Locke argues convincingly that liberating the talents of the "industrious and rational" few is the key to promoting economic growth. (And I would argue, more generally, that the key to promoting superior economic growth in Canada is to think long and hard about how to liberate the productive potential of *every* employee, as well as every manager, owner and entrepreneur.)

If we would only think more clearly about our liberal roots, we would see that they point us toward a thorough-going individualism that is not tainted or undermined by any sort of collectivist impulse. The Lockean solution is based on the belief that the success of the group depends on the success of the individual. And yet we persist in holding on to vestiges of the old colonial mentality, now useless and terribly outdated, that leads us to act on the premise that the success of the individual depends on the success of the group. We're paying for that harmful inversion of liberal thinking with a standard of living that is now 20% lower than America's.

Individuals, Groups and the Equal Opportunity Ideal

The value in the American belief that the success of the group depends on the success of the individual is that it supports the equal opportunity ideal, which has given the U.S. its great advantage in the race for talent and wealth. When a nation believes that the welfare of the whole is intrinsically linked to maximizing the potential of the individual, then it must ensure that everyone gets a chance at some point to show what he or she can do. And that, put rather simply, is the idea on which the equal opportunity principle is based.

The Canadian tendency to believe that the success of the individual depends on the success of the group effectively destroys the imperative of giving every person the chance to make his or her unique contribution, and thereby diminishes the productive power of the equal opportunity ideal. This point is a variation on the more general thesis that informs every chapter in this book; and, that is, that Canada's standard of living is declining because the group prevails over the individual in ways that undermine the equal opportunity ideal, and its natural companion, national prosperity. To summarize the main points:

> • The policy of multiculturalism, which asks us to think of the country as a coalition of groups, creates discord and prevents us from developing the united spirit that we need

to meet the challenge of developing the practices and polices that will promote the equal opportunity ideal and improve our standard of living.

• Employment equity creates group rights to employment opportunities and thereby utterly destroys the equal opportunity ideal.

• Pay equity subverts the equal opportunity ideal because it arbitrarily awards pay increases to groups, i.e., people in female-dominated occupational groups, without regard to whether individuals in those groups are truly adding value to their organizations.

• The failure to provide a constitutionally guaranteed right to private property compromises the equal opportunity ideal because it prevents us from affirming the values that the ideal promotes, namely, individualism, entrepreneurship and meritocracy.

• Based on the mistaken belief that Canadians have a social democratic bias, many of our political elites continue to promote socialistic policies, such as employment equity and pay equity, which subvert the equal opportunity ideal and undermine our wealth-creating potential.

• The leaders of the Compassionate Society spent recklessly to improve the plight of "disadvantaged groups" and thereby robbed the country of the revenue needed to sustain the social and economic conditions that support the actualization of the equal opportunity ideal for members of those groups.

• The overriding value placed on doing at the expense of thinking creates a workplace where group norms honor the routine performance of specialized tasks rather than the wealth-creating, individualistic creativity that an equal opportunity society is supposed to foster.

- The failure to embrace the basic liberal premise that the individual is the building block of society produces the pernicious belief that the success of the individual depends on the success of the group, which undermines the equal opportunity ideal and all its benefits.

We can measure all of these problems against the studies conducted by the Ontario Task Force on Competitiveness and Prosperity, the TD Economic Forum on Canada's Standard of Living, and the work of independent analysts and business people. These studies reveal that America's economic success and our economic decline can be traced to attitudinal advantages enjoyed by the United States. We would be well advised to adopt these attitudes if we hope to improve our standard of living; but we will never do so as long as we continue to endorse the policies and outlooks—reviewed in chapters 3 to 10—that have undermined the equal opportunity ideal.

Let's review America's attitudinal advantages and link them to the myths that are holding us back:

- Greater commitment to individual rights (and a corresponding rejection of group rights).

  If we continue to believe in the myths that employment equity promotes equal opportunity, pay equity secures equal pay, Canadians have a social democratic bias, and the success of the individual depends on the success of the group, we will continue to live with policies that promote group rights that undermine equality of opportunity and national prosperity.

- Greater belief in the power of the individual, greater belief in meritocracy, greater openness to "new talent" among immigrant groups.

  If we insist on believing that multiculturalism promotes peace and prosperity, employment equity promotes equal opportunity, pay equity secures equal pay, private property is not a fundamental right, Canadians have a social democratic bias, and the success of the individual depends on the success of the group, we will continue to undermine the notion of individual merit and the prosperity that it generates.

- Greater respect for private property, greater respect for markets and greater willingness to compete in global markets, higher tolerance for risk-taking.

  As long as we adhere to the myth that private property is not a fundamental right, we will continue to undervalue individualism, entrepreneurship and meritocracy, which are the values that promote these advantageous market-based beliefs.

- Greater belief in the benefits of theoretical research.

  As long we continue to believe that doing is more important than thinking, America will continue to enjoy this competitive advantage.

This project of calling into question the various myths that propel our political culture—and the policies associated with them—is absolutely essential if we hope to adopt the attitudes that America has so effectively employed to achieve its superior economic performance. This, as I said at the start, does not mean that we must mimic American political culture, and simply become a smaller version of the U.S. in order to improve our standard of living. We must, however, seriously consider how we can integrate American attitudes that promote equal opportunity and national prosperity with our own attitudes so that we can create a uniquely Canadian policy that will promote a national Renaissance. In effect, I am recommending that we imitate the best practices approach that temporarily made Japan a formidable economic power. We should take America's best practices and beliefs, and combine them with our own, to create a new outlook that will promote the equal opportunity ideal, and with it, the twin goals of meritocracy and national prosperity.

The alternative is simply to muddle through. And, if that's the choice we make, we had better be clear about the consequences: an accelerated decline in our standard of living, mediocrity as the norm, failing social programs, a second-rate educational system, the emigration of our most talented citizens to other parts of the world and, finally, the loss of hope.

ENDNOTES

Myth One

1. Ontario Institute for Competitiveness and Prosperity, "A View of Ontario: Ontario's Clusters of Innovation," Working Paper No. 1, April 2002, p. 9; Andrew Sharpe, "Rising Canadian Living Standards: A Framework for Discussion," Centre for the Study of Living Standards, p. 8; TD Forum on Canada's Standard of Living, see TD Economics at http://www.td.com/economics/standard/standard.jsp.

2. http://www.ipsos-na.com/news/pressrelease.cfm?id=2603.

3. Calculation based on OECD figures at http://stats.oecd.org/wbos/viewhtml.aspx?QueryName=6&QueryType=View&Lang=en.

4. See TD Economics at http://www.td.com/economics/standard/standard.jsp; Alex Law, "Canada's top-selling vehicles for 2004," available from Auto123.com; Dan Lienert, "The best-selling vehicles of 2004," available from MSNBC.com.

5. Jeffrey Simpson, *Star-Spangled Canadians: Canadians Living the American Dream*, (Toronto: HarperCollins Canada, 2000), pp. 139, 143-4.

6. Conference Board of Canada, "Addressing the Challenge: Deliberations at the TD Forum on Canada's Standard of Living," p. 3, TD Economics. See note 1.

7. The Auto Pact was preserved under the FTA and NAFTA but was abolished when the World Trade Organization dispute panel ruled in 2001 that the Pact unfairly discriminated against foreign manufacturers under rules contained in the General Agreement on Trades and Tariffs.

8. A. Charles Baillie, Address to the Canadian Club of Toronto, February 26, 2001, p 1, available from http://www.td.com/communicate/speeches/26feb01.jsp; "We Can Outdo U.S. Economy, Martin says," *National Post,* February 28, 2001, sec. A4; "Canada doesn't have to be an also-ran," Editorial, *National Post,* February 27, 2001, sec. A15.

9. Conference Board of Canada, "Recommendations from Author's Submissions," TD Economics. See note 1.

10. Modern political disputes are not so much about ends but rather the means of achieving them.

Myth Two

1. Internal document provided by the World Bank, July 2004.

2. Ontario Institute for Competitiveness and Prosperity, op. cit., p. 9; http:ocde.p4.siteinternet.com/publications/doifiles/302005041P1T007.xls; Institute for Competitiveness and Prosperity, "Closing the Prosperity Gap," First Annual Report, Nov. 2002, p. 14.

3. The real growth rate is the annual percentage increase in the GDP minus the annual rate of inflation.

4. Canada's average growth rate was 2.8%; the OECD average was 2.7%. Andrew Sharpe, op. cit., p. 8; Ontario Institute for Competitiveness and Prosperity, "A View of Ontario: Ontario's Clusters of Innovation." See note 1, Myth 1, p. 8.

5. From 1946 to 1973, the Canadian rate was 2.6%, the American 2.4%; from 1981 to 1989, the U.S. rate was 2.52%, the Canadian 1.85%; from 1990 to 1995, the U.S. rate was 1.02%, the Canadian .24%; from 1995 to 2001, the Canadian rate was 2.5%, the American 2.18%. Andrew Sharpe, op. cit., p. 7.

6. Ibid., pp. 6-7.

7. Ontario Institute for Competitiveness and Prosperity, "Measuring Ontario's Prosperity: Developing an Economic Indicator System," Working Paper No. 2, Aug. 2002, p. 19.

8. Ontario Institute for Competitiveness and Prosperity, "A View of Ontario," op. cit., pp. 10-11; "Investing for Prosperity," Second Annual Report, Nov. 2003, p. 15; Andrew Sharpe, op. cit., p. 9; Peter J. Nicholson, "The Growth Story: Canada's Long-run Economic Performance and Prospects," *International Productivity Monitor,* Number 7, (Fall 2003): p. 3 at 4-5, 7-9; Derek Burney, "The Way Ahead for Canada: A Question of Leadership and Skill," TD Economics, op. cit., p. 5-8.

9. According to Derek Burney, recently retired CEO of CAE (Canadian Aerospace Enterprises), the prosperity gap has been caused by three factors: the productivity gap, high taxes and structural differences. Burney argues that Canada's net after-tax income is 32% lower than that of the United States', and only one-third is attributable to the productivity gap. Of the remaining two-thirds, one-third is attributable to our higher tax burden, and one-third to three factors: (i) Canada has a higher unemployment rate than the U.S.; (ii) Americans work harder than Canadians; and (iii) the profitability of our natural resource sector was reduced by the fall in commodity prices during the 90s. Burney claims that the gap cannot be narrowed by adding back the benefits Canadians receive from public health care and public university education because most Americans, he argues, are covered by private, employer-funded health plans, and state schools have tuition fees very close to our own. Contrary to Burney's findings, the Ontario Task Force has determined that Canadians and Americans work almost the same number of hours per week, and that it's necessary to add back benefits from public health care and public education to calculate the net after-tax burden in Canada. However, adding those benefits does not eliminate the gap. Note that Peter Nicholson, special advisor to Prime Minister Paul Martin, believes Americans are working longer hours than Canadians. He claims that household surveys show longer hours than do the establishment surveys. Nonetheless, Nicholson doesn't contend that we can eliminate the productivity gap simply by working longer hours. Burney, op. cit.

10. Andrew Sharpe, op. cit., p. 16; Sharpe, "Why Are Americans More Productive Than Canadians?" Centre for Living Standards Research Report, March 2003, Charts 5-7; Nicholson, op. cit., p. 6; Pietro Catte, Peter Jarrett, David Rae, "Looking Forward Hopefully: What Canada Can Learn From Some Other OECD Countries' Growth Experiences," July 24, 2002, p. 5, TD Economics, op. cit.; Ontario Institute for Competitiveness and Prosperity, "A View of Ontario," op. cit., p. 6.

11. Andrew Sharpe, "Why Are Americans More Productive Than Canadians?" op. cit., p. 19.

12. The Global Competitiveness Report 2004-2005, World Economic Forum, Geneva, 2004, p. 582, table 9.01, p. 584, table 9.03.

13. Dr. Horace ("Woody") Brock, "Making Sense of Today's Global Economy," Strategic Economic Decisions, Inc., 2000, private research paper.

14. The creativity gap seems largely attributable to the rate of investment in research and development. The productivity gap seems to be related to other factors such as the rate of investment in capital (e.g., machinery or computer technology), improvements in quality control and improvements in workplace organization. Nonetheless, the productivity gap can also be

related to research and development that produces innovations in production technique, which are often manifested in the creation of new kinds of manufacturing equipment.

15. *OECD Factbook 2005: Economic, Environmental and Social Statistics,* see science and technology indicator, tables on gross domestic expenditures on R&D, available from www.oecd.org; Roger L. Martin, "The Demand for Innovation in Canada," Aug. 12, 2002, p. 2, TD Economics, op. cit.; Nicholson, op. cit., pp. 18-9.

16. Sharpe, "Why Are Americans More Productive Than Canadians?", op. cit., p. 19; Nicholson, op. cit., pp. 18-9.

17. Four of the centers are devoted to promoting innovation in specific fields: energy, information and communications technology, materials and manufacturing, and photonics. The fifth has a general mandate to promote all forms of innovation in the workplace. Martin, op. cit., pp. 3-4.

18. Ontario Institute for Competitiveness and Prosperity, "Measuring Ontario's Prosperity: Developing an Economic Indicator System," Working Paper No. 2, August 2002, p. 33.

19. Ontario Institute for Competitiveness and Prosperity, "Investing for Prosperity," op. cit., pp. 21, 24.

20. Ibid., p. 24.

21. Sharpe, op. cit., p. 20; Ontario Institute on Competitiveness and Prosperity, "Closing the Prosperity Gap," First Annual Report, Nov. 2002, p. 33. Business education accounts for 20% of the total weighted degrees in the United States; Martin, op. cit., p. 11.

22. Nicholson, op. cit., p. 9; Sharpe, op. cit., p. 20; Sharpe, "Raising Canadian Living Standards," p. 16; Burney, op. cit., p. 5; Institute for Competitiveness and Prosperity, "A View of Ontario," op. cit., p. 28. Note that Ontario's share of employment in ICT clusters is not much below the U.S. average (4% vs. 5.12%), but it is low compared to leading peer states; California's share is 31.26% and Massachusetts is 11.5%, as compared to 12% in Canada.

23. Ontario Institute on Competitiveness and Prosperity, "Closing the Prosperity Gap," op. cit., pp. 35-6; "Investing for Prosperity," op. cit., p. 26.

24. Ibid., p. 27.

25. Note, however, that an industry need not be high tech in order to enjoy cluster status; in the United States, IT is 14th on the cluster list, and clustered

high-tech industries of all kinds account for only 8% of cluster employment. Ontario Institute for Competitiveness and Prosperity, "A View of Ontario," p. 28.

26. In its report of November 2003, the Ontario Task Force speculated that Ontario's clusters suffer from a lack of inter-firm rivalry, because they are still in some measure protected from foreign competition; "Investing for Prosperity," op. cit., p. 39.

27. Ontario Institute for Competitiveness and Prosperity, "A View of Ontario," op. cit., pp. 16-28; "Investing for Prosperity," op. cit., p. 39.

28. www.taxtips.ca; www.taxpolicycenter.org.

29. Ontario Institute for Competitiveness and Prosperity, "Measuring Ontario's Prosperity," op. cit., pp. 32-7. Mintz has determined that the average total tax on labor in Ontario, at the highest marginal rate, is 59%. Ontario's rate is not much higher than its top rivals in productivity, Massachusetts and California, which are 52% and 53% respectively. While the *average rate* in Ontario is 31%, it's 26% in Massachusetts, 17% in California and Illinois, 16% in Georgia and 15% in Michigan. Ibid., p. 35. Even though Ontario residents receive greater benefits in the form of subsidies for health care and education, as compared to its main rivals, Ontario's overall higher tax burden offsets those gains, so that Ontario ends up with a higher average marginal tax rate on labor than its peers. Ibid., pp. 36-7.

30. Ibid., p. 37; "Investing for Prosperity," op. cit., pp. 36-8.

31. Ontario Institute for Competitiveness and Prosperity, "Measuring Ontario's Prosperity," p. 33. In the communications sector, the average marginal rate on labor in Ontario is 70%, and the average marginal rate on capital is 25%; whereas the American rate on labor is 25% and on capital 7%.

32. Mintz, for example, favors cutting all federal and provincial taxes so that the total tax burden for any individual does not exceed 50% of gross income. He also favors eliminating capital taxes, and lowering the combined provincial and federal tax rate to 30%. As well, he advocates raising the deduction limits for pension contributions and RRSP contributions. In line with Mintz's position, Derek Burney, former CEO of CAE argues that personal and corporate taxes should be reduced to American levels and that those reductions should be offset by an increase in consumption taxes to ensure that governments can pay for public goods and services. Peter Nicholson, special advisor to Prime Minister Martin, is not as adamant about tax cuts because he believes that taxes that fund public education and infrastructure can play an important role in promoting growth. Nonetheless, he is opposed

to taxes that "prop up inefficient enterprises" or "dampen" work incentives. He argues that "skepticism is warranted in respect of proposals to increase the size of government relative to the economy [because] on balance, there is likely to be a cost in terms of labor output." Jack Mintz, "Tax Policy as a Contribution to Canada's Economic Advantage," p. 10, TD Economics, op. cit.; Burney, op. cit., p. 11; Nicholson, op. cit., p. 14

33. Martin, op. cit., p. 8.

34. Ontario Institute for Competitiveness and Prosperity, "Investing for Prosperity," op. cit., pp. 27-30.

35. Ontario was America's third-largest trading partner after Japan and Mexico, with total trade coming in at around $360 billion. The figures for American imports were: Ontario at 74%, Quebec at 10%, the Prairies at 14%, B.C. at 6% and the Atlantic provinces at 1%. Ontario Institute for Competitiveness and Prosperity, "A View of Ontario," op. cit., p. 15.

36. This is not an exhaustive list of the solutions that have been proposed by the Ontario Task Force, the 50 commentators who submitted papers to the TD Economic Forum and other leading figures in the field of public policy. While I suspect that many in this community of experts would support these solutions, some place emphasis on alternative solutions such as national daycare, national public housing, a new approach to economic development in Aboriginal communities, a fundamental change in employment criteria or the adoption of a more positive attitude toward entrepreneurs. Then there are a host of microeconomic solutions that depend solely on the initiative of the private sector, such as commitments to continuous product improvement and continuous employee training. Derek Burney argued that to become truly competitive, a company must focus on talent and commit itself to attracting and retaining "a cadre of highly educated, creative people"; it must be committed to continuous improvement; and it must be offensively and defensively agile in investment and production strategies. Burney, op. cit., p. 10.

37. Nicholson, op. cit., p. 14.

38. Ibid., pp. 6, 20.

39. The closest Canada came to reaching this target was when it outgrew the U.S. by an average of .9% between 1966 and 1981. Sharpe, op. cit., p. 12.

40. Ibid., p. 15.

41. Ibid., pp. 12, 15. Roger Martin argues that Ireland's history isn't relevant due to its size; in his view, the same can be said of Norway, Switzerland and Denmark, as well as Luxembourg and Iceland, whose economies are smaller than the city of Hamilton. Martin, op. cit., p. 5.

Myth Three

1. Royal Commission Report on Bilingualism and Biculturalism, Vol. IV, Queen's Printer, p. 7.

2. *Equality Now!* Report of the Special Committee on Visible Minorities in Canadian Society, (Ottawa: Queen's Printer, 1984), p. 2.

3. Evelyn Kallen, "Multiculturalism: Ideology, Policy and Reality," *Journal of Canadian Studies*, 17(1) (1982): p. 53.

4. Wallace Brown, *The Good Americans: The Loyalists in the American Revolution*, (New York: William Morrow and Co., Inc., 1969), pp. 192, 195-7; Kenneth D. McCrae, "The Structure of Canadian Society," in *The Founding of New Societies*, ed: Louis Hartz, (New York: Harcourt, Brace and World, 1964), pp. 235-6, 245.

5. Michael Alexander, "The Portable Mosaic," *The Idler*, No. 11, Toronto, p. 22 at 23-4.

6. Statistics Canada website, 2001 Census, "Ethnic Origin (232), Sex (2) and Single and Multiple Responses (3) for Population, for Canada, Provinces, Territories, Census Metropolitan Areas and Census Agglomerations, 2001 Census—20% Sample Data; The Atlas of Canada (federal government website), Visible Minority Population, 2001, available from http://atlas.gc.ca/site/english/maps/peopleandsociety/visible_minority/vmin/1; Statistics Canada website, 2001 Census, Visible Minority Groups, 2001 Counts, for Metropolitan Areas and Census Agglomerations–20% Sample Data, p. 6. Note that if all Europeans are excluded from the total minority population, then the national figure for the population is around 14%.

7. Citizens' Forum on Canada's Future: Report to the People and Government of Canada, Canadian Government Publishing Centre, Supply and Services Canada, 1991, p. 85.

8 Equality in Employment, A Royal Commission Report, Judge Rosalie Silberman Abella, Commissioner, Minister of Supply and Services, Canada, 1984, pp. 9-10.

9. Ibid., pp. 46-7, 206.

10. Charles Taylor, *Multiculturalism and the Politics of Recognition: An Essay*, (New Jersey: Princeton University Press, 1992), pp. 25-6, 34, 36, 38, 60-1, 64; Michael Ignatieff, *The Rights Revolution*, (Toronto: House of Anansi Press, 2000), pp. 53, 66, 70, 86-9, 113, 124.

11. Ibid., pp. 63-6, 113-4.

12. Ibid., pp. 85-9.

13. Ibid., pp. 81-2.

14. Neil Bissoondath, *Selling Illusions*, (Toronto: Penguin Books, 1994), pp. 86-8, 191-2.

15. Clearly I am concerned about group outcomes as measured by shareholder return and GNP, since I've argued that Canada is failing to maximize its productive potential. However, that doesn't mean I don't care about individual outcomes. We need a new kind of individualism—one that liberates the productive potential of every citizen—if we hope to increase individual and collective wealth, and create a public surplus that will allow us to assist disadvantaged individuals so that they too can realize their productive potential.

Myth Four

1. National Library of Canada website, "Macdonald Introduces the National Policy, 1878," p. 1.

2. Equality in Employment, op. cit., pp. ii, 126.

3. Ibid., pp. 2, 8-9, 10.

4. Thomas Sowell, "*Weber* and *Bakke* and the Presuppositions of Affirmative Action," *Wayne Law Review*, Vol. 26 (July 1980): 1309 at 1314-8.

5. Equality in Employment, op. cit., p. 206.

6. Ibid., pp. 47, 103

7. Ibid., p. 46.

8. Ibid., pp. 7, 9, 205, 207.

9. Ibid., p. 10.

10. *Regents of the Univ. of Cal. v. Bakke*, 438 U.S. 265 (1978); 1978 U.S. LEXIS 5, at 26.

11. Equality in Employment, op. cit., p. 23.

12. Sowell, op. cit., p. 1336; www.pollingreport.com/race.htm; Richard Morin and Sharon Warden, "Americans Vent Against Affirmative Action," *Washington Post*, March 24, 1995, p. A 01.

13. *CNR v. Canada (CHRC)* [1987] 1 SCR 1114.

14. Ibid., p. 182.

15. *National Capital Alliance on Race Relations (NCARR) v. Canada (Health and Welfare)* [1997] C.H.R.D. No. 3.

16. R. Brian Howe and David Johnson, *Restraining Equality: Human Rights Commissions in Canada*, (Toronto: University of Toronto Press, 2000), pp. 125-6.

17. Equality in Employment, op. cit., pp. 48-51.

18. *R. v. Oakes* [1986] 1 S.C.R. at 136.

19. *Lovelace v. Ontario* [2000] 1 S.C.R. 950; 2000 S.C.R. LEXIS 40, at 17-9.

20. Ibid., pp. 11, 16-7.

21. Ibid., pp. 19, 29-30.

22. *Kalanke v. Bremen* [1995] E.C.R. 1-3051.

23. *Franks v Bowman Transportation* 424 U.S. 747 (1976) at 763.

24. In *United Steelworkers of America v. Weber*, 443 U.S. 193 (1979), 1979 U.S. LEXIS 40, which invoked this principle, Chief Justice Burger and Justice Rehnquist dissented from the court's decision on the basis that the clear wording and legislative history of Title VII of the *Civil Rights Act* prevented the adoption of any race-based remedies absent a specific finding of past discrimination practiced by an employer, and there was no such finding in this case. Furthermore, Justice Rehnquist characterized the plan as prohibited racial balancing undertaken in response to pressure from the Federal Office of Contract Compliance rather than a voluntary attempt to deal with past discrimination in the workplace. As well, he was concerned that the quota system would necessarily result in reverse discrimination against white employees. See LEXIS p. 20 (note 6), pp. 20-4, 35. Also see: *Johnson v. Transp. Agency, Santa Clara Cty., Cal.* 107 S.Ct. 1442 (1987) at 1460-5, 1470-1.

25. Equality in Employment, op. cit., p. 9; *Griggs v. Duke Power Co.*, 401 U.S. 424 (1971) at 431.

26. Bakke, op. cit., pp. 24, 32.

27. Ibid., pp. 33-5.

28. *Gratz v. Bollinger* 539 U.S. ____ (2003) (Slip Opinion), pp. 23, 25-8.

29. *Grutter v. Bollinger* 539 U.S. ____ (2003) (Slip Opinion), p. 20.

30. Ibid., p. 3.

31. Johnson, op. cit., pp. 1470-1.

32. *Metro Broadcasting, Inc. v. F.C.C.* 110 S.Ct. 2997 (1990) at 3011, 3026, 3028-9.

Myth Five

1. Steven E. Rhoads, *Incomparable Worth: Pay Equity Meets the Market*, (Cambridge University Press, 1993), pp 8-9; *Canada (Attorney General) v. Public Service Alliance of Canada (T.D.)* [2000] 1 F.C. 146; 1999 F.C. LEXIS 104, p. 5.

2. Government of Canada, HRSDC website, "Lessons Learned, Gender Equality in the Labor Market," October 2001, p. 1, available from http://www.hrsdc.gc.ca/en/es/sp/hrsdc/edd/reports/2001-002501/page07.shtml; Statistics Canada, "Women in the Workplace," Catalogue 71-534, p. 9.

3. Rhoads, op. cit., p. 10.

4. William Gairdner, *The Trouble With Canada*, (Toronto: General Paperbacks, 1991), p. 287.

5. Walter Block (chapter), in *Discrimination, Affirmative Action and Equal Opportunity*, ed: Walter Block and Michael Walker, (Vancouver: The Fraser Institute, 1982), pp. 108, 112-3; Sowell, op. cit., p. 1324; Gairdner, op. cit., pp. 286-7; Morley Gunderson, "Male-Female Wage Differentials and Policy Responses," *Journal of Economic Literature*, Vol. XXVII (March 1989): 46, p. 52.

6. Rhoads, op. cit., pp. 12-3.

7. Ibid., p. 13.

8. Gunderson, op. cit., pp. 52-3.

9. Canadian Federation of Independent Business, Interview, March 2005.

10. Rhoads, op. cit., p. 5.

11. Ibid., pp. 4-5.

12. *Service Employees International Union, Local 204 v. Ontario* (1997), 35 O.R. (3d) 508 at 529.

13. Ibid., pp. 534-6.

14. *PSAC*, op. cit., pp. 11-2.

15. Gunderson, op. cit., p. 54; Rhoads, op. cit., pp. 20, 27.

16. *American Federation of State, County and Municipal Employees, AFL-CIO (AFSCME) v. State of Washington*, 770 F.2d. 1401; 1985 U.S. App. LEXIS 22712, p. 8.

17. Rhoads, op. cit., pp. 2-3.

Myth Six

1. John Locke, *Two Treatises of Government* (New York: New American Library, 1965) Book 2, c. 2, para. 6, p. 311; Alexander Hamilton, James Madison and John Jay, *The Federalist Papers* (New York: New American Library, 1961), p. 78.

2. Pierre Elliott Trudeau, *Federalism and the French Canadians*, (Toronto: Macmillan, 1968), pp. 53, 56.

3. Locke, op. cit., c. 2, para. 4-15, pp. 307-8.

4. J. Locke, *Essay Concerning Understanding* (Oxford: Clarendon Press, 1984), p. 351 (c. xxi). The priority of duty in the Aristotelian understanding is supported by the idea that human beings are naturally fitted for the practice of virtue and also by the following related notion: since human beings can reach their end (i.e., virtue) only in and through civil society, the state has a prior claim on their activities on the ground of their own good; Aristotle, *The Politics*, trans: C. Lord (Chicago: University of Chicago Press, 1984), c. 1 and 2; L. Strauss, *Natural Right and History* (Chicago: University of Chicago Press, 1953), c. 4.

5. Locke, op. cit., c. 5, para. 34, 37, 40 at pp. 333, 336, 338.

6. Ibid., c. 5, para 43, p. 340.

7. John Locke, *Two Treatises of Government* (New York: New American Library, 1965), Book II, para. 6, 25–51, 72–3, 120, 139–42, 184.

8. *Kelo v. New London* 545 U.S. ____ (2005) (Slip Opinion) at 8-9, 10, 13-6; O'Connor dissent at 1-13; Thomas dissent at 1-5, 16-8.

Myth Seven

1. Selection of OECD social indicators: How does Canada compare? Available from http://www.oecd.org/dataoecd./34/38/34553342.xls.

2. Michael Adams, *Fire and Ice*, (Toronto: Penguin Books, 2003), p. 5.

3. Hamilton, Madison and Jay, op. cit., p. 51.

4. Patrick Malcolmson and Richard Myers, *The Canadian Regime*, (Peterborough: Broadview Press, 2002), p. 23.

5. Tracy Quan, "Is It Sexy to be Canadian? A Borderline View," p.2, available from http://www.digitaljournal.com/print.htm?id=3355.

6. Samuel Beer, *Modern British Politics* (Parties and Pressure Groups in the Collectivist Age), (New York: W and W Morton Co., 1982), pp. 4-5, 45; Gad Horowitz: "Conservatism, Liberalism and Socialism in Canada: An Interpretation," in *Party Politics in Canada*, ed: Hugh G. Thorburn, (Toronto: Prentice-Hall Canada, 1972), pp. 79-80; Robert M. Calhoun, *The Loyalists in Revolutionary America, 1760-1781*, (New York: Harcourt, Brace and Jovanovich, Inc., 1973), p. 228.

7. McCrae, op. cit., p. 235; Ramsay Cook, *The Maple Leaf Forever*, (Toronto: Macmillan of Canada, 1971), pp. 210-1; S.F. Wise, "Conservatism and Political Development: The Canadian Case," *South Atlantic Quarterly* (1970): p. 235.

8. See note 4, Myth 1.

9. Wallace Brown, *The King's Friends*, (Providence: Brown University Press, 1965), pp. 288-9.

10. Calhoun, op. cit., p. 231; W.H. Nelson, *The American Tory*, (Oxford: Clarendon Press, 1961), p. 22.

11. Brown, *The Good Americans*, p. 66.

12. See note 4, Myth 1.

13. McCrae, op. cit., pp. 238, 240; Brown, *The Good Americans*, pp. 196-7; George M. Wrong, *Canada and the American Revolution*, (New York: Cooper Square Publishers, Inc., 1968), pp. 437-8; S.M. Lipset, *The First New Nation*, (New York: Basic Books, 1963), p. 251; S.F. Wise, op. cit., pp. 231, 235; S.F. Wise, "Upper Canada and the Conservative Tradition," in *Profiles of a Province*, ed: Ontario Historical Society, 1967, p. 30.

14. Wise, "Conservatism and Political Development," p. 235; "Upper Canada and the Conservative Tradition," pp. 29-30, 32; McCrae, op. cit., p. 243.

15. Horowitz, op. cit., p. 83; Frank Underhill, *In Search of Canadian Liberalism*, (Toronto: The Macmillan Co., 1960), pp. xxi, xii; Walter D. Young, *Anatomy*

of a Party, 1932-1961, (Toronto: University of Toronto Press, 1969), pp. 31, 40, 44, 73, 134; Michael Horn, *The League for Social Reconstruction: Intellectual Origins of the Democratic Left in Canada, 1930-1942*, (Toronto: University of Toronto Press, 1980), pp. 21, 102, 149; Leo Zakuta, *A Protest Movement Becalmed*, (Toronto: University of Toronto Press, 1964), p. 36; Ivan Avakumovic, *Socialism in Canada*, (Toronto: McClelland and Stewart, 1978), p. 50.

Myth Eight

1. Allan Bloom, *Shakespeare's Politics*, (Chicago: University of Chicago Press, 1964), p. 4.

2. Alexis de Tocqueville, *Democracy in America*, (Garden City: Anchor Book) Vol. 2, pt. II, c. 10, pp. 459-65.

3. http://www.aip.org/history/einstein/quantum1.htm.

4. Tocqueville, op. cit., p. 462.

5. Ibid., pp. 460-1, 464.

6. Institute for Competitiveness and Prosperity, "Striking Similarities: Attitudes and Ontario's Prosperity Gap," Sept. 2003, Working Paper No. 4, p. 36.

7. Institute for Competitiveness and Prosperity, "Investing for Prosperity," op. cit., pp. 22-3.

8. http://www.careersintrades.ca/media/default.asp?load=faqs01.

9. Canada25, "Toward a New Magnetic North," TD Economics, op. cit., pp. 4-5.

10. Canada25, "A New Magnetic North," section 4.1-4.1.5, available from http://www.canada25.com.

11. Canada25, "Toward a New Magnetic North," op. cit., p. 3.

Myth Nine

1. Tom Axworthy, *Toward a Just Society*, (Toronto: Penguin Books, 1992), p. 358.

2. Tom Axworthy, *Canadian Forum 5*, Nov. 1984, p. 6.

3. Andrew Coyne, "Social Spending, Taxes and the Debt," available from www.andrewcoyne.com, http://www.andrewcoynecom/Essays/Trudeau%20book%20piece.rtfd/TXT.html, p. 1.

4. Ibid., p. 3. The real value of a dollar from year to year is based on the annual average rise in the prices of goods and services, i.e., the rate of inflation. If the rate of inflation is 3% in a particular year, then one dollar buys 3% less in goods and services than it did the year before. In the figure cited above, the point was to determine whether the amount of government revenue spent on each citizen in 1985 was equivalent to the amount spent in 1968. To make this comparison, the value of the 1985 dollar would have to be reduced by the percentage increase in inflation since 1968. So, if inflation averaged 3% per year during this 17-year period, then value of the 1985 dollar would have to be reduced by 48% (17 years times 3%) to give it the same value it had in 1968. Once the 1985 dollars are revalued this way, then a straight comparison of the total amount spent in 1968 and 1985 will yield a true comparison. Based on this kind of analysis, the figures cited above establish that the government spent twice as many "real dollars" on each citizen in 1985 as compared to 1968.

5. Gairdner, op. cit., p. 177.

6. Coyne, op. cit., p. 5.

7. Ibid., pp. 3-5.

8. Trudeau favored funding to these groups based on what he called a system of "counterweights," which was a bastardized version of the system of checks and balances on which American federalism was based. He felt it was necessary to empower minority groups so that they could compete for government largesse on an equal footing with other more established groups. (If the Canadian Manufacturers Association or the Canadian Bankers Association had lobby groups in Ottawa, why couldn't women and cultural minorities have their own groups there too?) While this was a nice idea, it certainly bore little resemblance to the American system of checks and balances. The American system was based on the idea that each branch of government would check the efforts of the other to increase its power; the result was limited government. In Trudeau's system, interest groups were given funds to lobby Parliament to increase its power; the result was unlimited government.

9. Gairdner, op. cit., pp. 167, 193.

10. Coyne, op. cit., pp. 7-8.

11. Gairdner, op. cit., pp. 166, 177.

12. Ibid., p. 181. In 1988, the federal expenditure on social programs was $60 billion but only $17 billion actually went to the poor. Ibid., p. 191.

13. Thomas Hobbes, *De Cive,* (Gloucester: Peter Smith, 1978), author's preface, p. 97.

14. Clifford Orwin, "Moist Eyes – from Rousseau to Clinton," *The Public Interest* (Summer 1997): 3 at 6-7; Arthur Melzer, "Rousseau's Moral Realism: Replacing Natural Law with the General Will," *American Political Science Review,* Vol. 77 (1983): 633 at 637-8.

15. Orwin, op. cit., pp. 14-9.

16. Tocqueville, op. cit., pt. III, c. 1, pp. 561-5.

17. Ibid., pt. II, c. 8, pp. 525-8.

18. Gairdner, op. cit., p. 194.

19. Jason Clemens, Joel Eves with Katrina Ward, "2001 Generosity Index: Comparing Canadian and American Charitable Giving," Fraser Forum, pp. 10-1, available from http://www.fraserinstitute.ca/admin/books/chapterfiles/Misused%20User%20Fees-dec01ff1.pdf#9.

20. See note 1, Myth 7.

21. Ibid., It's not entirely accurate to say that America spends less on the sick. In fact, OECD statistics reveal that American and Canadian governments spend almost exactly the same amounts on health care, as measured as a percentage of GNP (6.6% in the United States versus 6.7% in Canada). The difference is that fewer people are covered by the public system in the United States.

Myth Ten

1. *National Post,* July 24, 2003, sec. A3.

2. http://www.rbc.com/unique careers/index.html. [date 6/3/2005].

3. Burney, op. cit., p. 13.

INDEX